# Hegel's Naturalism

# Hegel's Naturalism

## *Mind, Nature, and the Final Ends of Life*

TERRY PINKARD

OXFORD
UNIVERSITY PRESS

# OXFORD
UNIVERSITY PRESS

Oxford University Press, Inc., publishes works that further
Oxford University's objective of excellence
in research, scholarship, and education.

Oxford    New York
Auckland   Cape Town   Dar es Salaam   Hong Kong   Karachi
Kuala Lumpur   Madrid   Melbourne   Mexico City   Nairobi
New Delhi   Shanghai   Taipei   Toronto

With offices in
Argentina   Austria   Brazil   Chile   Czech Republic   France   Greece
Guatemala   Hungary   Italy   Japan   Poland   Portugal   Singapore
South Korea   Switzerland   Thailand   Turkey   Ukraine   Vietnam

Published by Oxford University Press, Inc.
198 Madison Avenue, New York, New York 10016

www.oup.com

Oxford is a registered trademark of Oxford University Press

Library of Congress Cataloging-in-Publication Data
Pinkard, Terry P.
Hegel's naturalism : mind, nature, and the final ends of life / Terry Pinkard.
p.  cm.
ISBN 978-0-19-986079-1 (hardcover : alk. paper)
1. Hegel, Georg Wilhelm Friedrich, 1770–1831.   I. Title.
B2948.P457 2012
193—dc23      2011018598

1 3 5 7 9 8 6 4 2

Printed in the United States of America
on acid-free paper

*To Susan*

# CONTENTS

PART TWO

# ACKNOWLEDGMENTS

The book has, I am sure, many shortcomings. It would have had even more except for the help I received from several people who read earlier versions of it. Parts of the book are now very different from the manuscript they read precisely because of the questions they raised and the suggestions they made. In particular, I would like to thank Thomas Kuhrana, Charles Larmore, Katie Padgett-Walsh, Robert Pippin, Sally Sedgwick, Martin Shuster, and Christopher Yeomans for their comments and discussions. I also benefited from discussion with Daniel Warren and Hannah Ginsborg about some of the issues at stake.

Georgetown University and the Department of Philosophy provided both a good working environment and the sabbatical that made writing this book possible. In addition, I owe a debt of gratitude to the Wissenschaftskolleg zu Berlin for providing me with a year under their auspices. Reinhart Meyer-Kalkus was a valuable conversation partner about the topics discussed here.

I also wish to thank my long-standing philosophical discussion partner, Stan Sechler, for his comments and suggestions.

Susan Pinkard's comments and discussions were irreplaceable.

# PREFACE

Since Hegel developed his own very specialized vocabulary for carrying out his program, interpreting his works poses special problems. Not the least of the problems posed by Hegel's rigorous use of his nonetheless arcane terminology is the way it almost naturally fosters the suspicion that taking the trouble to understand Hegel's sometimes dense vocabulary may simply be too much work for too little payoff. Several dead ends appear in the attempt to devote so much time to it. If one talks just like Hegel in talking about Hegel, then, at least among a good many Anglophone philosophers, the response is often something along the lines of "Fine and good, but what you just said made no sense at all." On the other hand, if one does not talk like Hegel, then the response of quite a few Hegelians is often something along the lines of "Fine and good, but what you just said isn't Hegel."

There is something to be said for both these types of objections. If one is to do justice to them, one thus has to steer a middle course between a mere recitation of the texts in their original terms and a reconstruction of Hegel's views in non-Hegelian language. This means that one has to combine a sense of historical accuracy mixed with a good sense for anachronism—that is, a way of sometimes reading Hegel in light of terminology that was not his own that is nonetheless faithful to his texts and contexts.

I also happen to think that this also amounts to taking Hegel's own advice about at least one way of approaching the history of philosophy:

> But this tradition [of the history of philosophy] is not merely a house-keeper who preserves faithfully what she has received and transmits it unaltered to her successor. It is not a motionless statue; it is alive, swelling like a mighty river which grows the further it is pushed on from its

source. The content of this tradition is what the world of *Geist* has produced, and the universal *Geist* does not stand still.[1]

### Notes

I have slightly altered the translations of almost all the citations to preserve a certain consistency.

1. Georg Wilhelm Friedrich Hegel, *Introduction to the Lectures on the History of Philosophy*, trans. T. M. Knox and A. V. Miller (Oxford: Clarendon; New York: Oxford University Press, 1987), viii, 193 pp., p. 10. This is from the 1823 notes on the lectures. I added the *nicht*, which is present in the 1820 notes and makes more sense. Georg Wilhelm Friedrich Hegel and Walter Jaeschke, *Vorlesungen über die Geschichte der Philosophie* (Philosophische Bibliothek; Hamburg: F. Meiner Verlag, 1993), 7.

# Hegel's Naturalism

# Introduction

What we look for in philosophy, as Kant said, is orientation. In Kant's meta-phor, it is as if we are in a dark room where there are nonetheless some familiar landmarks, and we use those landmarks to make our way around the room.[1] ("If this is the desk, then the door has to be in this direction.") When we look at our lives from a vantage point removed from the contexts of our more immediate concerns, and we turn to pure reason for help, we find ourselves in a similar darkness. However, we are without any assurance there even are such land-marks, and we then look to many other activities—philosophy among them—to offer us points of orientation. That is, we look to them to offer us something like metaphorical objects we can grasp in the dark to get our sense of direction and some kind of grip on where we are and in what direction we are going. In this kind of darkness, when we are looking for such orienting points and we turn to philosophy, we are engaged in a distinctive form of inquiry that Kant called "speculation."[2]

For Kant, all such "speculation" leads to four questions. What can I know? What ought I do? For what can I reasonably hope? Answering all three, as Kant said later in his career, amounts to answering a fourth question: What is man?

As he announces in the first paragraph of the first *Critique*, in submitting itself to "speculation," pure reason inevitably goes in search of the "unconditioned." We start with a series of conditions, and we seek to know if the series has any end. Unfortunately, once uncoupled from empirical constraint, pure reason's specula-tive impulse can only lead to what Kant called irresolvable antinomies, that is, basic contradictions among the terms that are candidates for the "unconditioned." It encounters a whole array of conceptual dilemmas that admit no empirical answer but seem to appear and reappear and whose only limits seem to be those of human cleverness in devising new arguments for one side or the other of the antinomy. The traditional name for the deepest of those conceptual dilemmas was "metaphysics," but, in keeping with Kant's spirit, we could also call it, simply, "philosophy."

The short versions of Kant's answers to his four questions are easy enough to state, although, as even the most lackadaisical readers of Kant rapidly discover, each of these calls out for a fiendishly elaborate set of qualifications.

What can we know? We can know a lot about the world under the conditions with which we can experience it but nothing about the world as it exists in itself, apart from those conditions. What ought we do? We ought to do what reason commands any rational being to do, which is to act in terms of universal principles and to respect the infinite dignity of all those creatures who have that capacity. However, to believe we can actually do that, we must presume that we are free, but we have no good reason for thinking that in the world as we can possibly know it we really are free. For what can we hope? We can rationally hope for a world where our happiness marches along proportionately hand in hand with our virtue, although there is no good reason to think that must happen in the world in which we live. Who are we? We are natural creatures who are also rational and who must think of themselves as possessing a capacity for self-causation that defies everything else we know about the world.

One of the arguments that Kant gives for why we cannot know the world as it exists in itself is that when we try to think of the way the world is apart from the complicated set of conditions under which we can experience it, we inevitably run into those antinomies. Even though the natural sciences provide us with a breathtaking knowledge of the world as it must appear to us, we must nonetheless conclude that the natural world so understood is not equivalent to the world in itself.

In short: We are thus metaphysical mysteries to ourselves even if, in putting the problem this way, we do at least understand the terms of the mystery—the mystery arises out of our own metaphysical limitations.

On the one hand, this might look rather bleak, as if it were to say: At one point, many people had hoped that "pure reason" unburdened with empirical study—namely, "philosophy"—would make the world and our needs intelligible to us, but we can no longer reasonably expect any such thing. Since "philosophy" in that traditional sense would always amount to a collection of unsolvable conceptual puzzles, the enterprise of philosophy could only consist in creating proposed solutions to those puzzles so that other philosophers can come up with crippling criticisms of those solutions. The enterprise of philosophy itself would keep going, but it will most likely be sustained by the postulate that at some indeterminate time in the future, these problems will have been solved, even though in human time, they never will.[3]

Kant called the process in which such conceptual dilemmas are endlessly generated "dialectic." So did Hegel.

Like Kant, Hegel also thought that the history of metaphysics was at least in one important sense a failed enterprise. It had failed at least in the minimal sense in that what it had produced could indeed be construed, as Kant had done, as a series of philosophical positions that boiled down in effect to sets of antinomies. Like Kant, Hegel also thought the detachment of conceptual thought from empirical grounding was part of the diagnosis of this limited failure.

In terms of its ultimate ambitions, philosophy had thus failed to resolve most of its problems. However, like Kant, Hegel did not think that this implied that such problems were therefore meaningless or that, as insoluble puzzles, we need not worry about them. The very production of these antinomies itself had a deeper meaning to it that was already implicit in Kant's own rejection of the possibility of a pure metaphysics in the traditional sense.[4] Especially when the Kantian antinomies are used to draw a line between what thought can know and what is "beyond" thought's capacity to provide knowledge, on which side of the line is the thinker standing?[5] Some of Hegel's contemporaries concluded that wherever it was that they were standing, it could not be expressed in any direct way but only be "seen" through some kind of special faculty of something like "intellectual intuition."

Hegel disagreed with that and thought that what Kant had actually showed us in his doctrine of the antinomies is that what we are seeking in those dilemmas is a way of characterizing our own "mindedness" (to render Hegel's term *Geistigkeit* into uncomfortable English). More specifically, in our status as human agents, precisely because we are animals conscious of ourselves, we are also—to appropriate a term that Charles Taylor made famous—self-interpreting animals.[6] One of Hegel's more succinct versions of that claim occurs in his lectures on the philosophy of art, where he states his conception of "mindedness" in unmistakable Hegelian terms:

> Man is an animal, but even in his animal functions he does not remain within the in-itself as the animal does, but becomes conscious of the in-itself, recognizes it, and raises it (for example, like the process of digestion) into self-conscious science. It is through these means that man dissolves the boundary of his immediate consciousness existing-in-itself, and thus precisely because he knows that he is an animal, he ceases to be an animal and gives himself the knowledge of himself as *Geist* [spirit, mind].[7]

Moreover, because of this, the self-conscious animal produces itself. In Hegel's terms, spirit "gives itself" its own reality. Or as he also puts it, "spirit is essentially only what it knows itself to be."[8] If we are only as we know ourselves to be, and this kind of knowing is itself historical, then we are indeed "self-interpreting animals."

In a nutshell, this is also Hegel's view about the context of the final ends of life: We are natural creatures, self-interpreting animals, and our final ends have to do with how we are to give a rational account—or, to speak more colloquially, to make sense—of what, in general, it means to be a human being and what, in the concrete, it means to be a parent, child, friend, warrior, tribe member, employee of a corporation, medieval serf, and so on. Everything hangs on that. On the other hand, left merely at that, Hegel's thesis sounds altogether implausible, as if it were saying that if we merely interpreted ourselves to be angels, we would therefore be angels, or that there are no limits to our interpretations, and we can therefore interpret ourselves as we like. Much therefore depends on how that thesis is to be interpreted if it is to be more convincing than its initial statement makes it out to be.

In that light, the history of metaphysics, of philosophy itself, is the history of our attempts to come to grips with what it means to be, to use that uncomfortable translation of a Hegelian term, "minded" (*geistig*)—that is, what it means to *be* a human being, or, in Hegel's slightly denser jargon, what it means for *Geist* (spirit, mind) to arrive at a full self-consciousness. Unlike so many people in the nineteenth and twentieth centuries who came after him, Hegel did not think that metaphysics was in some strict sense meaningless—that it somehow supposedly violated some kind of basic or transcendental boundary on the meaningfulness of statements, such as "verifiability" or "criteria" of use. The conceptual dilemmas of metaphysics do indeed result in contradictions, he thought, but they are not, for all that, meaningless. Rather, they are essential to who we are. We cannot avoid dealing with such antinomies.

To summarize Hegel's views in some general terms that will require much more elaboration: Like Kant, Hegel holds that these kinds of conceptual dilemmas can never be finally solved in the way that other problems can be solved by appeal to a proof or appeal to a fact. "Why does ice float in nonfrozen water?" poses a problem that can be solved, but metaphysical or conceptual dilemmas are not like that. Like Kant, Hegel thinks that there is something special about such problems that makes their resolution seem pressing to those who reflect on them, but, like the later Wittgenstein, he is open to the idea that the impossibility of their resolution is not the threat to reason that it at first seems to be.[9] For Hegel, the "dialectic" consists in a movement from a set of conceptual dilemmas (or antinomies) in one way of speaking and experiencing to a different, more determinate context from which those antinomies cease to be as threatening to the very rationality of the system as they had originally seemed to be. The puzzles are not solved, seldom dissolved, but they are tamed.

To characterize this kind of move, Hegel notoriously puts the German term *Aufhebung* to use so that he can play on its two meanings of "canceling" and "preserving."[10] The threat is removed once the antinomies are viewed in the light of a different context in which their opposition no longer is the self-undermining threat it originally appeared to be. Since there is no good translation for the German term that captures its sense in English, Anglophone translators revived an older word that had gone out of use, *sublation*, to render Hegel's term into English. There are problems with this—it is, after all, an obviously artificial and rather nonintuitive solution—but reasons of economy recommend its continued employment.

It is a relatively separate, although important, issue, but Hegel also thought that he could give an account of how all these antinomies hung together. He thought he could show that the collection of all the classical conceptual dilemmas that are identified as "philosophical" dilemmas in fact have a kind of deeper logic to them, such that one can demonstrate how these dilemmas incite each other and how various groups of dilemmas both belong together and themselves incite the construction of other groups of dilemmas. Hegel's own demonstration of this came in the various versions of his *Science of Logic*, but even he expressed a certain modesty about how successfully he had carried out such a wildly ambitious program.

If so, then there can be within Hegel's own terms no a priori method that can state in advance whether any particular conceptual problem will in fact turn out to generate such antinomies. Although it is by now a widely discredited view that Hegel thought that everything proceeded along the lines of thesis-antithesis-synthesis, if in fact he had held anything even like that view (that is, that there was an a priori "method" that could be applied to all the material at hand), he would have put himself into a direct contradiction with everything else he held. The innovation that a new context brings with it cannot be predicted from or literally deduced from the dilemma that provoked it. One cannot predict conceptual innovation, since to predict the innovation is just to make it. Hegel's view was that there is a logic to the kinds of antinomies that philosophy in its history has put on display, but this logic itself can be demonstrated only after the fact, after the problems have already gathered themselves into what seems at first like an inchoate heap but can then be given an intelligible order—only after, to use his famous metaphor, the owl of Minerva has already flown.

Ultimately, following Hegel in his line of thought will take us to what Hegel at an early point in his 1807 *Phenomenology* claims is his central thesis: that the central claim that his philosophy seeks to develop is just that the truth must be comprehended "not merely as *substance* but also equally as *subject*."[11] For Hegel, to be an agent is to not to be made of any particular stuff (say, "mental" as distinct from "physical" stuff), since agents are, after all, natural creatures. To be an agent is to be able to assume a position in a kind of normative space, which, so it will turn out, is a kind of social and historical space.[12] To be able to do this, the natural creatures who are human beings are brought up within a form of life, and in doing so, they acquire an array of social skills, dispositions, and habits that function for them as a "second nature." In becoming "second nature" and not simply a nonnatural capacity to respond to norms, a form of life remains a form of "life," that is, part of the natural world but different from the forms of life of other natural creatures. In acquiring the ability to move within such a normative social space, each agent emerges as an organic animal "substance" reshaped into a self-conscious "subject" capable of guiding her actions by norms. This also turns out to involve what Hegel calls "recognition."[13]

Moreover, to comprehend the truth "also" as subject is also to comprehend the way in which the presentation of the dialectic up to this point in the story is itself one-sided. (Here, too, there is once again a rather cursory resemblance to some of the ideas of the later Wittgenstein. Like Wittgenstein, Hegel holds the view that "what people accept as justification shows how they think and live.")[14] To be an agent is to be an organic human animal who has a normative status conferred on her that she must then sustain through her own acts. As an agent moves around in this social space and learns to negotiate it, she also commits herself to making sense of what she is doing, and that involves giving and asking for reasons from others moving around in that social space.

This is part of yet another aspect of Hegel's conception of dialectic as that of an experiential and practical affair, a way in which an entire form of life can generate tensions within itself because of the way it collectively commits itself to certain conceptions of what for it counts as the "unconditioned." Such tensions can ultimately make the statuses that one occupies in such a social space only barely inhabitable or, in the extreme case, fully uninhabitable. For a status to be fully inhabitable is for one to be able to "settle into it" or "invest oneself" in the status.

One of the most well-known Hegelian metaphors is that of having the world as a home.[15] One of the few places where Hegel offers an extended explicit discussion of "being at home" is the introductory sections of his discussion of Greek philosophy in his lectures on the history of philosophy. Hegel raises the rhetorical question of why the Greeks are so important for us, and he answers his own query by remarking that it is only in recent times that "European humanity," after having passed through centuries of "the hard service" of the church and Roman law, has finally been "rendered pliable and capable for freedom." In this way, European humanity had therefore finally come to be in a position where it might be both "at one with itself" and "at home" with itself.[16] What therefore attracts contemporary—that is, eighteenth- and nineteenth-century—Europeans to ancient Greek life is that it was at that point that not only for the first time did "humans begin to be at home . . . they themselves made their world into a home, and it is the shared spirit of being-at-home that binds us to them."[17] Contemporary Europeans, Hegel thought, in the 1820s saw their own aspirations as having been actualized in some way or another in ancient Greek life.

For Hegel, what was particularly attractive about the way in which the Greeks (at least to the gaze of cultivated nineteenth-century European tastes) were "at home" with themselves had to do with how their own agency and nature existed for them in a kind of spontaneous harmony and thus beauty.[18] Unlike Hegel's imaginary "Orientals"—whom he mistakenly confused with real inhabitants of what Europeans call Asia and imagined had an overly monistic, stalled conception of their own agency in nature—and unlike the "moderns" (whom he describes as embodying the principle of "abstract subjectivity" characterized as "pure formalism," as empty, or as "having made itself empty"), the Greeks had both a naturalistic understanding of themselves and a normative understanding of their own "mindedness," spirituality, *Geistigkeit*. On Hegel's view, what is finally most attractive about them is that they not only thought of themselves as both free and as part of nature but also seemed to be actually free and to be actually at home in their world.

Moreover, so Hegel thought, after almost 1,800 years, European life was finally drawing itself closer to a more authentic understanding of Greek life than had been possible since the end of antiquity. Now, this idea that the Greek world was something of a model for the modern European world had been part of Hegel's repertoire since his student days at Tübingen, and it had become even part of a generational aspiration to show that in contrast with the Roman humanist tradition, the roots of the European form of life were in fact not Roman but Greek.[19] In other words, Europe's roots were not primarily Christian but pagan. Unlike some others, Hegel also thought that he could show how Christianity was in fact, when properly reinterpreted and recast, compatible with this Greek idea of the world, but the central idea remained of revivifying the Greek idea by means of a full reinterpretation of it.[20]

However, Hegel's other key idea—that the truth must be grasped not merely as "substance" (which is the Greek mode) but also as "subject"—meant that the Greek model cannot simply be revived or newly applied or even serve as an object of nostalgia. Greek ideas must be reargued, rearranged, and reinterpreted, and, despite their exemplary status for us, a hard look at them must make us realize just how irretrievable some key parts of their common life were and why trying to "retrieve" the Greeks is itself a hopeless and possibly dangerous fantasy.

To jump immediately to the end of the story: The truth of what first appears only as an endless procession of metaphysical dilemmas is that such dilemmas are the result of *Geist* grasping the way it is not at one with itself by virtue of its own activities of taking up positions in social space.[21] We try to make a home in the world, we fail at it, and the story to be told about this is not a purely psychological or austerely historical story but something else. Oddly, for a philosopher whose best known saying is "the true is the whole," Hegel thinks that this conclusion should be taken as a warning about the mistaken drive for certain kinds of wholeness.

Ultimately, the final end of our lives is self-comprehension, that is, knowing what it is to be a self-interpreting animal and knowing what follows from that. On its face, the sweeping feature of that claim surely is not likely to strike very many people as being very plausible. Whether it can be made plausible at all depends on how we construe Hegel's defense of that claim. That will take two parts. The first part concerns Hegel's conception of nature and his reworking of Aristotle to make his case. The second part concerns what Hegel takes this to imply about the conditions under which we are to realize that final end that is necessary if we are to lead satisfying, even if not happy, lives.

## Notes

1. Kant, "What Is Orientation in Thinking?" in Immanuel Kant, *Kant: Political Writings*, ed. Hans Siegbert Reiss (2nd enl. ed., Cambridge Texts in the History of Political Thought; Cambridge: Cambridge University Press, 1991), xv, 311 pp., pp. 40–242: "It is at this point, however, that the right of the need of reason supervenes as a subjective ground for presupposing and accepting something which reason cannot presume to know on objective grounds, and hence for orientating ourselves in thought—i.e. in the immeasurable space of the supra-sensory realm which we see as full of utter darkness—purely by means of the need of reason itself."

2. There is more to Kant's conception of speculation than this characterization alone, but delineating the exact contours of the specifically Kantian conception of speculation is not the issue here. Kant does say in the *Critique of Pure Reason*: "Metaphysics is a completely isolated speculative science of reason, which soars far above the teachings of experience, and in which reason is indeed meant to be its own pupil." See Immanuel Kant, *Immanuel Kant's Critique of Pure Reason*, trans. Norman Kemp Smith (London: Macmillan, 1929), xiii, 681 pp., p. 21.

3. What Kant has to say about human history would also be attributable to metaphysics or "philosophy" in this sense. "It may perhaps be moving and instructive to watch such a drama for a while; but the curtain must eventually descend. For in the long run, it becomes a farce. And even if the actors do not tire of it—for they are fools—the spectator does, for any single act will be enough for him if he can reasonably conclude from it that the never-ending play will go on in the same way forever." See I. Kant, "On the Common Saying: 'This May Be True in Theory, but It Does Not Apply in Practice,'" in Hans Siegbert Reiss, ed., *Kant: Political Writings* (Cambridge Texts in the History of Political Thought; Cambridge: Cambridge University Press, 1991), p. 88.

4. See the discussion of the relation of the Kantian antinomies to Hegel's dialectical approach in Paul Redding, *Analytic Philosophy and the Return of Hegelian Thought* (Modern European Philosophy; Cambridge: Cambridge University Press, 2007), x, 252 pp.

5. This kind of issue is redolent of Wittgenstein's remark in the preface to his *Tractatus* that "to set a limit to thought, we should have to find both sides of the limit thinkable (i.e., we should have to be able to think what cannot be thought). It will therefore only be in language that the limit can be set, and what lies on the other side of the limit will simply be nonsense." See Ludwig Wittgenstein, *Tractatus Logico-Philosophicus. The German Text of Logisch-Philosophische Abhandlung* (International Library of Philosophy and Scientific Method; London: Routledge & Kegan Paul; New York: Humanities Press, 1963), xxii, 166 pp., p. 3. Hegel's position, in distinction from both Kant and (the early) Wittgenstein, consists in his arguments to the effect that this idea of a limit itself demands its resolution in his conception of the space of reasons as the "absolute." Hegel notes: "Even if the topic is that of finite thought, it only shows that such finite reason is infinite precisely in determining itself as finite; for the negation is finitude, a lack which only exists for that for which it is the sublatedness, the *infinite* relation to itself." See Georg Wilhelm Friedrich Hegel, *Enzyklopädie der philosophischen Wissenschaften II*, ed. Eva Moldenhauer and Karl Markus Michel, 20 vols. (Theorie-Werkausgabe, 9; Frankfurt a. M.: Suhrkamp, 1969), §359; Georg Wilhelm Friedrich Hegel and Arnold V. Miller, *Hegel's Philosophy of Nature: Being Part Two of the Encyclopedia of the Philosophical Sciences (1830), Translated from Nicolin and Pöggeler's Edition (1959), and from the Zusätze in Michelet's Text (1847)* (Oxford: Clarendon; New York: Oxford University Press, 2004), xxxi, 450 pp., p. 385.

6. Charles Taylor, *Human Agency and Language* (Philosophical Papers; Cambridge: Cambridge University Press, 1985), viii, 294 pp. Fortunately, the terms *minded* and *mindedness* have been given a lease on life in English by Jonathan Lear, *Open Minded: Working Out the Logic of the Soul* (Cambridge, Mass.: Harvard University Press, 1998), 345 pp.

7. Georg Wilhelm Friedrich Hegel, *Vorlesungen über die Ästhetik I*, ed. Eva Moldenhauer and Karl Markus Michel, 20 vols. (Theorie-Werkausgabe, 13; Frankfurt a. M.: Suhrkamp, 1969), p. 112; Georg Wilhelm Friedrich Hegel, *Aesthetics: Lectures on Fine Art*, trans. T. M. Knox, 2 vols. (Oxford: Clarendon, 1988), p. 80.

8. Georg Wilhelm Friedrich Hegel, *Enzyklopädie der philosophischen Wissenschaften III*, ed. Eva Moldenhauer and Karl Markus Michel, 20 vols. (Theorie-Werkausgabe, 10; Frankfurt a. M.: Suhrkamp, 1969), §385; Georg Wilhelm Friedrich Hegel et al., *Hegel's Philosophy of Mind: Being Part Three of the "Encyclopaedia of the Philosophical Sciences" (1830)* (Oxford: Clarendon, 1971), xxii, 320 pp., p. 21.

9. There is yet another way in which his views overlap, at least superficially, with those of the later Wittgenstein. Wittgenstein was also obsessed with the way that conceptual concerns push us to questions with which we are burdened but cannot answer and (notoriously) noted almost in passing that "philosophical problems arise when language goes on holiday" (as the phrase is usually translated). ("Denn die philosophischen Probleme entstehen, wenn die Sprache *feiert*." See Ludwig Wittgenstein, *Philosophical Investigations = Philosophische Untersuchungen* (New York: Macmillan, 1953), x, 232 pp., ¶38.) This has often been taken to be the view that such reflection on such problems is excessive or unneeded, that it is engaged in the kinds of nonpractical and ultimately trivial pursuits that characteristically are assigned to vacations. However, if one translates Wittgenstein's phrase differently—that philosophical reflection takes place when language "celebrates" (*feiert*)—one has something closer to a Hegelian conception. On that view, such reflection comes about when we attempt to grasp the "unconditioned," the purely conceptual, something that cannot be settled by appeal to fact. Or to continue the personification of language, one could say that, pulling itself away from its practical pursuits, language engages in a "festival" (*die Sprache feiert*) of thought about its ultimate concerns.

10. The term *Aufhebung* also carries the sense of "raising something up," and this is almost always mentioned in any discussion of Hegel's use of the term. However, when Hegel gives his longest explanation of it in his *Science of Logic*, he speaks only of two meanings of the term and not of the third sense of "raising up": "Sublation (*Aufhebung*) has the two-fold sense in [the German] language so that it equally means preserving, conserving as well as ceasing to be, putting an end to it.... The two cited determinations of sublation can be lexically listed as two meanings of this word. However, it must be striking that a language has reached the point where one and the same word is used for two opposed determinations. It is gratifying for speculative thought to find words which have a speculative meaning in themselves." See Georg Wilhelm Friedrich Hegel, *Wissenschaft Der Logik I*, ed. Eva Moldenhauer and Karl Markus Michel, 20 vols. (Theorie-Werkausgabe, 5; Frankfurt a. M.: Suhrkamp, 1969), vol. 5, p. 114; Georg Wilhelm Friedrich Hegel, *Hegel's Science of Logic*, trans. A. V. Miller (Muirhead Library of Philosophy; London: Allen & Unwin; New York: Humanities Press, 1969), 845 pp., p. 107. The same reference to the two (and not three) meanings also occurs in Georg Wilhelm Friedrich Hegel, *Enzyklopädie der philosophischen Wissenschaften I*, ed. Eva Moldenhauer and Karl Markus Michel, 20 vols. (Theorie-Werkausgabe, 8; Frankfurt a. M.: Suhrkamp, 1969), §96, *Zusatz*; Georg Wilhelm Friedrich Hegel et al., *The Encyclopaedia Logic, with the Zusätze: Part I of the Encyclopaedia of Philosophical Sciences with the Zusätze* (Indianapolis, Ind.: Hackett, 1991), xlviii, 381 pp., p. 154. "It is worth remembering here the double-meaning of our German expression, '*aufheben*' (sublation). By 'sublation' we understand at one time sweeping away, negating and we say, for example, that a law, an institution, etc. is rescinded (*aufgehoben*). It also means preserving, and we say in this sense that something has been well preserved (*aufgehoben*). This linguistic usage with its double-sense, according to which the same word has at the same time a negative and a positive meaning, may not be viewed as simply accidental, nor a reason to reproach language as a source of confusion. We ought rather to recognize here the speculative spirit of our language, which goes beyond the 'either/or' of the understanding." The *Oxford English Dictionary* points out that "sublate" is a fairly old term that had more or less died out in usage in the middle of the nineteenth century. Originally imported from Latin in the sixteenth century, its primary meaning was that of "negating" or "removing." Hegel's translators more or less stipulated that it also meant "to preserve." In Hegel scholarship, how exactly one is to understand Hegel's use of the term has been a matter of some contention. Sublation is to be distinguished from "overcoming" (which in German would be an

*Überwindung*). It should also be distinguished from "superseding" or "transcending." It is also not the same as "subsumption" under a higher unity.

11. Georg Wilhelm F. Hegel, *Phänomenologie des Geistes*, ed. Eva Moldenhauer and Karl Markus Michel, 20 vols. (Theorie-Werkausgabe, 3; Frankfurt a. M.: Suhrkamp, 1969), p. 23 (¶17). Even Hegel notes his usage of "truth" throughout his works is idiosyncratic. First, most of his uses of "truth" have little to do with the more ordinary sense in which a statement, such as "the rose is red," is true if and only if the rose is red. Indeed, Hegel has no trouble at all with the idea that in the normal usage of "truth," things are made true by whatever it is that the statement is about. This is not the sense in which he is interested. For example: Hegel, *Enzyklopädie der philosophischen Wissenschaften II*, §246; Hegel and Miller, *Hegel's Philosophy of Nature: Being Part Two of the Encyclopedia of the Philosophical Sciences (1830), Translated from Nicolin and Pöggeler's Edition (1959), and from the Zusätze in Michelet's Text (1847)*, p. 13: "If the truth in the subjective sense is the agreement of the representation with the object, then this means that the true in the objective sense is the agreement of the object (*Objekts*), of the state of affairs (*Sache*) with itself, so that its reality (*Realität*) is adequate to its concept." Second, there is "truth" in what he calls the "deeper" sense, which is truth as a norm to which something may live up to or to which it may or may not conform. See, for example, Hegel, *Enzyklopädie der philosophischen Wissenschaften I*, §213, Zusatz; Hegel et al., *The Encyclopaedia Logic, with the Zusätze: Part I of the Encyclopaedia of Philosophical Sciences with the Zusätze*, 287: "On the other hand, the truth consists in a deeper sense in objectivity's (*Objektivität*) being identical with the concept. This deeper sense of truth is that of which we are speaking when it is an issue of, for example, that of a *true* state or of a *true* work of art. These objects are *true* if they are as they are supposed to be, i.e., if their reality corresponds to their concept. Taken in that way, the untrue is the same as what is otherwise also called the bad." Third, there is a sense of "truth" in which the problems that come to light in the use of a concept (along with its abstract inferential relations to other concepts and the concrete conditions of its employment) are themselves resolved in the new uses of the term that express the concept (which in turn affects the other concepts with which it is inferentially connected), or, if they are not resolved, when they are at least harmonized with each other.

12. I tried to make the case for this in Terry P. Pinkard, *Hegel's Phenomenology: The Sociality of Reason* (Cambridge: Cambridge University Press, 1994), vii, 451 pp.

13. The theme of recognition (*Anerkennung*) is vast and probably requires an entirely separate treatment. It forms the core of some of the non-neo-Platonist interpretations of Hegel. A representative but not exhaustive sample would start with, of course, Alexandre Kojève and Raymond Queneau, *Introduction to the Reading of Hegel* (New York: Basic Books, 1969), xiv, 287 pp. In addition: Robert B. Pippin, *Hegel's Practical Philosophy: Rational Agency as Ethical Life* (Cambridge: Cambridge University Press, 2008), xi, 308 pp.; Robert Brandom, *Tales of the Mighty Dead: Historical Essays in the Metaphysics of Intentionality* (Cambridge, Mass.: Harvard University Press, 2002), x, 430 pp.; Robert Brandom, *Reason in Philosophy: Animating Ideas* (Cambridge, Mass.: Harvard University Press, 2009); Pinkard, *Hegel's Phenomenology: The Sociality of Reason*; Dean Moyar, *Hegel's Conscience* (New York: Oxford University Press, 2010); Ludwig Siep, *Anerkennung Als Prinzip Der Praktischen Philosophie: Unters. Zu Hegels Jenaer Philosophie d. Geistes* (Reihe Praktische Philosophie; Freiburg [Breisgau]; München: Alber, 1979), 378 pp.; Axel Honneth, *The Struggle for Recognition: The Moral Grammar of Social Conflicts* (Cambridge, Mass.: Polity, 1995), xxi, 215 pp.

14. Wittgenstein, *Philosophical Investigations = Philosophische Untersuchungen*, ¶325 (Anscombe translation altered). "Was die Menschen als Rechtfertigung gelten lassen,—zeigt, wie sie denken und leben."

15. Michael Hardimon has made this into a central point of discussion of Hegel's philosophy, particularly his practical philosophy. See Michael O. Hardimon, *Hegel's Social Philosophy: The Project of Reconciliation* (Modern European Philosophy; Cambridge: Cambridge University Press, 1994), xiv, 278 pp.

16. "Germanic sturdiness made it necessary to pass through the hard service of the church, along with the law which came to us from Rome and to which we had to be disciplined. It was only in passing through such service that the European character was softened up and made capable of freedom. Since then, European humanity has come to be at home with itself (*bei sich zu Hause*), has looked to the present and has retired from what was historically given to it by what was alien to itself." See Georg Wilhelm Friedrich Hegel, *Vorlesungen über die Geschichte der Philosophie I*, ed. Eva Moldenhauer and Karl Markus Michel, 20 vols. (Theorie-Werkausgabe, 18; Frankfurt a. M.: Suhrkamp, 1969), p. 173.

17. Ibid., 173–74: "It was there that people began to be in their own home (*Heimat*). However, for us, what is nostalgic (*heimlich*) about the Greeks is that we find them to have made their world a home; the community spirit of being-at–home (*Heimatlichkeit*) connects us to them. With the Greeks, it is like it is in ordinary life [for us]—we feel good with people and families that are at home with themselves and are content with themselves and not with something above and beyond them."

18. Ibid., 176: "The other extreme term of abstract subjectivity (that of pure formalism) exists in emerging from out of itself, in being within itself, even if it still empty or, rather, has made itself empty—the abstract principle of the modern world. The Greeks stand in between both of them in the beautiful middle ground, which is the middle ground of beauty because it is at the same time natural and *spiritual*, but in such a way that *spirituality* remains the determining subject."

19. The biographical and historical aspects of this are discussed in Terry P. Pinkard, *Hegel: A Biography* (Cambridge: Cambridge University Press, 2000), xx, 780 pp.

20. More recently, Bernard Williams has also claimed that "in important ways, we are, in our ethical situation, more like human beings in antiquity than any Western people have been in the meantime. More particularly, we are like those who, from the fifth century and earlier, have left us traces of a consciousness that had not been touched by Plato's and Aristotle's attempts to make our ethical relations to the world fully intelligible." See Bernard Arthur Owen Williams, *Shame and Necessity* (Sather Classical Lectures; Berkeley: University of California Press, 1993), xii, 254 pp., p. 166. However, Williams also especially singled out Hegel as one of the people who, by Williams's lights, got in the way of this retrieval.

21. This point is also made by Robert Stern, who takes it, however, to show that Hegel's argument demands a kind of realism about concepts. The interpretation I am giving here tries to make the case that no such metaphysical commitment to metaphysical realism about concepts is implied by Hegel's system. See Robert Stern, "Hegel's Idealism," in Frederick C. Beiser, ed., *The Cambridge Companion to Hegel and Nineteenth-Century Philosophy* (Cambridge: Cambridge University Press, 2008), and Robert Stern, *Routledge Philosophy Guidebook to Hegel and the Phenomenology of Spirit* (Routledge Philosophy Guidebooks; London: Routledge, 2002), xviii, 234 pp.

# PART ONE

PART ONE

# 1

# Disenchanted Aristotelian Naturalism

## A: Hegel's Aristotelian Turn

By his own account, Hegel takes his views on Aristotle to have shaped his entire thinking about how best to conceptualize our own status as creatures with minds and how to think about the role that practical reason plays in human life.[1] Given what Hegel says about Aristotle's importance for his own views, a quick look at Hegel's own summary of Aristotle's practical philosophy can help us to orient ourselves in his thought.

It is a commonplace, although a highly contested one, to say both that the Greeks had no concept of the will and that the concept of the will was first introduced by the Christians (specifically, by Augustine).[2] Hegel obviously does not hold that view, since he notes that "the best thoughts we have...on the will, on freedom and on further terms such as 'imputing responsibility,' 'intention,' etc. are, all the way up to modern times, Aristotle's own thoughts on the matter."[3] (Again, it is striking that he gives Aristotle, and not Kant, credit for this, even though he is quite clear that he thinks that Aristotle's views need amplification about one very key aspect of the nature of freedom and the will.)

For Aristotle, the highest good, the final end that such willing aims at is, of course, *eudaimonia*, happiness (or what may also be rendered as "flourishing" or "getting along well in life"). Hegel gives his own interpretation of this by putting it into his own terminology (and thus giving us a clue as to how his own views on this are to be taken). Happiness, *eudaimonia*, is, he says, "the energy of the (complete) life willed for its own sake, according to the (complete) virtue existing in and for itself."[4] The energy of a whole life willed for its own sake involves two elements—that of reason and that of passion and inclination—and the two must exist in a unity for there to be virtue.[5] On Hegel's reading, Aristotle holds that the agent cannot act without such inclination: "Impulse, inclination is what drives the agent; it is the particular, which, with regards to what is practical, more precisely pushes for realization in the subject."[6] Thus, all the virtues involve a balance, a "mean" between the universally rational and the particular aspects of agency, a kind of "more or less" that cannot in principle be given a "pure"—that is, a priori—specification. That implies, of course, that at least for Aristotle (on

Hegel's reading of him), there can be no "pure practical reason" that can specify the virtues.

This also suggests that Hegel both accepts Aristotle's own framing of the issue and accepts what Aristotle takes to be the problems in such a view. Indeed, it seems to be that Hegel develops his own conception of freedom as a way of "being at one with oneself" (Beisichsein) out of Aristotle's conception of what counts as voluntary action.

Aristotle himself conceived of the voluntariness of an action as involving three aspects: First, an action is "voluntary" when the "moving principle" is within the agent; second, when the agent himself is the origin of the action, or, as Aristotle also puts it, when it is in accord with the agent's impulses;[7] and, third, when the action is not the result of an "external force."[8] Hegel restates the Aristotelian view in his own terms so that it comes out saying that the "inner, moving principle" becomes actualized, that is, when the "inner" formation of an intention, made in light of a responsiveness to reasons, is actualized in an "outward" action in conformity with the intention.[9] In its most succinct version, this view would hold that an action is in conformity with the intention when the content of both is the same (when the action just is the intention fully realized), and, as Hegel gradually fleshes out this idea, it becomes the claim that the interpretation of the whole complex of "intention-action" on the part of the actor must be in conformity with the interpretation given by others, who, for whatever reason, are called on or are in a position to assess the action.[10] How do we reach that conclusion, and what would it mean?

We are self-conscious, self-interpreting animals, natural creatures whose "non-naturalness" is not a metaphysical difference (as that, say, between spiritual and physical "stuff") or the exercise of a special form of causality.[11] Rather, our status as geistig, as "minded" creatures is a status we "give" to ourselves in the sense that it is a practical achievement. Indeed, our continuity with the natural world (specifically, with animals) is at the center of Hegel's Aristotelian conception of mindful agency more than it could possibly be for either Augustine or Kant (or any of their voluntarist comrades). In Hegel's terms, animals also have the capacity to be "at one with themselves" and even to have both "selves" and, as we shall see, "subjectivity."[12] However, Hegel holds that human agents, by virtue of thinking of themselves as animals, thereby become special animals, namely, self-interpreting ones, and, as we have already noted, that makes all the difference.

Hegel's discussion of animals is of great importance in figuring out what he means by calling his own philosophy an "idealism." "Idealism" is usually taken either to be the doctrine that all supposed physical objects are really just (somehow) subjective representations in somebody's mind or to be some kind of metaphysical doctrine to the effect that all that is genuinely real is some sort of spiritual or mental substance. Hegel has long been interpreted as a monist idealist of the latter sort who holds that all of the world should be interpreted as some kind of development of a spiritual substance, Geist.[13] That picture of Hegel's thought would have us believe that he subscribes to something like the view that everything from stars to rocks to animals to humans is an emanation from or a development of a single spiritual substance.

Yet when Hegel discusses animals, he also calls them "idealists." The language is striking. Animals, he says, are not "metaphysical realists," since when they encounter things, they do not take them to be merely mental in their constitution. Instead, they "take hold of them, grasp them and devour them."[14] If animals demonstrate the truth of idealism by devouring things, Hegel's own idealism cannot therefore consist in a denial of the materiality of nature. Indeed, one of the clues to Hegel's conception of his own idealism—although he himself seemed to prefer the term "speculative philosophy" as a label for what he was doing—is the way that, as he puts it, animals deny the "self-sufficiency" of worldly things.

The specific character of the idealism that is at stake emerges in Hegel's discussion of nature. Hegel's conception of nature in general is that of a disenchanted Aristotelian naturalism. (The term *disenchanted* is a bit overused, but no better term suggests itself.)[15] This comes especially to the forefront in his "philosophy of nature" (an inexact translation of what he called his *Naturphilosophie*).[16] First, Hegel has no quarrel with the natural sciences. Hegel, in fact, says that "not only must philosophy be in agreement with the experience of nature, but the *origin* and *formation* of philosophical science has empirical physics as its presupposition and condition" (a claim that, taken out of context, might sound as if it came from some twentieth-century adherent to Quine's naturalism).[17] The project of the natural sciences involves the construction of theories (which Hegel divides into mechanical, physical, chemical, and biological theories) that are to be tested against empirical observation. Nonetheless, even if the best conception of "nature" is to be considered as equivalent to whatever it is that the natural sciences determine to be the case, the issue still remains open as to whether *that* nature, as described by the results of the natural sciences, is the whole, is all there is to things. Or to put it in the other terms we have used, although mechanics may tell us all there is know about the determinations of matter in motion, do such determinations fully and without residue express the unconditioned or, to shift to the more exuberant language Hegel inherited from Schelling, the absolute?

Second, what thus distinguishes Hegel's *Naturphilosophie*, his "philosophy of nature," from physics itself is that the philosophy of nature aims at producing a metaphysics or, as Hegel calls it, the "diamond net" into which we make the world intelligible—a comprehension, in Wilfrid Sellars's famous phrase, of how things (in the broadest sense of the term) hang together (in the broadest sense of the term).[18] Not surprisingly, Hegel even rejects the idea that the real distinction between science and philosophy is that between the empirical and the a priori. After all, mechanics uses mathematics, which is the gold standard of all a priori disciplines. Even for the most seemingly a priori of his own works—the first two volumes of his *Science of Logic*—Hegel claims that his theory "is consequently...a critique which considers [determinations of thought] not in terms of the abstract form of apriority as opposed to the a posteriori, but rather considers them themselves in their particular content."[19] In fact, in his actual description of scientific practice, he accuses some of the natural sciences of his time of being too metaphysical and thus failing to be sufficiently empirical.[20]

Third, what Hegel takes from his immensely detailed study of the state of the art of the natural sciences in the early nineteenth century is that there are three different types of explanation for what is really at work (wirklich) in the natural world.[21] There are mechanical explanations, which explain the whole in terms of the causal interactions of its parts (each of which is identifiable outside of its position in the whole). However, mechanical explanations (or so he thought, basing his claim on the going physical theories of the time) cannot explain how different substances are generated. For that, one requires chemical explanations to account for how different substances have an affinity or lack of affinity for each other in various combinations (in which the chemical "whole" thus plays an explanatory role different from what it does in mechanical explanations). Finally, there are biological explanations that are teleological in a functionalist sense, where the parts (as organs) cannot be identified as organic functions outside of their place within the organic whole—that is, one cannot identify an eye as an eye without taking into account how it functions in the organism for sight. Each of these types of explanations runs into fundamental philosophical difficulty when it claims to be absolute, to be an explanation that requires no further explanation outside of itself (to be, in effect, the unconditioned). None of them runs into any a priori difficulty when they are taken to be the explanatory enterprises they are.

The philosophy of nature thus deals with the kinds of conceptual problems that arise when anything "finite" is asserted to be the "unconditioned." The philosophy of nature is an investigation of the antinomies produced by the key concepts of the natural sciences—if there are any antinomies there to be found.

A fully enchanted nature—one that is understood as the expression of some divine purpose or as the locus of unobservable potentials for perfection—is not one suitable for scientific investigation, although the reasons for this unsuitability emerged not primarily at first as the result of philosophical dissatisfaction with the concept of an enchanted nature. It was instead the success of natural science itself that showed that much of what had been considered to be an expression of the various perfections inherent in the natural order (such as the sharp distinction between movement in the sublunary and superlunary spheres) had been rendered obsolete by the construction of adequate scientific theories that were confirmed by empirical evidence.

This is not to say that Hegel simply cedes all authority to the natural sciences in interpreting nature. Rather, on his view, it is when we properly rethink the nature of our own mindful agency, Geist, that we come to see nature as the "other" of Geist. In Hegel's more dialectical terms, "we" as natural creatures make ourselves distinct from nature. This nature, from which we have distinguished ourselves, is not anything that stands, as it were, in a friendly relationship with us or that is an expression of the grand providential plan of the universe. Indeed, such a disenchanted nature as a whole threatens no longer to be understood as responding to human aspirations at all, and if so, nature and religion part ways. It is thus in disenchanting nature and coming to a new understanding of ourselves that we make way for a genuinely naturalist, scientific account of nature, and, in turn, the success of the natural sciences further underwrites this new conception of *Geist*.

The task of a *Naturphilosophie* thus is linking natural science with metaphysics in something like the following sense.[22] It has to show what nature as a whole must be like if nature is indeed the kind of object that is best studied by empirical natural science. However, that kind of study is not itself a natural scientific empirical look at nature but rather an interpretive and evaluative look at science's study of nature. It attempts to show whether, for example, the kind of law/event model of explanation that dominates post-Baconian and post-Galilean science (which supplanted the older rationalist model of explaining nature in terms of inherent properties accessible to pure reason alone) can in fact be taken to be a rational account of nature as a whole, that is, of what nature, interpreted as governed by the law/event model of explanation, must itself be like. It must also evaluate the claim as to whether the disenchanted nature investigated by the natural sciences is itself absolute. Likewise, it has to show how the metaphysical issue between those two models of explanation does not threaten the rationality of the scientific enterprise altogether. The "thing" that the law/event model studies is, after all, an independent thing, identifiable apart from all its other relations and thus the proper object of a rigorously empirical study that looks for its causal relations to other things. However, the thing as so studied is itself dependent for what it is on its causal relations to other things. The "thing" is thus both independent and dependent, but, so Hegel's thought goes, this contested metaphysical status does not threaten the rationality of empirical science.

Now, not surprisingly, developments in the natural sciences since Hegel's own time have at least thrown into question, if not entirely invalidated, a great many of his particular views on scientific issues, but the way they have done this is fully consistent with Hegel's own views about the nature of conceptual content.

One of the many places where Hegel's own *Naturphilosophie* runs into trouble has to do with Hegel's own ideas about how best to comprehend biological explanation. Hegel thinks that the only rational position to take in biology is a form of holism, a rather strong position that seems to violate his own strictures on introducing metaphysical constraints on scientific theory. Relying on his tripartite characterization of explanations in nature (mechanical, chemical, and biological), Hegel concludes that, unlike mechanical wholes, organic wholes are simply not analyzable into their parts, and thus there can be no mechanical or purely chemical explanation of life.[23] Now, to be sure, that restraint comes, for Hegel, from the way nature actually is and not because philosophy is imposing some kind of a priori restraints on what can count as biology. In arguing for this restraint, Hegel is claiming that this is what empirical biology has revealed about nature (that is, up until the 1820s). A *Naturphilosophie* must base its interpretation on those find-ings, not on some a priori scheme devised in advance of empirical biology.

In fact, to say that in principle there could never be any mechanical explana-tion of life unfortunately looks just like it is putting constraints on what empirical biology can find, a view that would violate Hegel's own views on the nature of conceptual content. Nonetheless, even if Hegel's claim is relativized into the more restricted view that, given the findings of biology in the 1820s, such explanation is impossible, it runs into a specific factual difficulty. In 1828, in Berlin—while Hegel was still alive and teaching (he died in 1831)—Friedrich Wöhler acciden-tally synthesized urea in his laboratory, thus demonstrating (although he had no prior intention to do so) that a discipline of organic chemistry was in principle possible. Wöhler's discovery set in motion a program for explaining the nature of organic matter in terms rooted in inorganic chemical and mechanical models.

Now, Hegel's particular discussions about the state of physics, chemistry, and biology have an unmistakable antiquarian tint to them, and it is fairly easy to keep adding to the list of scientific revolutions since Hegel's death in 1831, which heightens that tint even more. Since the invention of quantum chemistry in the twentieth century has thrown into question Hegel's own rejection of so-called mechanical models of explanation in chemistry, and since evolutionary theory after Darwin has reasonably shown that there are mechanisms at work in the origin of the species (natural selection and sexual selection), it thus seems odd to continue to deny that mechanical explanations can also have a perfectly good place in biological explanations of the world. Indeed, one way of reading Darwinian theory suggests that the equation of reductionism with mechanistic explanations (an implicit belief held by both Hegel and his Romantic counterparts) is itself not true. Robert Brandon, for example, has argued that it is surely an empirical question as to whether natural selection operates at the group level or the individual level, whereas metaphysical reductionism has to hold that any such group-level mechanistic explanation must be a priori reducible to lower level mechanistic workings.[24] To hold a priori that it must work at the individual level would thus amount to imposing metaphysical standards on the practice of empirical natural science, thus violating one of the crucial strictures Hegel him-self puts on such accounts. (Hegel's own opposition to evolutionary accounts of the distinctions among species is a special case.)[25]

Hegel's overall point is that the problem with nature as it is conceived on the scientific model and reconstructed in *Naturphilosophie* is that it is a disenchanted nature. On its own, nature is incapable of organizing itself into better and worse exemplifications of anything. Hegel calls this incapability the "impotence of nature."[26] Indeed, it is only when life appears in nature that it even makes sense to speak of better and worse since only organisms display the kind of self-directing, functional structure that makes the application of such terms meaningful. However, even at the level of organic life, the stage of natural development at which the terms *better* and *worse* begin to become meaningful, nature remains impotent since nature on its own cannot organize itself into something like the best version of a lion, a rose, or a trout, much less organize itself as a whole into a better whole.

As a whole, nature aims at nothing, even if there are some creatures in the natural order that do aim at some things.[27] In fact, taken as a whole, nature does not constitute a genuine "whole" at all, at least in the sense that nature "as a whole" cannot be made fully intelligible to pure reason. The intelligibility of nature as a whole is only partial, and the true understanding of nature thus requires not merely conceptual analysis but hard empirical work—the work of the natural sciences. This is a problem with nature—it is not in league with us—but it is not a problem, as it were, for nature itself. It is only when human mindful agency arrives on the planet that the issue arises about what it means for that kind of creature to be the best it can be, and that issue can only be formulated in terms of the human form of life as self-consciousness, where we, as self-interpreting animals, have a historically developing conception of what it is to be the best exemplifications of the agents we are and thus where we are in the position of actually aiming at realizing such a conceptions in our lives. Nature "as a whole" is present only to such self-conscious creatures in thought, which is to say "nature as a whole" is "ideal."[28] Nature does not deal with itself as a whole. Nature has no problems with itself. It is we who have problems with nature.

## 1: Animal Life

The philosophical problem with organic life (and animal life in particular) is that reflection on it in terms of the natural sciences and our own experience of nature seem to lead in us opposite directions. As is often the case, Kant's formulation of the problem points the way for Hegel. On the one hand, the world as we must experience it requires a mechanical explanation. On the other hand, we cannot make sense of organic life without bringing in the conception of teleology (of what an organ is for). As with several of Kant's other antinomies, his solution was to say that although we find it unavoidable to ascribe purposes to organisms, we nonetheless cannot make sense of that within the way we must think of the world as a causal system. Our ascription of purposes has only subjective validity, something "we" must do in studying things—which we find unavoidable—and is not a feature of the things being studied.

Against the grain of many of the views prevailing in his own time, Hegel held that animal life must be understood in terms of having a kind of subjectivity on its own, a mode of self-relation as self-maintenance, and that this is not a matter of mere subjective validity. The animal organism, that is, is to be conceived as having a kind of self-contained striving within itself and thus as having a kind of self-relation in that it regulates itself by a series of mechanisms so that it can accomplish what is appropriate for it to accomplish as the animal that it is. As Hegel puts it, this gives us the first step in understanding what his idealist thesis is all about, and it is not the thesis that everything is mental or spiritual in its makeup. Animal life is the first step in moving to idealism since—and it is important to underline Hegel's decidedly anti-Cartesian understanding of animal life here[29]—we recognize that animals have subjectivity in that we must speak of them as having an "inside" and an "outside" that are not merely that of "inside the skin" and "outside the skin."[30] All organisms develop what Hegel calls a center in that the mechanical and biochemical processes of the organism are oriented around the organism's preserving and reproducing itself, and this is all the more pronounced in animal organisms.

Animals have an inwardness, and the animal must also do things to stay alive. Now, this inwardness is not that of a realm of special private mental facts accessible only to the animal, but a mode of registering both itself and its environment for the sake of its own preservation. The animal registers its environment through what Hegel calls sensation, *Empfindung* (which also carries the connotations of "feeling").[31] For the animal, its environment is thus something "outer" to its own purposes (where the purposes are taken as the various organic functions working together to keep the animal alive and to reproduce itself). In Hegel's terms, the environment is the negative of the animal's inwardness in that it sets the limits against which the animal's own inwardness is determined. In this context, what that means is that the subjective interiority of an animal life-form can be genuinely determined only as demarcated from what it must sense as "outer" to itself. (We should also note that although it is we, not the nonlinguistic animal, who fully articulate the "outer" of the animal's "inner," it is not "we" who determine what counts as the animal's functioning well.)

The existence of the animal is not that of a nonorganic thing, like a stone. Through its nervous system, the animal establishes a self-relation different from inorganic things.[32] Although the stone may indeed respond to its environment by, say, dissolving in humid conditions, and although it is in the nature of the stone to decompose by virtue of exposure to, say, salty water, the stone does not do anything to accomplish this.[33] On the other hand, by virtue of having a nervous system, the animal establishes a relation to itself that gives it an "inner" that is not merely, as we mentioned, spatial in character (not merely "inside the skin").[34] For Hegel, very importantly, animals may thus be said to be the subjects of their lives. Whereas the stone simply is, the animal is what it is by maintaining itself and therefore sustaining a different kind of self-relation.

This is what it means for the animal to have a teleological structure to itself— that is, that there are some things (organs) in it that can be said to work well or badly, given the animal's needs—and thus there are things that can be said to be good or bad for the animal. For this reason, with the appearance of organic life on the planet, disease also enters the picture, since for each animal or plant there is some way in which some organ or part of itself can be interfering with the plant's or the animal's achieving the goals that are built into that life-form. Because of this kind of self-relation, all animals (obviously including self-interpreting ones) can become ill, can fail to function well, whereas the stone, as Hegel says, cannot become sick.[35] The way in which the concept of disease functions in our under-standings of animal life shows that, first of all, we seek to explain it in purely physical terms—that the animal is in a certain state because of x, y, z factors—but its being in certain states interferes with its natural functioning when the animal is taken as a whole (as a distinct substance). To speak of diseases in plant and animal life is thus not merely a matter of subjective validity, of our having to describe things in this or that way because we have trouble doing otherwise. It is a matter of whether the plant or animal really is diseased, that is, really is in a state that interferes with its proper functioning.[36] If that is true, then there are functions "in" nature, although this does not imply any kind of metaphysical vitalism or require the postulation of new forces to explain the existence of such functions. Purposiveness exists in nature, even if nature as a whole is not purposive.

## 2:  The Inwardness of Animal Life

The animal acts on its environment in light of its sensation, that is, its inward sensing of its outer environment. Hegel makes a terminological distinction bet-ween this meaning of *sensing* (as registering within itself the unity of itself and its environment) and *representation* (*Vorstellung*), which he reserves for self-reflective human consciousness. Hegel claims that the animal does indeed have experiential content in its sensing but that this content is not in the same shape as that which appears in human reflective consciousness (although Hegel also says that the content in an animal's sensation may be regarded as only possible content, in that it cannot serve as a ground for further inference).[37]

The responsiveness an agent displays toward the world (the physical world and other agents) thus has various "moments" that can be distinguished although not separated from each other, each of which manifests a kind of self-presence. There is what Hegel calls the "soul," the level of embodied engagement with the world and others in which a variety of animal motor skills are at work. At this level of engagement, one should expect that there will be far more at work in guiding and shaping behavior than what will be fully present to a subject in his most fully self-conscious life. However, exactly how such motor skills function (if and when they function at all) is a matter for empirical research, not for philosophical argument. (That prereflective grasp of things also means that we will not always be self-consciously responsive to reasons in our behavior, since there is more in our processing the world than appears in our conscious life. Our limited awareness of the world around us involves what Hegel calls an "infinite periphery.")[38] This is again only an animal-level of normativity infused with a capacity for fully self-conscious normative behavior. In the terms of this level of speaking about agency, one cannot yet speak of there being a fully drawn distinc-tion between the normative and the nonnormative (or the subjective and the objective) at work. More like Merleau-Ponty's conception of the agent's "phenomenal body" in his *Phenomenology of Perception*, Hegel's conception involves a prior form of self-acquaintance that, as Merleau-Ponty puts it, is that of a "subject-object," a body perceived from the "inside" of subjective quasi animal awareness that projects outward its intention to act in the world.[39] Our presence to ourselves is undeveloped at this point, consisting in a set of circumstances having to do with tasks to be performed and goals to be achieved. As Hegel puts it, that kind of knowledge, even when it has to do with highly abstract matters for which a reflective capacity is a necessary condition, itself involves a fluency that "consists in having the particular knowledge or kind of activities immediately to mind in any case that occurs, even, we may say, *immediate in our very limbs*, in an activity directed outwards."[40]

On Hegel's account, the difference between animal and human mentality does not rest on the idea that the former is nonnormative (or that it is merely sentient, in Robert Brandom's phrase) whereas human mentality is also normative (or what Brandom calls sapient).[41] In the Hegelian view, there is a normativity already at work in nature in the sense that for organic life, there can be goods and evils for plants and animals—and thus reasons for plants and animals to respond in one way or another. In animals, the concept of an action takes shape in that the animal (depending on the complexity of, for example, its nervous system) can form plans, take steps to satisfy those plans, in some cases reevaluate the plan in light of new information, and so forth. Hegel notes (with an explicit reference that he is following Aristotle on this point) that the difference between human mindful agency and animal action is that the animal nonetheless does not "know his purposes as purposes."[42] To appropriate some terminology from John McDowell, the animal cannot respond to reasons *as* reasons since the animal lacks the capacity to make judgments that can then serve in inferences.[43] The animal response to normativity exists only *an sich*, in itself, because the goals at work in animal life cannot be entertained *as* goals. The animal does not entertain possibilities for living its life one way as opposed to another.[44] Animals may have reasons, but they do not respond to reasons "as" reasons.[45]

Moreover, the animal does not have the power (so far as we can tell) to figure out a way to actualize the possibility of understanding its reasons as reasons. The animal has no other goal than itself. It exists ultimately to reproduce itself, but even there, it has no conceptual awareness—no developed negativity, in Hegel's terminology—of itself as a member of a species. The lizard, the dog, and the dolphin reproduce themselves, but (at least on all the evidence we have) none of them can entertain the question of whether, for example, it is overall a better thing that there be, say, more dolphins. The animal encountering another animal of its species for reproductive purposes is aware not of the species per se but only of the particular other animal as an individual, and it encounters it in terms of satisfying a goal that it has by virtue of its organic nature, although it cannot entertain that goal *as* a goal. The animal "only senses the species and does not know of it. In the animal, the soul is not yet for the soul, the universal is not yet as such for the universal."[46] In this way, the animal is literally an end in itself (a *Selbstzweck*), since the animal's whole existence is exhausted by itself and the goals internal to its form of life.

Humans and animals both have inner lives, but the animal's inwardness is not itself a matter of awareness *as* inwardness. The animal strives for something but is not aware of its striving as a striving.[47] There is a strong continuity between animal experience and human experience in that both have meaningful content within their experience, but there is also a sharp break between animal and human awareness in that only humans can take up this content in a fully conceptual way by virtue of the more complicated human form of self-relation as self-consciousness. How does Hegel think he can manage that distinction?

Hegel's proposal is that the move from our animal life to our fully self-conscious lives should be conceived in terms of stages lying between the kind of goal-directedness characteristic of animal life and the rational character of self-conscious life, and these stages should not be interpreted as separable stages of self-conscious life (as if the later stages could exist apart from the earlier stages). They are, to be sure, distinguishable from each other, but that does not imply that each of them occurs independently of the others or that each stage succeeds the other in time. In this respect, the unity of the stages replicates what Hegel thought Kant should have said about the unity of concepts and intuitions in the critical system: They are distinguishable but not separable from each other.[48]

Thus, we have to think of how such human awareness incorporates within itself this kind of animal life as a series of stages that mediate each other. Now, there are several caveats that have to be entered about Hegel's reflections on this. Given his own view about how the *Naturphilosophie* is to be carried out, much of what he has to say about this should, on Hegel's very own terms, be out of date, since the meaning of the concepts at work in natural science—such as "mass" or "species"—cannot be established (except very abstractly) apart from the use that is made of them in the theories in which they appear. That in turn means that any *Naturphilosophie* will be intimately entangled with whatever the going theories are at the time and likewise will be entangled with whatever deeper errors were at work in them. It would be surprising even to Hegel if the sciences since his own time had not made any changes to the way key terms were put to use since the late-eighteenth and early-nineteenth centuries.

## B: From Animal Subjectivity to Human Subjectivity

Hegel distinguishes, as we noted, between this kind of animal awareness (or animal soul) and that of representational (*vorstellende*) consciousness. The relation between subject and world requires a differentiation between the ways in which an animal, in pursuing its own goals, senses the world and its own states and the way it gathers this kind of sensing into an organic whole. In moving to human consciousness, there must also be a way of distinguishing ourselves from those sensings so that they become representations (*Vorstellungen*) capable of conveying truth or falsity (in the more ordinary and not the fully inflated Hegelian sense of truth). The stage of animal awareness is only a content "in itself" in the sense that the animal—depending on how developed its neuromotor system is—can use such awareness to form beliefs (or some kind of analogue of belief, depending on how one wishes to restrict the term *belief*) about its world (such as "the prey is now in striking distance") and then, as factors in its environment or itself change, adjust its behavior in light of those goals.[49] To go back to Hegelian language, the animal cannot actualize this set of contents "in itself" into full fodder for inference—it cannot separate the belief from the ground of the belief. Or to put it another way while remaining within Hegelian terms, the animal cannot relate the abstract meaning to the concrete meaning.[50] For the animal, the world is a unity of the subjective and the objective, and thus animals do not have an objective world confronting them since they cannot distinguish the objective from the subjective as such—even if some animals can perhaps make something like that distinction when, for example, they hunt for food or flee from predators.

To draw the distinction between the subjective and the objective and to have the distinction itself be present to oneself as a matter of avowal, one requires self-consciousness. Or to put the same point differently, self-consciousness precisely is having that distinction present to oneself. If Hegel would have had to contend with something like a Darwinian evolutionary theory instead of the pre-Darwinian theories he in fact rejected, he would no doubt have been pressed by the empirical evidence to note that in the evolution of animal subjectivity—in life's establishing a practical relationship to itself that qualifies as "innerness"—the perceptual system would have to have developed a kind of accuracy or correctness built into it such that animals could track their environments in a way that would fit their goals, and, with the development of self-conscious animals, that earlier form of accuracy in, for example, stalking prey or avoiding predators would develop into a full-fledged conception of truth and falsity. That much would be consistent with Hegel's views, although by no means identical with the ones he actually espoused.

Thus, Hegel thinks that at least three distinctions have to be drawn when one speaks of animal subjectivity. One must distinguish the specific ways in which the animal registers the world—as we have seen, Hegel calls this "sensing" and not "representing"—from the way the animal organizes its feeling of itself and its environment in light of these various sensings.[51] (Hegel calls the latter "feeling," even while noting that ordinary German does not itself draw such a sharp distinction between "sensation," *Empfindung*, and "feeling," *Gefühl*.)[52] The first has to do with the way in which the organism registers the world and is attracted to some things while being repelled by others. The second distinction has to do with the way in which animal life learns to put its "sensings" into order and, in the cases of the so-called higher animals, forgo certain attractions to better satisfy its inherent goals.

The third distinction has to do with what it would mean to speak of the actualization of the "soul." The soul, our animal existence, is, in Hegel's own terms, the "ideal simple being-for-itself (or self-relation) of the bodily as *bodily*," whereas in self-conscious life there is the practical distinction established between one's self and one's body.[53] A self-conscious agent both is his body (since the person is an animal) and is not his body since the agent establishes a practical distinction between himself and his body.[54] (This "is and is not" marks a fundamental tension in human experience, which as both Kant and Hegel diagnose the matter, can mislead us into thinking that mind and body must therefore be two separate "things" or separate "substances.")[55]

What animals and agents have in common is not some form of "givenness" of sensation, as one might imagine (that is, the idea that in our seeing something blue, we are having the same qualitative sensation that the color-sighted animal is having).[56] Both humans and animals are characterized in terms of the type of self-relation they maintain, and what is different between them is the kind of self-relation that marks the distinction between the animal soul and human agency. For the human agent, experience is that of a world of objects that exist independently of us and that appear to us from our different perspectives. That difference—the object as it is apart from us and our perspective on the object—is a distinction that is present to a self-conscious agent, even if the distinction itself is not always explicitly made. Moreover, at the level of the soul (that of animal awareness), such a distinction can in principle be practically put to use—although it is an empirical issue as to which animals, if any, actually do put it to use—even though the distinction as such cannot be drawn solely from within the sphere of animal awareness itself.

Once again, we see Hegel's background reworking of Aristotle being put to Hegel's own use—that is, being rendered into his own "sublation" of Aristotelian thought.[57] The "actual soul" (the realized soul) has to do with a form of life—human life—that can have that distinction between its experience of the object and the object itself exist as an explicit distinction. As Hegel notes, this difference is marked by the fact that the soul can acquire habits, and for human agency as such, "the soul brings into its bodily activities a universal mode of action, a *rule*, to be transmitted to other activities."[58] In doing so, our animal awareness moves from its animal normativity to something more full-bloodedly normative in its orientation instead of only having the sheer normativity of goal-directed behavior. The soul thus becomes present to itself *as* soul, that is, *as* an inwardness of animal consciousness that now takes its inwardness *as* inwardness.[59] This inwardness is constituted by the animal organism's assuming a relation to itself mediated by its nervous system that puts it into a different kind of relation to itself and its environment than is the case with nonanimals and especially with nonorganic things.[60] (Hegel also holds that fully submitting ourselves to such rules also requires a recognition by other such agents and ultimately a kind of locating ourselves in social space constituted by norms, but introducing that point here would be jumping ahead in the story.)

The actual soul is thus not a correlation between two independent realms (the inner and the outer). It is "this identity of the inner with the outer, where the latter is subjected to the former."[61] The behavior of the animal is to be explained as an expression of its various "inner" states, but the animal remains at one with itself in these expressions. As such an actualized soul—as a human animal life that assumes a normative stance to itself and entertains not only its goals as possibilities but also its own stance to itself as yet another possibility—the actual soul is no longer really a soul at all but a feature of self-conscious agency. With that, a different kind of practical establishment of a self-relation thus comes to be at work in the organism. The human animal now distinguishes itself (as leading a life) from its perspectives on the world it inhabits, and in doing so, it subjects itself to norms that constitute what it is for such a act of making distinctions to take place at all. The freedom it embodies is, as Hegel puts it, both a "freedom from and a freedom in" the natural world, not a dualist account of freedom as involving nonnatural powers.[62]

Hegel's account of the actual soul is thus a nondualist account that stresses the element of inwardness in subjectivity by seeing it as emerging in animal life as having to sustain itself by directing itself to the achievement of goals. Human subjectivity emerges as a kind of reflexive complication of this kind of organic, animal self-relation, not as something radically other than animal life.

Hegel's commitment to this kind of disenchanted Aristotelian naturalism is strong enough for him that, as he puts it, if our theoretical choices really were indeed restricted to either a purely naturalist-materialist account of mindful agency or a dualist account, we would have to opt for the naturalist-materialist account. In his lectures on the subject, he put it this way: The "point of view of materialism" is a view we should in fact "honor" as a way of articulating the unity of mind and nature and overcoming all the dualisms associated with it.[63] Likewise, if we thought that our only alternatives were subjective idealism—the view that nature is somehow only a construct out of our own subjective experience—or non-Aristotelian naturalism, then we would have to choose naturalism (or, for that matter, even dualism) over the "belief in miracles" that subjective idealism seems to force on us. Indeed, as Hegel wryly puts it, it would be "in order to avoid [such] miracles...to avoid the dissolution of the steady course of nature's laws, that we would prefer to stick with either materialism or with inconsistent dualism."[64]

## C:  Animal Life and the Will

In his own notes for his popular lectures on the philosophy of history, Hegel states his own views about the will in a way that both replicate and extend his own statements about Aristotle's views in other contexts:

> Laws and principles have no immediate life or validity in themselves. The activity which puts them into operation and endows them with real existence has its source in the needs, impulses, inclinations, and passions of man. If I put something into practice and give it a real existence, I must have some personal interest in doing so; I must be personally involved in it, and hope to obtain satisfaction through its accomplishment.[65]

In putting his point this way, Hegel is transforming Aristotle's own system—with its substantialist and essentialist metaphysics of potentialities and actualities—into a theory of how "the concept" realizes itself. Thought and the will, Hegel says, are "not two separate faculties; on the contrary, the will is a particular way of thinking—thinking translating itself into existence, thinking as the drive to give itself existence."[66] That is, the activity of willing something is a mode in which the conceptual is shown to be already at work in reality—in which it is, in Hegel's updating of Aristotelian terminology, *wirklich*, actual, effective.[67] Saying that the will is "thinking translating itself into existence" is Hegel's way of saying that the conceptual is actualized in bodily doings. Moreover, for the will to actualize thought, there must be a mediation between principle and passion: For general principles to have any grip on an agent, they must appeal to the singularity of the agent's life, be reasons for him or her as a singular entity to act.

Hegel contrasts this view of the will—as the capacity of thought to give itself existence and thereby actualize itself—with what he takes to be the more received and therefore ordinary view of willing. That view sees the will as a special faculty on its own, a separate part of the mind, the lever one pulls to put deliberative judgment into practice.[68] On Hegel's diagnosis, this conception arises naturally out of the ordinary ways in which we reflect on our lives. Our very language itself suggests to us that the difference between the "inner" (thought) and "outer" (bodily movement) is a difference between two separate "things"—mental states and bodily movements—and since there is often and obviously a discrepancy between what we thought we were doing and what somebody (others or even ourselves) took to be what we actually did, we are very naturally led to the view that the two realms "must be" distinct from each other.

The natural tendency of that view, when philosophically articulated, develops into the more Augustinian, non-Aristotelian voluntarist conception of freedom as the result of an "inner" act of will producing an action through some type of nonstandard causality in that the will (seen as one "thing") causes another "thing" to occur (the bodily movement). However, in the terms of Hegel's more Aristotelian conception, the relation between intention and will should not be seen as a relation between two "things" at all but in the relation of the contents—the meanings—of the "inner" intention with the contents (the meaning) of the "outer" bodily movements. This is why Hegel prefers the metaphor of "translation" in speaking of the relation between the "inner" and the "outer" to other metaphors of, say, pushing or pulling. The "inner" content is "translated" into "outer" content. The metaphor of "translation" is better suited to bring out the different ways in which intentions-actions as a whole can be reinterpreted in various ways. (An intention-action complex is like a text in that it is as capable of reinterpretation as any other text; sometimes the meaning is rather clear, and at other times it is more up for grabs. The metaphor of the text dovetails nicely with Hegel's own metaphor of translation: Sometimes, translations are perfect in that the original and its translated expression match up, but very often, the translation changes the original.)

In Hegel's metaphor of translation, the inner intention and the outer action are two sides of the same coin, and in Hegelian language, each is said to be a moment of the other. For something to be a "moment" in the Hegelian sense is for it to be a distinguishable but nonseparable component of what is supposed to be conceived as a whole. The intention is thus not a separate "thing" from the action. Rather, an intention (the "inner") is an "action on the way to being realized," and an action (the "outer") is a "realized intention." In keeping with Hegel's language, one could put it this way: The intention is the action in its inner "moment," and the action is the intention in its outer "moment."[69] It probably goes without saying that intentions can fail to be realized in actions, and sometimes for the most obvious reasons: One changes one's mind, one forgets, one is prevented from acting, and so forth. However, if one sees the intention as an "action on the way to being realized," one is not tempted to think of the intention as some separable, determinate mental state that is merely to be correlated with an action.

To have a will, therefore, is to have a conceptual capacity that has as a "moment" of itself an embodied agent located in a natural and social world, and that element of embodiment in both the physical world and the social world is a component of the spontaneity of thought-as-willing.[70] Since the will is a "form of thought," what distinguishes having a will from what one might describe as a merely animal response to any perceived good or evil is, in Hegel's language, to grasp the goal as a goal (or the reason *as* a reason) and to grasp the reason *an sich*—in itself, or "as such"—something that does not automatically specify what it would mean to realize that reason.

When an agent successfully unites the affective and the cognitive, she achieves a kind of practical truth, that is, not only a grasp of some isolated propositional truth (which would only be "abstract" in Hegel's sense) but also an affective relation to that truth. The free agent manifests this practical truth by knowing what she must do and doing it.[71] Without the relation to "needs, impulses, inclinations, and passions," no action will take place, and the agent will have shown that, however sophisticated her grasp of the propositions at stake, she is not in possession of practical truth.

In doing that, one gives shape to one's will in resolving to do this and not that, that is, in putting limits on one's willing, in moving oneself to do one thing and not another.[72] For self-conscious creatures, the "moving principle" at work is not that merely of animal motion—which basically has to do with the preservation of itself as an individual and with the preservation of the species—but the series of social reasons "out there in the social world," which themselves go beyond the merely natural goods of self-preservation and propagation (for example, the various ways one might think, say, of honoring a friendship or of choosing a career), however much these social reasons might have some basis in those principles of animal motion.[73] Animals may have reasons for action (such as fleeing from a predator, going after something for food, taking this as a mate, etc.), but only self-conscious agents have the capacity to understand these goals as goals, reasons *as* reasons.

*Notes*

1. For example, Hegel himself notes: "The books of Aristotle on the soul, along with his discussions of its special aspects and states, are for this reason still by far the most admirable, perhaps even the sole, work of speculative interest on this topic. The main aim of a philosophy of mind can only be to reintroduce the conception as such into the cognition of mind, and so reinterpret the lesson of those Aristotelian books." Hegel, *Enzyklopädie der philosophischen Wissenschaften III*, §378; Hegel et al., *Hegel's Philosophy of Mind: Being Part Three of the "Encyclopaedia of the Philosophical Sciences"* (1830), p. 3. This is not to claim that Aristotle is the only philosopher who influenced Hegel; the point here is not the historical issue of who and what influenced Hegel at what time—an issue that is both fascinating in its own right and always vexatious with Hegel, since he seems to have been influenced by everybody. Hegel's systemic and philological relation to Aristotle's work has been admirably explored by Alfredo Ferrarin, *Hegel and Aristotle* (Modern European Philosophy; Cambridge: Cambridge University Press, 2001), xxii, 442 pp. Hegel's praise of Aristotle's theory of the mind as the touchstone for much of his own thought is not something that has gone unnoticed. See, for example, Michael Wolff, *Das Körper-Seele Problem: Kommentar Zu Hegel, Enzyklopädie* (1830), §389 (Frankfurt a.M.: Klostermann, 1992); Robert B. Pippin, *Hegel's Practical Philosophy: Rational Agency as Ethical Life* (Cambridge: Cambridge University Press, 2008), xi, 308 pp. G. R. G. Mure had already some time ago put the relation to Aristotle front and center in his work on Hegel: G. R. G. Mure, *A Study of Hegel's Logic* (Oxford: Clarendon, 1950), viii, 375 pp. In his celebrated study of Hegel's ethical theory, Allen Wood drew attention to the very Aristotelian character of many of Hegel's claims; see Allen W. Wood, *Hegel's Ethical Thought* (Cambridge: Cambridge University Press, 1990), xxi, 293 pp.
2. For a summary of the debate, see T. H. Irwin, "Who Discovered the Will?" *Philosophical Perspectives*, 6 (1992), 453–73. Irwin claims that the Greeks did in fact have all the elements of a concept of the will. What they did not have, he argues, is the more specifically Augustinian "voluntarist" conception of it.
3. Georg Wilhelm Friedrich Hegel, *Vorlesungen über die Geschichte der Philosophie II*, ed. Eva Moldenhauer and Karl Markus Michel, 20 vols. (Theorie-Werkausgabe, 19; Frankfurt am Main: Suhrkamp, 1969), p. 221: "The best that we have on psychology, all the way up to the most recent times, is what we have from Aristotle—likewise with what he thought about the will, freedom and the further determinations of imputation, intention, etc." Whereas although in Hegel, *Enzyklopädie der philosophischen Wissenschaften III*, §482; and Hegel et al., *Hegel's Philosophy of Mind: Being Part Three of the "Encyclopaedia of the Philosophical Sciences"* (1830), p. 239, he does say that "the Greeks and Romans, Plato and Aristotle, did not have it [the Idea of freedom]" in its "actuality," he also clearly does not deny that Aristotle had a concept of the will, only that he failed to attain the full "Idea" of freedom, since he also endorsed slavery.
4. Hegel, *Vorlesungen über die Geschichte der Philosophie II*, p. 222.

5. Ibid., pp. 222–23: "From a practical consideration [Aristotle] distinguishes a rational and an irrational part in the soul; in the latter, νοῦς [spirit] is only δυνάμει [potentiality], and what befits it are sensations, inclinations, passions, and affects. In the rational side of the soul, there is intellect (Verstand), wisdom, level-headedness, knowledge—all of which have their place. However, they do not yet constitute the virtues. The virtues first exist in the unity of rational with the irrational side. We call those things virtues when the passions (inclinations) comport themselves to reason in such a way that they do what reason commands. If insight (λόγος) is bad or not even present but passion (inclination, the heart) acquits itself well, then good-heartedness can very well be at work, but there is no virtue because the ground (λόγος, reason) is lacking, [that is,] the νοῦς, that is necessary for virtue."

6. Ibid., p. 223: "What is impelling is impulse and inclination. That is, the particular, with a view to the practical, is closer to the subject that is on the way to actualization. The subject is particularized in his activity and it is necessary that he be identical therein with the universal."

7. "The voluntary would seem to be that of which the moving principle is in the agent himself, he being aware of the particular circumstances of the action." Aristotle, The Nicomachean Ethics, trans. W. D. Urmson, J. O. Ross, and J. L. Ackrill (The World's Classics; New York: Oxford University Press, 1998), xxxvi, 283 pp., p. 52.

8. See Susan Sauvé Meyer, "Aristotle on the Voluntary," in Richard Kraut, ed., The Blackwell Guide to Aristotle's Nicomachean Ethics (Malden, Mass.: Blackwell, 2006), 137–58.

9. "But actions and states of character are not voluntary in the same way; for we are masters of our actions from the beginning right to the end, if we know the particular facts, but though we control the beginning of our states of character the gradual progress is not obvious any more than it is in illnesses; because it was in our power, however, to act in this way or not in this way, therefore the states are voluntary." Aristotle, The Nicomachean Ethics, p. 63.

10. This reconceived Aristotelian conception is thus in the same family as what Charles Taylor calls an "expressivist" conception of action, although it is not identical with it; Hegel certainly does not conceive of action as merely the expression of an already determinate meaning; the action as a whole—intention and action—realize a meaning. It also fits with much of both Allen Wood's and Robert Pippin's characterization of Hegel's conception of action. See Wood, Hegel's Ethical Thought, and Pippin, Hegel's Practical Philosophy.

11. On Hegel's understanding of freedom as not requiring any special form of causality, see also Paul Redding, Hegel's Hermeneutics (Ithaca, N.Y.: Cornell University Press, 1996), xvi, 262 pp.; and Pippin, Hegel's Practical Philosophy.

12. There are numerous passages where Hegel speaks of animals as having "selves." Here are two representative ones. Hegel, Enzyklopädie der philosophischen Wissenschaften II, §371 Zusatz; Hegel and Miller, Hegel's Philosophy of Nature: Being Part Two of the Encyclopedia of the Philosophical Sciences (1830), Translated from Nicolin and Pöggeler's Edition (1959), and from the Zusätze in Michelet's Text (1847), p. 429: "The organism exists then in the opposed forms of being and of the self, and the self (just as what is for itself) is the negative of itself." Hegel, Enzyklopädie der philosophischen Wissenschaften III; Hegel, Enzyklopädie der philosophischen Wissenschaften II, §351, Zusatz: "With animals, the self is for the self, and the reason is the following: the universal of subjectivity, the determination of sensation (Empfindung), which is the differentia specifica, is the absolutely distinguishing feature of the animal.... This ideality, which constitutes sensation, is in nature the highest wealth of existence, because everything is compacted therein."

13. The most thoroughgoing contemporary "spiritual monist" interpretation is that offered by Frederick Beiser in Hegel (Routledge Philosophers; New York: Routledge, 2005), xx, 353 pp. In contrast to a "spiritual" monism, Rolf-Peter Horstmann, Die Grenzen Der Vernunft: Eine Untersuchung Zu Zielen Und Motiven Des Deutschen Idealismus (Frankfurt a.M.: Anton Hain, 1991), sees Hegel as offering a "monism of reason," a view that the entire world is produced by a kind of cosmic rationality working its way out.

14. Hegel, Enzyklopädie der philosophischen Wissenschaften II, §246; Hegel and Miller, Hegel's Philosophy of Nature: Being Part Two of the Encyclopedia of the Philosophical Sciences (1830),

*Translated from Nicolin and Pöggeler's Edition (1959), and from the Zusätze in Michelet's Text (1847)*, 9: "There is a metaphysics which is all the rage in our time, which holds that we cannot know things because they are completely closed off to us. One could put it this way: Not even the animals are as stupid as these metaphysicians, for they go directly to the things, seize them, grasp them and consume them." See also Georg Wilhelm Friedrich Hegel, *Grundlinien der Philosophie des Rechts*, ed. Eva Moldenhauer and Karl Markus Michel, 20 vols. (Theorie-Werkausgabe, 7; Frankfurt a. M.: Suhrkamp, 1969), 20 v., §44; Georg Wilhelm Friedrich Hegel, *Elements of the Philosophy of Right*, ed. Allen W. Wood, trans. Hugh Barr Nisbet (Cambridge Texts in the History of Political Thought; Cambridge: Cambridge University Press, 1991), lii, 514 pp., p. 76: "The free will is consequently the idealism which does not consider things as they are to be existing in and for themselves, whereas realism declares those things to be absolute, even if they are found only in the form of finitude. Even the animal does not subscribe to this realist philosophy, for it consumes things and thereby proves that they are not absolutely self-sufficient." Hegel, *Phänomenologie des Geistes*; Georg Wilhelm Friedrich Hegel, "Phenomenology of Spirit" (trans. Terry Pinkard), at http://web .me.com/titpaul/Site/Phenomenology_of_Spirit_page.html (¶109): "Nor are the animals excluded from this wisdom. To an even greater degree, they prove themselves to be the most deeply initiated in such wisdom, for they do not stand still in the face of sensuous things, as if those things existed in themselves. Despairing of the reality of those things and in the total certainty of the nullity of those things, they, without any further ado, simply help themselves to them and devour them. Just like the animals, all of nature celebrates these revealed mysteries which teach the truth about sensuous things."

15. As is well known, the term *disenchanted* stems from Max Weber. For the history of Weber's own use of the term, see Hartmut Lehmann, *Die Entzauberung Der Welt: Studien Zu Themen Von Max Weber* (Bausteine Zu Einer Europäischen Religionsgeschichte Im Zeitalter Der Säkularisierung Bd. 11; Göttingen: Wallstein, 2009), 149 pp.

16. The term *Naturphilosophie* is probably better translated as "nature-philosophy" rather than as philosophy of nature. On this sense of *Naturphilosophie*, see Terry Pinkard, *German Philosophy 1760–1860: The Legacy of Idealism* (Cambridge: Cambridge University Press, 2002), x, 382 pp.

17. Hegel, *Enzyklopädie der philosophischen Wissenschaften II*, §246; Hegel and Miller, *Hegel's Philosophy of Nature: Being Part Two of the Encyclopedia of the Philosophical Sciences (1830), Translated from Nicolin and Pöggeler's Edition (1959), and from the Zusätze in Michelet's Text (1847)*, 6.

18. Hegel, *Enzyklopädie der philosophischen Wissenschaften II*, §246; Hegel and Miller, *Hegel's Philosophy of Nature: Being Part Two of the Encyclopedia of the Philosophical Sciences (1830), Translated from Nicolin and Pöggeler's Edition (1959), and from the Zusätze in Michelet's Text (1847)*, 11. Wilfrid Sellars, "Philosophy and the Scientific Image of Man," in *Science, Perception, and Reality* (International Library of Philosophy and Scientific Method; New York: Humanities Press, 1963), 366 pp., p. 35.

19. Hegel, *Wissenschaft Der Logik I*, p. 62; Hegel, *Hegel's Science of Logic*, p. 64: "The objective logic is consequently the genuine critique of those determinations—a critique which considers them not in accordance with the abstract form of apriority as opposed to the a posteriori, but rather considers them themselves in their particular content."

20. On this topic, see especially Sebastian Rand, "The Importance and Relevance of Hegel's Philosophy of Nature," *Review of Metaphysics*, 61/2 (December 2007), 379–400. One of the examples of this type of criticism on Hegel's part is that of the a priori, nonempirical idea that there must be some kind of nonobservable caloric "stuff" that explains heat. Hegel, *Enzyklopädie der philosophischen Wissenschaften II*, §305; Hegel and Miller, *Hegel's Philosophy of Nature: Being Part Two of the Encyclopedia of the Philosophical Sciences (1830), Translated from Nicolin and Pöggeler's Edition (1959), and from the Zusätze in Michelet's Text (1847)*, 153: "Specific heat-capacity, associated with the category of *matter* and *material* (*Stoff*), has led to the representation of *latent, indetectable, fixed heat-material*. As something not perceivable, such a determination does not have the warrant of observation and experience, and as

disclosed, it rests on the presupposition of a material self-sufficiency of heat (cf. Remark to §286). This assumption serves in its way to make the self-sufficiency of heat as that of matter empirically irrefutable, precisely because the assumption is not empirical. If the disappearance of heat, or its appearance is shown to be in a place where it previously was not present, then the disappearance is explained as the concealment or *fixation* of heat, and the appearance is explained as the emergence from indetectability. The metaphysics of self-sufficiency is *opposed* to that experience. Indeed, it is presupposed a priori."

21. See Rand, "The Importance and Relevance of Hegel's Philosophy of Nature." See also Wolfgang Neuser's helpful discussion in his contribution to Herbert Schnädelbach, Ludwig Siep, and Hermann Drüe, *Hegels Philosophie: Kommentare zu den Hauptwerken*, 3 vols. (Suhrkamp Taschenbuch Wissenschaft; Frankfurt am Main: Suhrkamp, 2000), 139–205; Wolfgang Bonsiepen, *Die Begründung einer Naturphilosophie bei Kant, Schelling, Fries und Hegel: Mathematische versus spekulative Naturphilosophie* (Philosophische Abhandlungen Bd. 70; Frankfurt am Main: V. Klostermann, 1997), 651 pp.; Georg Wilhelm Friedrich Hegel, *Hegel's Philosophy of Nature*, ed. Michael John Petry (Muirhead Library of Philosophy; London: Allen & Unwin; New York: Humanities Press, 1970).

22. One of the more troublesome issues in interpreting Hegel has been how to interpret the move from his *Science of Logic* (or the first book of the *Encyclopedia of the Philosophical Sciences*, which more or less recapitulates it in abbreviated form) to the philosophy of nature and then to the philosophy of *Geist*. At least in the terms sketched out here, that transition should be understood in terms of Hegel's own statement that the transition is no real transition at all. ("This determination is not a 'having-been' and a transition [*Übergang*]...in this freedom, no transition takes place." Georg Wilhelm Friedrich Hegel, *Wissenschaft der Logik II*, ed. Eva Moldenhauer and Karl Markus Michel, 20 vols. [Theorie-Werkausgabe, 6; Frankfurt a. M.: Suhrkamp, 1969], 573; Hegel, *Hegel's Science of Logic*, 843.) That is, if it is true that Hegel has no a priori method to apply to the content, and if sublation involves the act of moving to a different context that tames the oppositions of a prior context involving the assertion of the unconditioned (the absolute), then there can be no logical transition (in the narrower sense of Hegel's use of "logic") between the *Science of Logic* and the philosophy of nature. The problem for Hegel is analogous to the problem Kant faced in creating the "transcendental deduction of the categories" in his first *Critique*: Would it be possible for experience to present us with something that did not conform to the categories? At least one way of taking Kant's answer is: No, since we, or at least the structure of human mentality, shaped all experience in terms of the categories, nothing could appear there that was not in conformity with them. Hegel takes up the issue of nature and our experience of nature in the same way—could the philosophy of nature itself confront us with something that contradicted the categories of the *Logic*?—but he clearly could not rely on the idea that we shaped our experience to make nature conform to them. We thus had to investigate the experience of nature and the theories of nature neither with an a priori assurance that everything found there would be in conformity with the more rarified categories of the *Logic*, nor with any advance assurance that the dilemmas would arrange themselves in the same way. This approach to the *Logic* is criticized by Stephen Houlgate, who takes more of a conceptual realist stance toward the book. Stephen Houlgate, *The Opening of Hegel's Logic: From Being to Infinity* (Purdue University Press Series in the History of Philosophy; West Lafayette, Ind.: Purdue University Press, 2006), xix, 456 pp. Other similar conceptual realist stances are given in Robert Stern, "Hegel's Idealism," in Frederick C. Beiser, ed., *The Cambridge Companion to Hegel and Nineteenth-Century Philosophy* (Cambridge: Cambridge University Press, 2008); and in Kenneth R. Westphal, *Hegel's Epistemology: A Philosophical Introduction to the Phenomenology of Spirit* (Indianapolis, Ind.: Hackett, 2003), xvi, 146 pp.

23. Hegel, *Enzyklopädie der philosophischen Wissenschaften II*, §337 *Zusatz*; Hegel and Miller, *Hegel's Philosophy of Nature: Being Part Two of the Encyclopedia of the Philosophical Sciences (1830), Translated from Nicolin and Pöggeler's Edition (1959), and from the Zusätze in Michelet's Text (1847)*, 274: "Life is the unification of opposites in general, not merely that of concept and reality. Life is where the inner and the outer, cause and effect, end and means, subjectivity

and objectivity are one and the same. The genuine determination of life is that, with the unity of concept and reality, this reality does not any longer exist in an immediate way, not in the manner of self-sufficiency as a plurality of properties existing alongside one another. Rather, the concept is the utter ideality of indifferent durable existence. Since here the ideality that we had in chemical processes is posited, so too individuality is posited in its freedom. The subjective, infinite form exists now also in its objectivity, which it was not yet in its shape [as chemical process], because in that shape the determinations of infinite form still have a fixed existence as matters. The abstract concept of the organism, on the contrary, is that the existence of particularities (since they are posited as transient moments of one subject) are adequate to the unity of the concept, whereas in the system of the heavenly bodies, all the particular moments of the concept are freely existing, self-sufficient bodies which have not yet returned into the unity of the concept. The solar system was the first organism, but it was only in itself organic, not yet an organic existence.... What is there is only a mechanical organism.... The individuality of the chemical body can be overpowered by an alien power, but life has its other within itself, is in its own self one rounded-out totality—that is, it is own end (*Selbstzweck*)."

24.  See Robert N. Brandon, *Concepts and Methods in Evolutionary Biology* (Cambridge Studies in Philosophy and Biology; Cambridge: Cambridge University Press, 1996), xiv, 221 pp.

25.  It was not, of course, Darwin's theory that Hegel opposed. Hegel died in 1831, and Darwin's book appeared in 1859. He opposed the view that there had to be an externally teleological explanation of the origin of the species as "completing the series." This was, he thought, empirically vacuous. His own views were influenced by those advanced by his French contemporary, Georges Cuvier, who argued that each organism is an internally structured whole that exists in such a close harmony with its environment that changing any small part of it would damage its ability to survive in that environment. Although Hegel accepted the fact that the earth had a rather violent history of several million years, that there was once a time when there was no life on earth, and that many species of plant and animal life had become extinct, he also believed that empirical biology and comparative anatomy—as practiced by Cuvier—had ruled out evolution as a satisfactory explanation of the origin of the different species. See Hegel, *Enzyklopädie der philosophischen Wissenschaften II*, §339; Hegel and Miller, *Hegel's Philosophy of Nature: Being Part Two of the Encyclopedia of the Philosophical Sciences (1830), Translated from Nicolin and Pöggeler's Edition (1959), and from the Zusätze in Michelet's Text (1847)*, 283–84. In keeping with his own views, Hegel had no theory of his own about the origin of the species except for the general idea that the various species had to precipitate out of some kind of "life process," and he thought that it made more sense to think of each species, more or less, arriving on the scene as fully formed. Thus, in Hegel, *Phänomenologie des Geistes*, 141 (¶171), he says, "Within the universal fluid medium, life in its *motionless* elaboration of itself into various shapes becomes the movement of those shapes, that is, life becomes life as a *process*.... As such, it is life as *living things*....The simple substance of life is thus the estrangement of itself into shapes and is at the same time the dissolution of these durably existing distinctions. The dissolution of this estrangement is to the same extent itself an estrangement, that is, a division of itself into groupings." On evolution, he says, in Hegel, *Enzyklopädie der philosophischen Wissenschaften II*, §249, Zusatz; Hegel and Miller, *Hegel's Philosophy of Nature: Being Part Two of the Encyclopedia of the Philosophical Sciences (1830), Translated from Nicolin and Pöggeler's Edition (1959), and from the Zusätze in Michelet's Text (1847)*, 21: "The way of evolution, which starts from the imperfect and formless, is as follows: at first there was the liquid element and aqueous structures, and from the water there evolved plants, polyps, mollusks, and finally fishes; then from the fishes were evolved the land animals, and finally from the land animals came man. This gradual alteration is called an explanation and understanding. It comes from the philosophy of nature, and it still flourishes. However, although this quantitative difference is of all theories the easiest to understand, it does not really explain anything at all." It is thus not completely implausible that this part of the Hegelian system could be excised without doing much harm to the rest, and if it were, the apparent opposition between

Hegelian idealism and Darwinian evolutionary theory would itself dissolve, leaving the field open for a reconsideration of the links between the two. See James Kreines's speculations on the issue: James Kreines, "Hegel's Metaphysics: Changing the Debate," *Philosophy Compass*, 1/5 (September 2006), 466–80; James Kreines, "Metaphysics without Pre-Critical Monism: Hegel on Lower-Level Natural Kinds and the Structure of Reality," *Bulletin of the Hegel Society of Great Britain*, 57–58 (2008), 48–70; James Kreines, "The Logic of Life: Hegel's Philosophical Defense of Teleological Explanation of Living Beings,"in *The Cambridge Companion to Hegel and Nineteenth-Century Philosophy*, ed. Frederick C. Beiser (Cambridge: Cambridge University Press, 2008).

26. "...die *Ohnmacht* der Natur," in Hegel, *Enzyklopädie der philosophischen Wissenschaften II*, §250; Hegel and Miller, *Hegel's Philosophy of Nature: Being Part Two of the Encyclopedia of the Philosophical Sciences (1830), Translated from Nicolin and Pöggeler's Edition (1959), and from the Zusätze in Michelet's Text (1847)*, 23.

27. As Hegel sums this up: Hegel, *Enzyklopädie der philosophischen Wissenschaften II*; Hegel and Miller, *Hegel's Philosophy of Nature: Being Part Two of the Encyclopedia of the Philosophical Sciences (1830), Translated from Nicolin and Pöggeler's Edition (1959), and from the Zusätze in Michelet's Text (1847)*, 418 (§370): "The forms of nature are thus not to be brought into an absolute system, and the species of animals are exposed to contingency."

28. The very nature of idealism has to do with Kant's claim that the world as a whole cannot be apprehended in sensuous intuition and is thus only available to thinking creatures, who must therefore construct concepts and theories of what nature as a whole must be like. "Nature as a whole" is thus an "ideality," a "concept," not an individual existing "thing" available to any kind of perceptual intuition. It is in fact a philosophical (and therefore idealist) issue as to whether nature as a whole should be conceived as simply the set of all natural things, as something more than the set of all natural things, or even as something very different from that set. Idealism is thus the stance that a purposive creature would take to individual natural things, namely, to locate them within a purposive whole. In Hegel's admittedly playful language, animals are idealists in that they locate their food sources as playing a role in their own reproduction—and thus display an orientation to a greater whole than their immediate perceptions—but animals are, as it were, failed idealists in that they cannot have a conceptual sense of any greater whole than that of themselves as individual organisms experiencing various drives. Indeed, the very idea of animal's good is itself vague. It is not developed at this level, and it cannot be better developed, since what is good for the animal cannot be separated from what is good for its species. The goal of idealist philosophy is thus to have a true concept of nature as a whole—a concept that obviously outstrips the immediate empirical evidence on which such concepts are based. Hegel's version of idealism thus does not hold that natural, material objects are (to use an admittedly slippery term) reducible in any kind of way to mental or spiritual objects.

29. It is impossible not to notice the slightly scornful dismissal Hegel gives to Descartes' conception of animal life in Georg Wilhelm Friedrich Hegel, *Vorlesungen über die Geschichte der Philosophie III*, ed. Eva Moldenhauer and Karl Markus Michel, 20 vols. (Theorie-Werkausgabe, 20; Frankfurt a. M.: Suhrkamp, 1969), 155: "There are a few particular assertions which need to be mentioned, which have in particular contributed to Descartes's fame—particular forms which were otherwise noted in metaphysics, also by Wolff. One emphasizes: α) that Descartes saw the organic, animals as machines, that they are set in motion by an other and do not have the self-active principle of thought within themselves—a mechanical physiology, a determinate thought of 'the understanding,' which is of no real importance. With the sharp distinction between thought and extension, thought is not regarded as sensation, in the way that sensation can isolate itself. The organic, as the body, must be reduced to extension. What follows is thus a dependency on the first determinations."

30. Hegel's stance would thus seem to be at odds with McDowell's view that animals do not have subjectivity but only protosubjectivity and thus have no inner or outer experience, only sentience. John Henry McDowell, *Mind and World* (Cambridge, Mass.: Harvard University Press, 1994) x, 191 pp. (It's of course also not entirely clear whether these might not be

merely semantic differences between the McDowellian and the Hegelian stances.) For Hegel, animals have an "inner," and they are subjects of a life. However, they do not (because apparently they cannot, given the states of their organic neuronal systems) develop their subjectivity into a fully actualized, *verwirklichte* subjectivity.

31. Thus, Hegel says, in Hegel, *Enzyklopädie der philosophischen Wissenschaften III*, §381 *Zusatz*; Hegel et al., *Hegel's Philosophy of Mind: Being Part Three of the "Encyclopaedia of the Philosophical Sciences" (1830)*, 10: "Sensation is just this omnipresence of the unity of the animal in all of its members, which communicate each impression to the whole, which in animals is a whole that begins to be for itself. It lies in this subjective inwardness that the animal determines itself through itself, from the inner outwards, and is not merely determined from the outside, i.e., the animal has both impulse and instinct."

32. Hegel, *Enzyklopädie der philosophischen Wissenschaften II*, §352 *Zusatz*; Hegel and Miller, *Hegel's Philosophy of Nature: Being Part Two of the Encyclopedia of the Philosophical Sciences (1830), Translated from Nicolin and Pöggeler's Edition (1959), and from the Zusätze in Michelet's Text (1847)*, 356: "Since the animal organism is the process of subjectivity, relating itself in externality to itself, here the rest of nature is present as external nature, because the animal preserves itself in this relationship to the external."

33. Robert Brandom, *Making It Explicit: Reasoning, Representing, and Discursive Commitment* (Cambridge, Mass.: Harvard University Press, 1994), xxv, 741 pp. See Redding's critique of Brandom's conception of reliably differential responsive dispositions: Paul Redding, *Analytic Philosophy and the Return of Hegelian Thought* (Modern European Philosophy; Cambridge: Cambridge University Press, 2007), x, 252 pp. Pippin also argues against Brandom's view in Robert B. Pippin, "Brandom's Hegel," *European Journal of Philosophy*, 13/3 (December 2005), 381–408.

34. See Sebastian Rand's important discussion of this in Sebastian Rand, "Animal Subjectivity and the Nervous System in Hegel's Philosophy of Nature," *Revista Eletrônica Estudos Hegelianos*, 11 (2010).

35. Hegel, *Enzyklopädie der philosophischen Wissenschaften II*, §371; Hegel and Miller, *Hegel's Philosophy of Nature: Being Part Two of the Encyclopedia of the Philosophical Sciences (1830), Translated from Nicolin and Pöggeler's Edition (1959), and from the Zusätze in Michelet's Text (1847)*, 429: "The stone cannot become diseased, because it comes to an end in the negative of itself, is chemically dissolved, does not endure in its form, and is not the negative of itself which expands over its opposite (as in illness and self-feeling). Desire, the feeling of lack, is also, to itself, the negative. Desire relates itself to itself as the negative—it is itself and is, to itself, that which is lacking."

36. Not all things that interfere with its functioning are diseases. The concept of disease, like that of most such hybrids of the empirical and the normative, is elastic. Moreover, the environment can change on the animal and interfere with its functioning, even though this is not a disease on the part of the environment or the animal. Likewise, the animal can suffer injury and thus fail to function well, but this is not a disease. The possibility of disease or injury as the intrusion into the animal's functioning well already takes it as a fact that the animal as a whole has a way of functioning, and that is the key idea.

37. Hegel, *Enzyklopädie der philosophischen Wissenschaften III*, §381 *Zusatz*; Hegel et al., *Hegel's Philosophy of Mind: Being Part Three of the "Encyclopaedia of the Philosophical Sciences" (1830)*, 10: "That which senses (*das Empfindene*) is determined, has a content, and thereby a distinction within itself. This distinction is at first a still wholly ideal, simple distinction that is sublated in the unity of sensation. The sublated distinction enduring in the unity is a contradiction, which is thereby sublated in such a way that the distinction is posited as distinction. The animal thus will be impelled from out of its simple relation to itself and into the opposition towards external nature." However, in Hegel, *Enzyklopädie der philosophischen Wissenschaften III*, §402; Hegel et al., *Hegel's Philosophy of Mind: Being Part Three of the "Encyclopaedia of the Philosophical Sciences" (1830)*, 90, he says: "In this totality, or ideality, in the timeless indifferent inner of the soul, however, the sensations which are displacing each other vanish but not without leaving a trace. Rather, they remain therein as sublated, and

the content therein acquires its enduring existence as, at first, a merely possible content, which then first achieves its passage from possibility to actuality in that it comes to be for the soul, that is, within the content, this sensation comes to be for itself." Likewise, he notes that there are ways in which the content of animal awareness and human awareness are the same, except that human awareness actualizes the potential of normativity within itself. See Hegel, *Enzyklopädie der philosophischen Wissenschaften III*, §400; Hegel et al., *Hegel's Philosophy of Mind: Being Part Three of the "Encyclopaedia of the Philosophical Sciences" (1830)*, 74: "Although the characteristically human content belonging to free spirit takes on the form of sensation, yet this form as such is still the form that is common to animal and human souls and is consequently not adequate to that content. What is contradictory between spiritual content and sensation consists in the former being in and for itself a universal, something necessary, objective—sensation, on the other hand, is something singularized, contingent, one-sidedly subjective."

38. See Hegel, *Enzyklopädie der philosophischen Wissenschaften III*, §402 *Zusatz*; Hegel et al., *Hegel's Philosophy of Mind: Being Part Three of the "Encyclopaedia of the Philosophical Sciences" (1830)*, 90.

39. Maurice Merleau-Ponty, *Phenomenology of Perception* (Routledge Classics; London: Routledge, 2002), xxiv, 544 pp.

40. Hegel, *Enzyklopädie der philosophischen Wissenschaften I*, §66; Hegel et al., *The Encyclopaedia Logic, with the Zusätze: Part I of the Encyclopaedia of Philosophical Sciences with the Zusätze*, 115. In the passage cited, Hegel goes on to add, "In all these cases, immediacy of knowledge not only does not exclude mediation, but the two are so bound together that immediate knowledge is even the product and result of mediated knowledge."

41. Brandom, *Making It Explicit*.

42. Hegel, *Enzyklopädie der philosophischen Wissenschaften II*, §360; Hegel and Miller, *Hegel's Philosophy of Nature: Being Part Two of the Encyclopedia of the Philosophical Sciences (1830), Translated from Nicolin and Pöggeler's Edition (1959), and from the Zusätze in Michelet's Text (1847)*, 389: "Since the impulse can only be fulfilled through wholly determinate actions, this appears as instinct, since it seems to be a choice in accordance with a determination of an end. However, because the impulse is not a known purpose, the animal does not yet know its purpose as a purpose. Aristotle calls this unconscious acting in terms of purposes φύσις."

43. John Henry McDowell, *Having the World in View: Essays on Kant, Hegel, and Sellars* (Cambridge, Mass.: Harvard University Press, 2009), ix, 285 pp. See particularly the discussion on pp. 128–46 ("Conceptual Capacities in Perception"). Hegel's point is that the ability to see reasons *as* reasons grows out of the self-conscious animal's ability to entertain his goals as possibilities. Hegel himself seems to note this same point when in his lectures on Aristotle, he renders the Greek, "*Logos*," as both "*Grund*" and "*Vernunft*." This does not prejudge whether the capacity to see reasons as reasons is not itself something that might exist on more of a continuum with ordinary animal life than has been previously recognized. Perhaps there are some animals that can exhibit a bit of reflexivity about their reasons, such as entertaining in some primitive way something like the thought, "Must we really flee these predators, or are there enough of us to resist them?"

44. This distinction finds voice in two very different contemporary accounts of goods in nature. Alasdair C. Macintyre, *Dependent Rational Animals: Why Human Beings Need the Virtues* (Paul Carus Lecture Series; Chicago: Open Court, 1999), xiii, 172 pp.; Michael Thompson, "The Representation of Life," in Rosalind Hursthouse, Gavin Lawrence, and Warren Quinn, eds., *Virtues and Reasons: Philippa Foot and Moral Theory* (Oxford: Clarendon; New York: Oxford University Press, 1995). Thompson explicitly puts Hegel to work for some of his ideas on life, although he and Hegel part ways on several key points.

45. Hegel's nice metaphor for the way full-blown human normativity develops out of our animal normativity is that, as he says, *Geist* can be viewed as "asleep" in nature. The particular skills necessary for human normativity have not been developed yet and will not be developed except in the conditions in which humans put their natural makeup to work in social settings and institute normative statuses. "The Idea, or spirit existing in itself, sleeping in

nature, thus sublates externality, singularization and the immediacy of nature. It produces in its own eyes an existence adequate to its inwardness and universality, and it comes to be spirit reflected within itself, spirit existing for itself, the self-conscious, awake spirit, that is, spirit as such." Hegel, *Enzyklopädie der philosophischen Wissenschaften III*, §384, *Zusatz*; Hegel et al., *Hegel's Philosophy of Mind: Being Part Three of the "Encyclopaedia of the Philosophical Sciences" (1830)*, 19.

46. Hegel, *Enzyklopädie der philosophischen Wissenschaften III*, §381; Hegel et al., *Hegel's Philosophy of Mind: Being Part Three of the "Encyclopaedia of the Philosophical Sciences" (1830)*, 10: "This animal senses merely the species and does not know it. In the animal, the soul does not yet exist for the soul, the universal does not exist as such for the universal."

47. Hegel, *Enzyklopädie der philosophischen Wissenschaften III*, §401; Hegel et al., *Hegel's Philosophy of Mind: Being Part Three of the "Encyclopaedia of the Philosophical Sciences" (1830)*, 82: "Already we have seen in the observation of this relation that what is inner in the sensing being is not entirely empty, not completely indeterminate, but rather is to a greater degree something determinate in and for itself. This counts already for the animal soul and to an incomparably greater degree for human inwardness. Thus, what therein turns up is a content that is, on its own, *(für sich)* not an external but rather an inward content."

48. Hegel took one of Kant's mistakes to be the suggestion that since the distinction between concepts and intuitions was crucial, that meant that they were separable items. See Robert B. Pippin, "Concept and Intuition: On Distinguishability and Separability," *Hegel-Studien*, 40 (2005). To be sure, in claiming a "speculative identity" for the two—that is, that each was an inseparable moment of a whole—Hegel practically invited those unfamiliar with his arcane although nonetheless precise terminology to construe him as denying the difference between concepts and intuitions and thus setting himself up for the criticism that he was something like a holist gone mad who no longer had any way of conceiving of objects in the world as offering standards for the judgments about them. However, even before John McDowell had made the phrase "frictionless spinning in the void" a suitable metaphor for all such views that deny the way in which experience can provide genuine reasons for belief, Hegel himself scornfully employed a similar metaphor to speak of those who deny the existence of independent standards of judgment: See Hegel, *Phänomenologie des Geistes*, 293 (¶396), where Hegel speaks of a deficient conception of mentality as having "the appearance of the movement of a circle, which, within a void, freely moves itself within itself, and which, unimpeded, now enlarges and now contracts, and is fully satisfied in playing a game within itself and with itself."

49. On the role of animal awareness and emotions in German idealism in general and Hegel in particular, see the important work by Paul Redding, *The Logic of Affect* (Ithaca, N.Y.: Cornell University Press, 1999), x, 204 pp.

50. Thus, in Hegel, *Enzyklopädie der philosophischen Wissenschaften III*, §400; Hegel et al., *Hegel's Philosophy of Mind: Being Part Three of the "Encyclopaedia of the Philosophical Sciences" (1830)*, 74, Hegel goes into one of his usual warnings about the danger of thinking that the kind of animal immediacy of sensation could be used to justify anything. "However, that feeling *(Empfindung)* and the heart are not the form by which something is justified as religious, ethical, true, righteous, etc. The appeal to the heart and to feeling is either merely saying nothing—or is to an even greater degree saying something bad. This is not at all something about which we need to be reminded."

51. Although most twenty-first-century writers on animal awareness are far more likely to use the term *representation* to refer to the animal's sensing its environment, they would by and large agree that animals do not "represent" in Hegel's use of the term.

52. Hegel, *Enzyklopädie der philosophischen Wissenschaften III*, §402; Hegel et al., *Hegel's Philosophy of Mind: Being Part Three of the "Encyclopaedia of the Philosophical Sciences" (1830)*, 88: "For sensation *(Empfindung)* and feeling *(Fühlen)* there is no ordinary linguistic usage that makes a thoroughgoing distinction between them. Yet one still does not speak of a sensation for law, a sensation of oneself, etc. but rather of a feel for the law, or a "self-feeling." Sensation and sensitiveness belong together. One can therefore take the position that

sensation emphasizes more the aspect of the passivity of finding that one feels, i.e., the immediacy of determinateness in feeling, whereas feeling at the same time has more to do with the self-hood (*Selbstischkeit*) that is therein."

53. In Hegel's usage, unlike the usage to which Jean-Paul Sartre later put the terms, "being-for-itself" is not the simple opposite or counterpart of "being-in-itself." Translated fairly literally, *being-for-itself* is what something is "on its own," whereas the *being-in-itself* of anything is, in its Hegelian usage, what it is in its concept, which itself must then be articulated and developed in practice. Thus, its most abstract sense, *being-for-itself* means that which is "on its own," independent in the sense that it seemingly can in principle be characterized without having to contrast it with anything else or without having to refer it to something else. In the dialectic of mastery and servitude, for example, the master seeks a being-for-itself in his attempts to live the life of an agent who, as it were, entitles himself and others but is entitled to do so by nobody else. In the normative sphere in which agents live, this attempt at self-entitlement cannot simply come about passively. An agent's being-for-itself can only come about through his own activity, his own relating-to-himself. However, Hegel does not restrict, as Sartre does, being-for-itself to self-consciousness; the object of perception, for example, is said by him to be something we at first take to be something existing "on its own" without our having to relate such a thing to other things that form its limit, a task that proves to be impossible. (The object of perception turns out to be something supposedly independent from other things, but its very existence is dependent on its relations to other things, a dependency that becomes apparent only in reflection on the nature of the otherwise independent perceptual object.)

54. Hegel, Georg Wilhelm Friedrich Hegel, *Vorlesungen über die Ästhetik II*, ed. Eva Moldenhauer and Karl Markus Michel, 20 vols. (Theorie-Werkausgabe 14; Frankfurt a. M.: Suhrkamp, 1969): "Spirit and soul are essentially to be distinguished. The soul is only this ideal, simple being-for-itself of the bodily as *bodily*, but spirit is the being-for-itself of conscious and *self-conscious* life with all the sensations, representations and purposes of this self-conscious existence."

55. Hegel's diagnosis of this failed inference is a topic in Wolff, *Das Körper-Seele Problem: Kommentar Zu Hegel, Enzyklopädie (1830)*, §389.

56. Hegel, *Enzyklopädie der philosophischen Wissenschaften III*, §411 Zusatz; Hegel et al., *Hegel's Philosophy of Mind: Being Part Three of the "Encyclopaedia of the Philosophical Sciences" (1830)*, 148: "At the conclusion of the main section of the 'Anthropology' in §401, what was under consideration was the involuntary corporealization of inner sensations, and this is something that people have in common with animals. On the other hand, what is now to be discussed are the corporealizations that happen freely. These impart a characteristically spiritual stamp on the human body so that this stamp distinguishes the human from the animals much more than any natural determinateness could do. In accordance with his purely bodily aspect, the person is not that distinct from an ape."

57. See Aristotle, *Parts of Animals*, trans. William Oggle, 645b 14–20. "As every instrument and every bodily member subserves some partial end, that is to say, some special action, so the whole body must be destined to minister to some plenary sphere of action.... Similarly, the body too must somehow or other be made for the soul, and each part of it for some subordinate function, to which it is adapted." Aristotle and Richard Mckeon, *The Basic Works of Aristotle* (New York: Random House, 1941), xxxix, 1487 pp., p. 658.

58. Hegel, *Enzyklopädie der philosophischen Wissenschaften III*, §410, Zusatz; Hegel et al., *Hegel's Philosophy of Mind: Being Part Three of the "Encyclopaedia of the Philosophical Sciences" (1830)*, 146.

59. See Hegel, *Enzyklopädie der philosophischen Wissenschaften III*, §409; Hegel et al., *Hegel's Philosophy of Mind: Being Part Three of the "Encyclopaedia of the Philosophical Sciences" (1830)*, 140: "But this abstract being-for-itself of the soul in its embodiment is not yet the I, not the existence of the universal existing for itself. It is embodiment brought back to its pure ideality, which is appropriate to the soul as such...in that way, that pure being, which, since the particularity of embodiment, i.e., immediate embodiment, is sublated within it, is

being-for-itself, a wholly pure, unaware act of intuiting, which is, however, the foundation of consciousness into which it inwardly turns (*in sich geht*). It does this since it has sublated into itself that embodiment, whose subjective substance it is and which is for it a barrier. In that way, it is posited as a subject for itself."

60. On this point, see especially Rand, "Animal Subjectivity and the Nervous System in Hegel's Philosophy of Nature."
61. Hegel, *Enzyklopädie der philosophischen Wissenschaften III*, §411; Hegel et al., *Hegel's Philosophy of Mind: Being Part Three of the "Encyclopaedia of the Philosophical Sciences" (1830)*, p. 147.
62. Georg Wilhelm Friedrich Hegel et al., *Vorlesungen über die Philosophie des Geistes: Berlin 1827/1828* (Vorlesungen / Georg Wilhelm Friedrich Hegel; Hamburg: F. Meiner, 1994), xxx-viii, 321 pp., p. 19: "We have said that *freedom* is to be asserted as the basic essence of spirit, the freedom *from* and *in* the natural, which, however, must not be taken as arbitrary choice (*Willkür*) but rather as law-like freedom"
63. Ibid., p. 16.
64. Ibid., p. 20; Georg Wilhelm Friedrich Hegel and Robert R. Williams, *Georg Wilhelm Friedrich Hegel: Lectures on the Philosophy of Spirit 1827–8* (Hegel Lectures Series; Oxford: Oxford University Press, 2007), vi, 287 pp., p. 70. (This alters for emphasis Williams's translation.)
65. Georg Wilhelm Friedrich Hegel, *Lectures on the Philosophy of World History: Introduction, Reason in History*, ed. Johannes Hoffmeister (Cambridge Studies in the History and Theory of Politics; Cambridge: Cambridge University Press, 1975), xxxviii, 252 pp., p. 70; Georg Wilhelm Friedrich Hegel, *Vorlesungen über die Philosophie der Weltgeschichte: Berlin 1822/1823*, ed. Karl-Heinz Ilting, Hoo Nam Seelmann, and Karl Brehmer (Vorlesungen / Georg Wilhelm Friedrich Hegel; Hamburg: F. Meiner Verlag, 1996), x, 626 pp., p. 82.
66. Hegel, *Grundlinien der Philosophie des Rechts*, §4, *Zusatz*; Hegel, *Elements of the Philosophy of Right*, 35.
67. The term *actuality* is the accepted translation for the German *Wirklichkeit*, even though it means "reality" in ordinary German. However, Hegel has a term *Realität* that he contrasts with *Wirklichkeit*, so translators have on the whole shied away from rendering *Wirklichkeit* as "reality." In addition to that difficulty, there are some more systematic reasons for using "actuality" as an accepted translation. The term is a technical term in Hegel's system, and it is the preferred term for rendering Aristotle's concept of *energeia* (actuality) into German. Hegel himself notes in several places the link between the concept of *Wirklichkeit* ("actuality") and *Wirken* (to have an effect). The clearest statement of this is in the *Science of Logic*: "What is actual is what is efficacious (*was wirklich ist, kann wirken*)." A. V. Miller translates the relevant phrase as "what is actual can act." Hegel, *Wissenschaft der Logik II*, p. 208; Hegel, *Hegel's Science of Logic*, 546. In his early works, Hegel also defined *Wirklichkeit* as the "possibility of efficaciousness." Georg Wilhelm Friedrich Hegel, *Jenaer Schriften*, ed. Gerd Irrlitz (Philosophische Studientexte; Berlin: Akademie-Verlag, 1972), liii, 526 pp., p. 185; Georg Wilhelm Friedrich Hegel, *Hegel and the Human Spirit: A Translation of the Jena Lectures on the Philosophy of Spirit (1805–6) with Commentary*, ed. Leo Rauch (Detroit: Wayne State University Press, 1983), 183 pp. The phrase used is *"Möglichkeit des Wirkens."* Another instance occurs in Hegel, *Grundlinien der Philosophie des Rechts*, §82; Hegel, *Elements of the Philosophy of Right*, 116: "For actuality (Wirklichkeit) is that which has an effect (was wirkt) and preserves itself in its otherness, whereas what is immediate is receptive for negation." The French have a better solution for the problem of translating the term, having chosen *"l'effectif"* and *"effectivité"* as the translation of *"Wirklichkeit."*
68. Thus, in Hegel, *Grundlinien der Philosophie des Rechts*, §12; Hegel, *Elements of the Philosophy of Right*, 46, Hegel speaks of resolving (*beschließen*) to do something, which he identifies with bringing the "inner" into the sphere of the "outer." In §8, he makes it clear that the dialectical conception of the will only applies to that account that tries to combine the commitment to an objective world with an equal commitment to subjectivity. Not everything that has to do with willing is "dialectical" or "speculative" (his other term for the same thing). Ordinary practical reasoning is thus not "dialectical." As he puts it in Hegel,

*Grundlinien der Philosophie des Rechts*, §8; Hegel, *Elements of the Philosophy of Right*, 43: "The consideration of the will's determinacy is the task of the understanding [*des Verstandes*, the intellect] and is not primarily speculative."

69. The two taken together, intention and action, stand in what Hegel calls a relation of "speculative identity"; in fact, the "intention/action" complex is almost a paradigm case of what Hegel means by a "speculative identity," namely, a whole with distinguishable but nonseparable components, which leads to various conceptual dilemmas when the components are each treated as parts possessing their own determinate identity.

70. Hegel, *Grundlinien der Philosophie des Rechts*, §11; Hegel, *Elements of the Philosophy of Right*, 45: "The will which is free as yet only *in itself* is the *immediate* or *natural* will. The determinations of the difference which is posited within the will by the self-determining concept appear within the immediate will as an *immediately* present content: These are the *drives*, *desires*, and *inclinations* by which the will finds itself naturally determined." See also Hegel's notes for his lectures on the philosophy of history: "The first thing we have to notice is this: that we have hitherto called the principle, or ultimate end, or destiny, of the nature and concept of the spirit in itself, is purely universal and abstract. A principle, fundamental rule, or law is something universal and implicit, and as such, it has not attained complete reality, however true it may be in itself. Aims, principles, and the like are present at first in our thoughts and inner intentions, or even in books, but not yet in reality itself. In other words, that which exists only in itself is a possibility or potentiality which has not yet emerged into existence. A second moment is necessary before it can attain reality—that of actuation or realization; and its principle is the will, the activity of mankind in the world at large. It is only by means of this activity that the original concepts or implicit determinations are realized and actualized." *Lectures on the Philosophy of World History: Introduction*, 69–70.

71. See the discussion of Aristotle's conception of practical truth in Gabriel Richardson Lear, *Happy Lives and the Highest Good: An Essay on Aristotle's Nicomachean Ethics* (Princeton, N.J.: Princeton University Press, 2004), viii, 238 pp., p. 106.

72. Hegel divides animals from people not on the religious ground that animals do not have souls—on Hegel's account, they do have souls—but on the ground that they cannot *think*, that is, cannot entertain reasons as reasons in the sense mentioned previously. To illustrate this, here are three among many examples that could be cited: Hegel, *Grundlinien der Philosophie des Rechts*, §4, *Zusatz*; Hegel, *Elements of the Philosophy of Right*, 35: "Spirit is thought itself, and the person distinguishes himself from animals through thought." Hegel, *Grundlinien der Philosophie des Rechts*, §42, *Zusatz*; Hegel, *Elements of the Philosophy of Right*, 74: "The animal can intuit (*anschauen*), but the soul of the animal does not have the soul as an object in its own eyes. It is rather something external." Hegel, *Enzyklopädie der philosophischen Wissenschaften III*, §468; Hegel et al., *Hegel's Philosophy of Mind: Being Part Three of the "Encyclopaedia of the Philosophical Sciences" (1830)*, 468: "However, in truth as we have just seen, thought determines itself into will and remains the substance of the latter, so that without thought there can be no will, and even the uneducated person wills only insofar as he has thought. On the other hand, because the animal does not think, it is also incapable of possessing a will."

73. In its subjectivity, the animal thus does not distinguish itself from the species, whereas we do. See Hegel, *Enzyklopädie der philosophischen Wissenschaften II*, §322; Hegel and Miller, *Hegel's Philosophy of Nature: Being Part Two of the Encyclopedia of the Philosophical Sciences (1830), Translated from Nicolin and Pöggeler's Edition (1959), and from the Zusätze in Michelet's Text (1847)*, 220: "In the organic, it is the genus, the inner universal, which brings about the loss of the individual." In Hegel, *Phänomenologie des Geistes*, 143 (¶173), Hegel notes: "But this other life for which the *genus* as such exists and which is the genus for itself, namely, *self-consciousness*, initially exists in its own eyes merely as this simple essence and, in its own eyes, is an object as the *pure I*."

# 2

# Self-Consciousness in the Natural World

## A: Animal and Human Awareness

At the level of the account of agency in terms of the animal soul, the animal moving itself in light of its own goals is at one with itself (the animal is, to use Hegel's description, *beisich*) and is thus free in a limited sense but still in a sense partly continuous with full human freedom. Hegel's views on animal freedom, as in other places, tracks Aristotle's own view of the voluntary (or perhaps we should say, tracks the implications of Aristotle's views).[1] Likewise, in carrying out a variety of ordinary tasks, the embodied human agent is also at one with himself in this more or less straightforward animal sense.[2]

However, with the introduction of self-consciousness, the human animal, unlike the other animals, ceases to be immediately at one with itself. For such an animal, what it means to act in light of its own purposes becomes an issue.

As we have already noted, to say that the animal soul is actualized in human agency does not, in Hegel's view, commit one to postulating a new realm of entities in the world (namely, private mental facts on which human agents report). Human agency actualizes the animal soul in that it develops the kind of self-relation already at work in animal life and, as it were, turns it on itself. The human animal does not merely monitor itself and the world in seeking its goals. It practically establishes a new type of self-relation that constitutes consciousness of an object and not merely an animal awareness of it. This involves not merely sensing the object and tracking, say, its location relative to oneself (as many animals with even rudimentary perceptual systems can do). It involves grasping one's own experience of the object as necessarily containing within it a distinction between the object as the object is fully independently of one's view of it and one's own experience of the object. It involves, that is, both the object and an awareness of one's perspectival grasp of the object.

In the *Critique of Pure Reason*, in what Hegel called one of the "most correct" and the "deepest" thoughts of that book, Kant said that the "I think must be able to accompany all my representations."[3] We must be able—that is, we have the capacity, even if we do not always exercise it—to recognize of any representation that we might only be thinking it, that our experience might turn out not to be

45

the truthful awareness we took it to be. Any awareness of objects in the world requires for its own possibility the consciousness of an identical subject of experience who holds the experiences together as representations of an object in the sense that there must be a doubled awareness of the object both as viewed from a perspective and of the object as independent of any perspective. The awareness of oneself is thus not a monitoring of a special set of private entities. Rather, it is a way of taking a normative stance toward one's own experience that becomes articulated in statements that contrast the way things are with the way they seem to be. Reporting what one thinks turns out not to be just reporting. It is just as much one's taking a position on things.

As such, this kind of awareness is, in Hegel's terms, infinite, in that it determines itself in its distinguishing itself (as "my perspective") from its object. If it were finite, it would be distinguished as an act of consciousness only by contrasting it from the outside with something it is not. Thus, in Hegel's rigorous (but rather obviously nonstandard) terminology, the finite is always that which is intelligible in terms of or is explained by its reference to something else, its "negation." For something, x, to be finite, means that it can only be grasped in terms of its contrast with y. Likewise, for something to be infinite in the true sense means that it is comprehended as what distinguishes itself from itself, and, so it turns out, only "mindful agency," *Geist*, fulfills the conditions for "true infinity." However, even that claim itself must be qualified.

Self-consciousness is infinite in that it is not the consciousness of some determinate thing that is itself simply given to us. Hegel's picture of self-consciousness is not that of a self that is conscious of an object and that then turns the light back on itself. The self is conscious of itself as conscious of itself and its object together, and it sets the terms of that relationship itself. Self-consciousness is not a causal relation between two entities but a kind of ordering relation among states of the same entity.[4] If indeed self-consciousness were a relation between two different "things"—a self and an object—then there would be an infinite regress at work in such a conception, since for the self to be aware of itself, either there would have to be a self that was not aware of itself while being aware of the others, or there would have to be an infinity of selves each taking note of each other.

As all readers of Hegel know, he distinguishes between the "bad" infinite and the "true" infinite. The bad infinite arises in all those cases where one reaches for the unconditioned as a "thing," as a final member of a series, and in doing so, one is pushed into some kind of infinite regress in explanation.[5] The only way to avoid such a regress is something that would ultimately be self-explicating, and the only candidate that can fit that criterion is the space of reasons itself as both explicating itself and correcting itself in historical time. It is *Geist* as historically developing within the space of reasons that meets the standard of infinity.

Although still difficult to phrase in gentler terms than he himself uses, Hegel's point is that self-consciousness should not be understood, at least primarily, as an observation of oneself—again, not as one thing looking at another thing—but more in terms of an agent's making a commitment to something, or taking a stance toward some claim.[6] To use non-Hegelian language, at one level, self-consciousness involves a kind of transparency toward itself. There is no distance between committing oneself to a claim and wondering if the claim is true.[7] The distinction between me as aware of myself and me as the object of awareness is, as Hegel often likes to say, the distinction that is no distinction at all. (This distinguishes it from third-person accounts of taking a stance, where the claims that "So-and-so believes P" and "So-and-so thinks that P is false" pose no problem of internal contradiction.) The kind of self-presence in self-consciousness is thus bound up with the ability to be able, minimally, to undertake commitments. The difference between first-person and third-person points of view is more of a difference in the type of commitment one undertakes, as distinct from the commitments others might ascribe to you. It has to do, that is, with the stance one takes to oneself and on one's standpoint on other matters, and in that respect, such transparency often evaporates. To know one's commitments, one must be able to interpret them from within the social space in which one moves, and thus one's stance toward one's own commitments may be relatively or even fully blind; in many cases, one will not be able to understand that to which one is committed until one knows the meaning of one's commitment, and one will not be able to know the concrete meaning of the commitment until it after it has been actualized. We will find ourselves to have commitments that are our own but that we can neither control nor completely survey.

Being self-conscious in this sense does not mean that the agent actually articulates his own stance as that of undertaking commitments. (For that, he would also have to have studied Hegelian philosophy.) However, for such commitments to be at work—to be actual, *wirklich*—in an agent's life, they must become part of the agent's dispositional makeup, a part of "second nature" (a term Hegel also adopts from Aristotle).[8] As such, one's standing commitments as "second nature" take the shape of habits (that is, regularities of behavior and dispositions) or rules—which appear as the "given" (or, in Hegel's nineteenth-century usage, "positive") rules of one's social world—that are usually subjectively experienced by people from within the naturalized dispositions of "second nature" more as normative facts to which conformity must be given.

That self-consciousness is a matter of avowing one's commitments, taking a stance, assuming a standpoint and, as such, is a feature, in Hegel's terms, of its ideality (that is, normativity) is thus not a natural fact about oneself. Animal life, as one natural thing among others in nature, establishes a relation to these other things by relating itself to them via its own self-established inwardness. "Idealism," as Hegel says, "begins with...the organism being *stimulated* by *external potencies* rather than being *affected by causes*."[9] However, the capacity for reflection—as one natural thing taking a normative stance to other natural things—constitutes having a consciousness of the world instead of a merely animal awareness of it. Therefore, in "consciousness," one does not have a new Aristotelian substance making its appearance in the world but something else: a subject of a life that is not merely aware of itself *in* occupying a position in that world (which is animal awareness) but aware of itself *as* occupying a position in that world. Hegel's own metaphor for this makes his point: The subject is like "the light that manifests both itself and others," and this kind of consciousness of oneself *as* occupying a position in the world is both "one side of the relationship and the whole relationship" itself.[10] The human agent, by virtue of certain biological characteristics having to do with its brain and its nervous systems (among other things), actualizes something that is already in play in animal life but that, as put to work in that way, becomes fundamentally different from it. That this feature is in play in animal life is, however, not something of which the animal itself, as animal, can be aware. The agent is, in Hegel's sense, the truth of animal life.

From the standpoint of the subject of a conscious life precisely as conscious of itself as occupying a position in social space, the subject has an immediate (non-inferential) relation to itself. That is, an agent is an animal that is, in Hegel's terms, "certain" of itself in that it establishes a relation to itself as occupying a position in the world, and this establishment of such a relation is not an inference it makes from something else. Rather, establishing that relation constitutes its being an agent—a subject of conscious life—in the first place. To be certain in this sense is to take oneself to be a subject, to stand within a social space of various entitlements and commitments, even if one is not in a position to articulate that stance to oneself in just that way. "Certainty" in this sense has to do with undertaking commitments, not in reporting certain inner, psychic states.

In putting his point in that way, Hegel also sets up an obvious distinction between self-certainty and truth. "Certainty" in Hegel's works has to do with the commitments one undertakes where one also takes these commitments not to require any defense or to be even beyond defense. The certainties of one's life are, as it were, the anchoring points of one's social space, the place where asking for reasons runs out, and one simply avows what seem like blind commitments— reasons for which there do not seem to be other reasons. To draw on yet another metaphor from Wittgenstein, such blind commitments indicate from the agent's point of view that "I have reached bedrock, and my spade is turned. Then I am inclined to say: 'This is simply what I do.'"[11]

To speak at this level of abstraction is nonetheless to speak only of the "formal ideality" of agency, namely, that it must submit itself to norms, and not to speak of which norms it must submit itself to.[12] What is actually at work in such an abstract conception of agency cannot be determined without considering what is required for such an agent to act and to lead a life characterized by the possibility of reflection. One of Hegel's central theses is that subjectivity is always determinate, located in a form of life with certain norms that are fundamentally authoritative for it and that form, as it were, the outer edges of intelligibility of that form of life, but that can also historically break down or go dead under pressures from their own internal shortcomings and contradictions. Certainty breaks down under the pressures of seeking truth. Which of these blind commitments can then be sustained under the pressure of being actualized, that is, can be statuses that the agent can genuinely inhabit?[13]

# B: Consciousness of the World

Why we should think that such self-presence is always a figure of conscious life at all? What is wrong with a simpler conception of consciousness as the state that an organism has when it distinguishes at the most basic level its own states from those of the object it takes those states to represent (or bring before its conscious life)? If there is to be anything like empirical truth—any meaningful conception of our experience as offering us genuine reasons for belief about things in the world—then one must at least minimally take it for granted that there is a normative line to be drawn between our awareness of an object and the object itself, and that it must be the object itself that makes our awareness (or a statement expressing our awareness or based on our awareness) true.

What appears is not always what is the case, and the agent has to learn how to discriminate what is real from what only seems to be. It is this line that separates the "inner" from the "outer" (although the animals cannot be aware of that line as such a line), and the object becomes not merely the object in the world in which the agent occupies a position but the object "external" to the agent's awareness. As involving a conception of truth in the ordinary sense, this sense of "external" is a normative, not a natural, distinction between what is in the mind ("what seems to be") and outside of the mind ("what really is"). Putting it like this, of course, suggests a certain picture of the relation between mind and world that Hegel labels as "finite."[14] On one version of that picture, the mind would be one "thing," which would be what it is only in its distinction from another "thing" (say, a physical object of which it forms a representation).

Drawing that line cannot consist simply in any kind of immediate conscious awareness of singular items of sense—what Hegel calls "sense-certainty"—since the capacity to discriminate those singular things in any kind of way that licenses normative claims about them relies on our contrasting them with each other in various ways.[15] (This is irrespective as to whether the items are taken to be singular things, like stones, or singular inner states, like sensations.)[16] Any awareness of any singular thing that can serve as the basis of any kind of claim (as something that can be true or false) requires a corresponding capacity to discriminate normatively one thing from another. For us to make claims about the singular entities of such putative "sense-certainty," we must also acknowledge that they already stand in relations of determinate contrast and exclusion with each other (for example, if a thing is red, it is not also green).[17]

Metaphorically speaking, where are "we" standing when "we" draw that line? To be sure, the animal organism can also make such distinctions and can exhibit in its behavior an awareness of a contrast among things, but it cannot make claims about these things since it cannot (as far as we know) articulate the distinction between "it seems" and "it is," even if it can direct some of its behavior on the basis of something like that distinction. The initial assertion itself—that an agent perceives a singular thing without having to draw any such line—looks like a self-sufficient claim, but in fact it requires a third element, some standpoint within which the distinction itself is being drawn. If all meaningfulness in experience boiled down to some ground-level claims about empirical awareness of singular items, claims that supposedly can be made without having to draw such contrasts, then one would be faced with some kind of self-referential nonsense: One would be saying something about these claims that is not itself an empirical claim about sensuous objects, and if all meaningfulness is based on rock-solid claims about empirically available singular objects, then that claim about the claim would have to be met with a denial that it is meaningful. That is, putting the idea of sense-certainty into practice shows us that the "abstract meaning" of "sense-certainty" is, when taken outside of the larger context in which it has its home, self-contradictory.[18]

Hegel's own way of doing this—notably different from typical Anglophone philosophical practice—is to use such characterizations as "sense-certainty" or "consciousness" as a shorthand for a more general philosophical claim. Thus, when put in more sloganlike form, "sense-certainty"—now taken as the generic name for this kind of position—is a reflectively formulated philosophical stance toward the meaningfulness of our own experience, which, in articulating itself as a claim about the nature of experience or evidence in general, undermines the very claim to the nonconceptuality and nonreflectedness embedded in the stance of "sense-certainty" itself. (For that reason, I persist in keeping it in quotation marks to indicate its status as a general position.)

It is not as if Hegel is asserting that there is simply no such thing as "sense-certainty" (as if he were claiming that anyone making claims based on "sense-certainty" would have to deny the existence of an empirical awareness of distinct, singular things). Hegel's point is that it is only when "sense-certainty" is taken to be absolute, to be the most basic, self-sufficient expression of the "ideality" involved in subjectivity, that it turns out to be self-undermining. That one sees a singular object (for example, a red ball) need not be self-undermining.

That "sense-certainty" as absolute is self-undermining is one point. There is another, dialectical point to be made. The self-undermining character of sense-certainty shows that its pretense to being absolute—to being a self-sufficient claim about what is normatively authoritative in our experience—quickly dissolves into a different type of claim. One's commitments in asserting anything like "sense-certainty" turn out not to be commitments to the idea that such an act of sensing a singular object is the normative bedrock for other assertions (where "one's spade is turned"). Rather, that to which one commits oneself is the claim that one is perceiving an enduring singular object in one's experience and that this object can have different properties in time. If the awareness of singular things is not possible without bringing in something else that is not itself part of the way in which "sense-certainty" formulates itself, then we have already admitted that we are in effect "placing" (or, in Hegel's terms, "positing") things within the field of our experience and not, as it were, simply reading them off the experience itself. Within experience, normative lines are being drawn (between "seems" and "is the case"), and that brings us back to the original question. Who or what is drawing the lines? Or is that the wrong question to ask?

If experience is to provide any evidential ground for our assertions about the world, then it must be the case that "the *singular* things of sensuous apperception are supposed to constitute *the ground* of universal experience."[19] Such a view is crucial to any view of knowledge of the world that would claim that perceptual contact with objects provides a basis for knowledge of the world. Just as "sense-certainty" is the reflective claim that the evidential basis of knowledge lies in the immediate sense-perception of singular items, "perception" is Hegel's shorthand for the reflective claim that is its successor, namely, that perceptual experience of individual objects in the world offers us reasons for belief that we can entertain as reasons. (Or, to put it slightly differently, the truth of sense-certainty is that it is really a more complex perceptual experience.)

However, more is given in perception than merely the particular perceived object itself. It is part of perceptual experience that it purports to be an experience of particular objects as instantiating more general properties (such that one not only can identify a particular object but also can reidentify it over time). The enduring things of sense experience are what are supposed to justify our having certain sensuous experiences. Why, then, is it not enough to rely on the animal perceptual system (which human agents share at least in part with other animals) to make all the points that need to be made? After all, some animals also seem to be able to track a singular object even as it goes in and out of their perceptual field and thus in some sense to identify and reidentify it.

Perceptual evidence *as* evidence thus oscillates between two conceptions of what constitutes a reason for belief. On the one hand, one has reason to believe that there is a particular object (say, a stone) confronting oneself because of one's perception of the particular stone. Likewise, one could be said to have a reason to believe that it is a stone confronting you because of the general features perceived of the individual stone. Although perceptual experience involves what "sense-certainty" claims was the bedrock of knowledge—sensations of singular items—the failure of "sense-certainty" to sustain its claim to being the absolute shows that it, "sense-certainty," turned out to be only an abstraction from out of the context of perceptual experience of the world. Likewise, although one can certainly learn to focus on the smells, sights, and tastes of perceptual experience apart from any of the claims that perceptual experience makes, focusing on such sensations is itself an act that abstracts these elements out their primary role in enabling perceptual experience of worldly objects.[20] On the other hand, for the perceptual

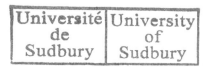

experience to have any cognitive import, to serve as evidence for assertions, it must be capable of being taken in terms of the reasons—the "universal"—it embodies. Thus, perceptual experience as a basis for claim making or as fodder for further inference involves more than merely the sensuous apprehensions of singular things. On that view, the sensuous apprehension of things is used as a vehicle for the grasp of things external to the sense experience itself, and the more general features of experience, which, in general, are not directly encountered in any sensuous sense, are, as Hegel notes, "supposed to be the ground, the essence, of universal experience."[21]

Perceptual experience thus involves a different and more complex line being drawn between the way things appear to us and the way things are apart from their appearance to us.[22] The line drawn in making an "inner-outer" distinction is thus that of not only distinguishing between "in the mind" and "external to the mind" but also distinguishing between "in appearance" and "outside of appearance." Or to put it in the Kantian terms, Hegel is clearly invoking both sensibility and "the understanding" (the intellect, *der Verstand*) must be at work together if perceptual experience is to have any cognitive import for a conscious animal.[23] For perceptual experience to do the work it is supposed to do in the reflective structure of "perception," the appearing world must provide evidence for the world as it is. Thus, there must be an "inner" to the appearing world that is not exhausted by the way it de facto appears to us at any given time, which is also supposed to explain why it is that the world appears to us as this way and not that (and for which the appearing world is the evidence). This "inner world"— behind, as it were, the perceptual world—is necessary because of the very instability of the concept of the perceptual object itself. The perceptual object is supposed to have a kind of independence from other perceptual objects, and this independence enables observers to establish correlations among objects of perception (such as the distinct perception of the lit match being applied to the paper and the distinct perception of the burning paper). However, as we construct causal explanations of perceptual objects in terms of the "inner world," we also come to understand that the perceptual object is what it is because of the causal relations in which it stands. The singular objects of "perception" thus are what they are because of the relations in which they stand. Perceptual objects are both the terminus of perceptual judgments, in that they make those judgments true and bring an end to the asking for reasons, and conceptually puzzling mixes of independence and dependence.

This "inner world," in the terms of "perception," cannot be something we observe via the sensory aspect of experience but instead must be that aspect of experience that manifests our conceptual capabilities at work, to be *wirklich*, in the experience itself.[24] There are the observations of singular things in perception, but the consciousness of the distinction between the object as appearing to oneself and the object as it is apart from the appearance is itself a line that is not drawn by the sensory aspect of the experience alone. Direct observation thus involves drawing a quasi-metaphysical line between appearance and the "inner" of appearance—between appearance and what appears—and that line is drawn within experience itself by our conceptual capacities as linked to our sensory capacities, not by our sensory capacities alone.[25]

If so, then we are once again driven to ask the question as to whether this line is drawn from within the terms of "perception" itself or from some standpoint outside of "perception." The object as it appears is perspectival, our perspectives on it shift as we change our locations, and we perceive the object in its various perspectives as the same object. In perception, we thus operate with a distinction that functions within experience as a distinction between myself as perceiving a world and that world as independent of me but nonetheless disclosed to me in perception. Making that claim itself is an act of judgment and not a perceptual observation itself.

Hegel concludes that in judging this way, "the I has an object which not differentiated from itself—[it is judging about] *itself*—[it is] *self-consciousness*."[26] That is, the subject-object distinction itself is a line drawn from "outside" of or "above" the subject-object distinction. It is the line drawn in understanding ourselves as occupying a position in the world and as undertaking commitments based on our experiential encounters with ourselves and the world. In understanding ourselves as perceivers, we understand ourselves as undertaking commitments and issuing entitlements based on those perceptions *as* reasons for belief, and we thus cease to be simple perceivers.[27] If the terms of perception formed the "unconditioned," our experience would be from the reflective point of view incoherent.

## C: Self-Consciousness

### 1: Being at Odds with Oneself in Desire

Since consciousness (as distinct from animal awareness) consists in maintaining a subject-object distinction as operative within perceptual experience itself, all consciousness involves drawing a nonempirical line between "appearing" (or "seeming") and "really is the case." (Such a line is nonempirical in the sense that the line cannot be an observable fact about oneself or one's observations.) This line between subject and object does not exist in nature apart from creatures practically drawing that line. When Hegel says that "all consciousness of another object is self-consciousness," he does not mean that every consciousness of an object carries with it a corresponding self-reflection (as if he were saying that every perception of, say, a green plant is accompanied by a corresponding reflection on the fact that one is seeing a green plant).[28] The self-conscious subject has "no reality (*Realität*), for it itself, in being its own object, is [thus] not an object at all, since there is no distinction present between itself and its object."[29]

Hegel also says that self-consciousness is "the truth of consciousness" and is the "ground" of consciousness.[30] The human organism as a subject (or agent) consists in the unity of the stances it takes toward objects so that in the realization of any act of consciousness of an independent object, the agent is locating himself within a space of reasons that is the basis for drawing the line between the "inner" and the "outer" in the first place. To actualize that self-consciousness, the agent must be able not merely to draw the line but to draw it in particular ways, and that requires a more specific determination of what is the case. The abstract meaning of "consciousness"—as a distinction between awareness of an object and independently existing objects themselves—involved the agent's awareness of himself as not merely occupying a position in the world but *as* occupying a position in that world. Although "consciousness" (as the general term for a set of certain types of reflective claims) at first looks like more of a metaphysical description of the agent-world relationship, it turns out instead to involve the normative stance that an agent assumes toward the world. It is in formulating the distinction itself between subject and object that one further commits oneself to the view, in Hegel's words, "that I have in *one and the same* consciousness *myself* and the *world*, that in the world I re-encounter myself again, and, conversely, in my consciousness have what *is*, what possesses *objectivity*."

That involves a dilemma. "Consciousness" commits one to a robust sense of objectivity, but "self-consciousness" seems to undermine this very robust commitment, since it involves committing oneself to the claim that it is "I" or "we" who draw the normative lines involved in "consciousness." (Hegel is less cautious on this point and calls this kind of rift an outright contradiction.)[31]

His discussion of this once again brings his particular uses of "negation" and "negativity" into play. In "consciousness," we take the limits of what we can with authority claim to know to be set by the objects themselves. These objects form the (determinate) "negative" of any conscious awareness, since one can determine what counts as an awareness only by distinguishing that awareness from something other than itself. (What an awareness is can be determined only by distinguishing it from something not itself, the object of awareness, and it is thus, in Hegelian terms, finite.) The negative of something is its limit, what demarcates it from something else, that is, the point where it ceases to be what it is or, even more important, where it ceases to exercise the authority it otherwise has. Hegel calls this "determinate negation" to indicate where the limit of something is not simply everything it is not (which would be everything else, full stop) but is what the item would become if, as it were, it stepped over its limit. (There may, of course, not be one thing but many different things that an item stepping over its limit could become; red could become green, or blue, or so on, but not sweet.) It is the negativity of the initial objects themselves in the (at first) naïve assertion of their status as the unconditioned that pushes us to such self-undermining reflection in the first place.

This kind of self-consciousness is also "abstract" in that, as characterized, it consists in nothing more than both the full awareness of the distinction between one's experiences of a thing and the thing itself and marking that as a distinction made within experience itself. The "I" in question that undergoes the experience is itself abstract when it is taken as merely the identity of the self over time, that is, the unity of the self that has the experiences. As drawing the line between itself and the world of which it is aware—that is, as drawing the line between "my experience of X" and "X as it is apart from my experience"—it is, as Hegel puts it, "inwardness devoid of any distinction."[32] For the subject to have anything to itself other than merely being "that to which experience is ascribed," it must actualize this abstract meaning in practice.

Abstract self-consciousness thus is that of a subject that has a life but does not yet lead that life in that although it is aware of its distinguishing itself from that of which it is aware (as being a subject that undertakes commitments), it cannot, at that point, have any criterion as to which commitments it is to undertake except for those that have as their aim "truth" or "objectivity" (themselves equally abstract goals).[33] To reconcile its understanding of itself as undertaking commitments, assuming a stance, as drawing the lines between what appears to itself and what is the case, such a subject needs, to put it in Hegelian terms, a conception of objectivity that reconciles itself with its own sense of subjectivity.[34]

To resolve that rift, Hegel speaks of this as self-consciousness "giving itself objectivity," which, he notes, is the other side of fully acknowledging the subjectivity of our encounters with the world.[35] He also speaks of this as a "goal to be achieved," but this is misleading.[36] Hegel is not claiming that any given agent actually has this reconciliation as an explicit goal for himself, as if this were, say, a hidden but always present desire on the part of any agent. Rather, it is a matter of following out the logic of self-consciousness once the tension between agency as "consciousness" and as "self-consciousness" has become more open. That "logic," in Hegel's terminology, has to do both with the finitude of "consciousness"—as involving the idea that thoughts (or speech-acts such as individual assertions) can be justified only by appeal to something else that is distinct from them and that from the standpoint of "consciousness" must be taken as given—and with the infinity of self-consciousness as involving the notion that ultimately it must set its normative limits itself. This very idea of the full self-determination of thought, that it can only obey a law that it sets for itself, seems to be itself contradictory, since it demands that thought set a normative standard for itself without any appeal to a normative standard by which it could claim in any non-question-begging way that the standard it sets is not arbitrary. Without therefore "giving itself objectivity," self-consciousness is straightforwardly at odds with itself, but it is not at first clear how "giving itself objectivity" is supposed to clear that up.

The fact that an agent is at odds with himself does not imply that the agent has to recognize that tension or even be motivated to clear it up. On the one hand, the agent can see those normative limits as themselves simply "given" and thus "give himself objectivity" by submitting himself to the dictates of reason. If the agent is to submit himself in any kind of norm-governed way—if he is to be an agent, a conscious and self-conscious being—something like the independent dictates of reason will have to be presupposed. He obviously cannot simply argue himself into accepting the dictates of reason without already having accepting those dictates, since without having already accepted the authority of reason, he would have no reason to do so. (The "bad infinite" as the infinite regress would immediately make its appearance. He would have to argue himself into accepting the argument to submit to the dictates of reason, and he will have to argue himself into that, and so on.) Thus it seems that the dictates of reason simply define the rules of the game, and if one is not playing the game by those rules, one is not playing the game at all. For that matter, it is probably even misleading to speak of playing the game, since that suggests that one is accepting the rules (as one might in a real game), whereas in the space of reasons, one cannot initially accept the rules at all without presupposing that one is already playing by the rules. Thus it might well seem that something like an immediate rational insight into the dictates of reason (perhaps something like Fichte's or Schelling's idea of "intellectual intuition") is required, but that is, or so Hegel thinks, a nonstarter. It transfers what Wilfrid Sellars calls the "myth of the given" from the realm where it has been at home in classical empiricism— namely, the idea that without having to know anything else, we know about internal mental states that can then serve as the grounds of further knowledge—to the realm of rational insight.

Suppose, however, that the agent actually is at least a partial reader of Hegel (or Kant or Fichte), and he accepts the idea developed up to this point that at this level of articulation there seems to be a contradiction between "consciousness" and "self-consciousness." Why should he care about resolving that contradiction? Once one is in the space of reasons, there are obviously lots of paradoxes and issues about infinite regresses that make their appearance (hares and tortoises, single barbers in a village that shave all those who do not shave themselves, and so forth), and one can certainly make it through life quite successfully not only without having resolved any of those paradoxes but also without even having worried about them at all (although one cannot successfully negotiate certain careers involving mathematics or logic without taking them seriously). Even assuming that the agent is playing the reasoning game, it is not entirely clear that he or she must resolve those paradoxes before acting.

In acting within the space of reasons and in treating reasons as reasons (and not as mere stimuli or ignition points for behavior), the agent is acting in terms of laws that constitute agency. (A fully nonrational agent is simply not an agent.) Thus, in responding to reasons *as* reasons, the individual agent may be said to be acting in terms of laws (or a law) that constitute the nature of the kind of entity of which the subject is self-consciously aware.[37] What, then, does such self-consciousness "giving itself objectivity" bring in its wake?

To answer this, we need to back up a bit. To resort again to Hegelian terminology: "Self-consciousness" is the sublation—the *Aufhebung*—of the soul, which means that the soul is preserved in self-consciousness. Although what it means to be an animal shifts when one begins to speak of self-interpreting animals, one's animality does not, for all that, simply vanish. A self-interpreting animal remains an animal. The self-conscious animal grasps himself as a singular organic subject to which different experiences and different actions are ascribed.

That self-consciousness is in this sense the sublation of the soul leads to perhaps the most familiar tension within all reflections on agency, that between our animal nature and our agency. As an animal, the agent lives in subjection to impulses, urges, and drives (what Hegel in his German simply calls a "*Trieb*") and their satisfaction. In the paradigm case, the urge (*Trieb*) is something "inner" to the animal, and it seeks something "outer" to satisfy the impulse. One of the things any adequate *Naturphilosophie* has to note is that the various principles that supposedly govern animal life have to do with the circumstances or the environment in which the animal lives. (That the best explanation for this would be Darwinian natural selection was, as already noted, not an intellectual tool available to Hegel.) Not surprisingly, animals and plants find what is necessary to nourish themselves and reproduce in their own environments, and, equally obviously, what is nourishment to one organism may be poison to another. When the animal and its environment match up, animals are thus at home in their worlds, and they are at one with themselves. Their subjectivity is expressed in the form of impulses and urges that more or less lead them to do what is required of them in their respective contexts. (It is a separate issue, but Hegel obviously had too placid a view of the stability of organic life and its environment, something not shared by Darwinian evolutionary accounts; alas for Hegel, the facts are on the side of the latter, not the former.)

As desiring animals, humans thus find themselves partly at home in their world. They find, for example, that many of their desires are appropriate to the objects of their desires without their having to reflect on that appropriateness.[38] Once again, this illustrates Hegel's otherwise puzzling claim (which he reiterates over and over) that animals are idealists. The appropriateness of animal desire and the object of desire is only one more illustration of the underlying "speculative identity" of subjectivity and objectivity in general and the "speculative identity" of mind and world in particular.[39] Moreover, Hegel seems to think that such desires may serve to motivate such self-interpreting animals independently of their being taken up by us in any kind of more reflective way or even being part of our self-consciousness.[40] The satisfaction of this kind of desire is a form of animal *Selbstgefühl*, that is, animal self-feeling or self-assurance. The animal has an urge, and as intelligence rises in animal behavior, it adopts different behaviors to achieve its goals or, for some animals, even alters the goals to achieve satisfaction of its goals.

Thus, even in animal behavior, there is already a kind of meaning at work in the animal's life in which the animal is potentially at odds with itself in that it may have an urge that it cannot fulfill. Nonetheless, the animal acts in terms of the principles of its own nature, and in doing so, it thus acts in a way that is at least minimally at one with itself. That certain objects (paradigmatically, food) serve to satisfy that desire illustrates that being at one with oneself is an ideal with its roots in animal life. The animal's self-feeling is an immediate awareness of itself as *this* animal responding to its environment in terms of the way that environment is registered by its internal systems. In satisfying his desires, the self-conscious agent also experiences the same kind of animal self-feeling, a feeling of itself as orienting itself in the world according to its own nature.

However, the self-feeling on the agent's "inner side" is different from that of mere animal self-feeling. Like any other organic being, a self-conscious agent, in acting consonantly with its own nature, would be following the goals set by its own nature. But what exactly are those goals, and what exactly is "its own nature"?

Some of the goals are obviously those that emerge from its animal nature. However, it is the very nature of a self-conscious agent to be potentially at odds with its own nature. In his discussion of the role of desire, Hegel characterizes animal desire as an example of "bad infinity." This might seem to follow from the means-end structure built into the fulfillment of desire. It can progress to "bad infinity" in the sense that if the means are justified in terms of the end, and the end is then itself justified as a means to a further end, the progress threatens to extend into infinity.

But this cannot be Hegel's real point, since on his own terms, there cannot be an a priori proof that there could never be such a thing as a desire that seeks only a limited end for its own sake. Hegel's real point thus seems to be something like this: The desire (say, for nourishment) requires its object (as food) for its satisfaction. The satisfaction of the desire is thus dependent on—or is distinguishable by (but again only "by us")[41]—its "negative," its determinate other (not just any other but only food consistent with the organism's nature will satisfy the desire), and the nature of the desire is thus set by the principles governing the organism itself. Now, one desire arises, is satisfied, and is then followed by another desire, and even a desire that seeks a particular end that is desirable for its own sake would be finite in Hegel's sense. What, if anything, would be misguided about seeing agency as a sum total of such finite desires?

Since the animal itself is, for itself, an end in itself, a *Selbstzweck*, the finitude of desire is thus not a problem for animal life. For animal life, its end is set by its nature, and it consists in the reproduction of the species and in keeping itself alive until such reproduction is carried out (or until the process is set into motion). The various objects the animal encounters therefore possess a normative standing for the animal—are good, bad, or indifferent—only in terms of how they fit into its own purposes as determined by its nature. Its own status as an end in itself is a status for it alone. For other animals, it may be simply be a means. In the natural world, although the prey may frustrate the predator by escaping or fighting back, it nonetheless cannot challenge its status as prey.

The self-conscious subject faces a different problem. The human agent is an end in itself, also a *Selbstzweck*, but as self-conscious, the agent can entertain the normative *as* normative in a way that the animal cannot. For the self-conscious agent, all other objects (with one obvious set of exceptions) lack a self (they are *selbstlos*, in Hegel's terms), and hence they offer no "resistance" (*Widerstand*) to its activities. By "resistance," Hegel clearly does not mean that human agents have special spiritual powers over objects that defy physical law (like magicians in fairy tales or heroes in action movies).[42] Rather, the lack of resistance on the part of objects indicates that the object can enter into no normative dispute with the agent. The prey still cannot challenge its status as prey, however much it may resist being reduced to it.

The object as object, that is, is insufficient on its own to challenge the way it fits into the complex web of ends that the agent has *as* an agent (including his urges and impulses as an animal). The object's value depends on the contribution it makes to the agent's ends. For Hegel, all goods are relative to some characteristic function of an entity, and thus an animal's good depends on what is necessary for that particular animal's life to go well. Likewise, the goods of agency depend on what, to use Aristotelian terms, would be the characteristic function of agency. Since all such goods will derive their value from what is the agent's overall good, there must be an unconditional end (or good) for agents as agents, for otherwise, it would remain indeterminate how good the ends that are subordinate to that end really are.[43] (These considerations, of course, leave it open for the moment as to whether the unconditional good of agency is an inclusive collection of different goods or a monistic good.)

The ordinary objects of desire cannot serve as the unconditional goods for agency, since as self-conscious, the agent himself can ask of any desire whether that desire itself—even a desire for a limited good that is itself desirable for its own sake—is a desire that should be fulfilled. In so taking himself, the subject thus is nonidentical with his own desires—that is, he is not fully absorbed into his desires—and, as nonidentical with those desires, he is the "other" to himself (in that he is now the other "thing" that raises the questions of what standards he, as an embodied agent, should follow). But what does it mean to say that the agent is now "other to himself"? And why should the agent take himself to be nonidentical with such desires?

If there were one unconditional good for agency—leaving it open for the moment as to how to characterize that good—then such a good would be in Aristotle's sense self-sufficient. That is, it would make the life organized around it worth choosing, and such a life would lack nothing—not in the sense that such an agent would have everything he could want but in the sense that, no matter what vicissitudes life throws at him, he would not have to look beyond that good for a basis for the choices he would have to make in order to make his life valuable.

Is such a good "objective" (as something that can be apprehended) or "subjective" (as having a status somehow conferred on it by desire)? Hegel's argument is to the effect that no matter how the individual agent, as individual, can think he is to resolve that issue, the issue will still remain essentially unresolved if left at the level of such individuality. He has two reasons for thinking this. The first (which is not itself really explicated either in the sections of the *Encyclopedia* on "self-consciousness" or in the sections on "self-consciousness" in the 1807 *Phenomenology*) is that there can be no appeal to given objects or to anything like "pure practical reason" to resolve that issue. The self-conscious agent remains an individual—an *Einzelnes*, a singular entity—and although *as* self-conscious, he has the capacity to distinguish himself from any of his desires (which, of course, does not mean that he really does so at any given time), he still remains an individual, desirous creature.[44]

This singularity of agency plays itself out in two ways. First, without some independent grasp of a space of reasons, the agent has no reason for choosing one desire over another except in terms of other desires. The singular agent requires something at least seemingly nonsingular to carry out such an activity. (Stated baldly like that, this is bound to be unconvincing to, among others, either Aristotelians or Kantians, since they would hold that right from the outset the space of reasons is both rich enough and present in such a way that is always available to such agents.) Second, the space of reasons he inhabits is itself bounded by time and place. It is itself a singular space of reasons, not one that automatically can command universal assent.

Hegel's second reason has to do with the implications of the way in which the self-conscious individual requires some kind of normative standard for the evaluation of desire, that is, the way in which he requires a standard that expresses his nature as an agent or, in Aristotelian terms, his characteristic function. In its attraction to the flower, the bee follows its nature and is, as it were, at home in the world, at least as far as the symbiosis between its makeup and its environment will permit. However, the self-conscious agent makes himself not at home in that world by virtue of the stance of "negativity" he assumes toward his world and himself. He both has claims made on him by his nature as a desirous organism and distinguishes himself from the claims themselves made on him by his own desirous nature. (As Hegel puts it in his 1807 *Phenomenology*, "consciousness suffers this violence at its own hands and brings to ruin its own restricted satisfaction.")[45] The "nature" of a self-conscious agent is that it need not be at one with itself, and this way of existing is a way of living that the rest of organic life does not share. His nature is not to have what is natural be definitive for him.

Thus, no matter what type of good the agent chooses as his final end (whether a single, monistic good or a pluralist conception of competing goods), it is a possibility that he or she may find himself or herself confronting another self-conscious agent who challenges that good and who is, moreover, willing to stake his life on making that challenge count for something. At that point, where one individual is willing to stake his life on the validity of his entitlement to decide what the good is, it does not matter what other claims the first set of agents make. Although this is only a possibility, Hegel will argue that such a confrontation turns out to be a necessary component for thinking about how there can be a move in history from a state of relative nonfreedom to freedom proper.

What is at stake in such a challenge has to do with what Hegel calls the "highest contradiction" between these two agents. Each is an individual with an "abstract self-consciousness" who confronts another such "abstract self-consciousness" as another embodied particular in the world, who also challenges the normative self-sufficiency of the other.[46] Each has what he takes to be a self-sufficient conception of what makes a life worth choosing, what sacrifices, and so forth need to be made for it, but one of them demands that the other recognize him as not merely having such a conception but as being the source of all entitlements to such conceptions. Each is an "abstract self-consciousness" in that he appears to the other both as a singular thing (like all other singular things that present possible obstacles to the fulfillment of desire) and as someone who makes normative demands on the other (and thus appears as someone who possibly disputes the norms by which one guides oneself). Although the animal confronts its world as something that can present obstacles to it (food can run out, predators can cut its life short, others of its species can prevent it from mating, and so on), the animal is not at odds with itself in those difficulties. It still acts in terms of a law that is its own law. The self-conscious agent, on the other hand, can be at odds with its world not merely in terms of the same kinds of obstacles that all animals face but in terms of how, in being at odds with himself and his social world, he can be at odds with himself in that he may not be clear to himself what his own law even is.

As Hegel frames the issue, there is nothing to rule out a priori the possibility that a collection of such agents could live out their common lives in complete harmony with each other.[47] However, at least when one of them or a group of them, even perhaps provoked by perfectly contingent circumstances, challenges the authority of whatever had been the basis of agreement that the others have previously accepted, and when these challengers are willing to stake their lives on the outcome, the former authorities are thrown into question. Insofar as the only conception of their agency remains that of "abstract self-consciousness," that is, of agency as self-conscious organic life, such clashes are practically unavoidable.[48] Among finite agents in a contingent natural world, the desires of particular agents (desires for nourishment, prestige, mates, and the like) will be thwarted by others, and the issue will arise as to what principles, if any, should govern such instances (that is, whether what is at issue are not merely the obstacles to satisfaction but which norms should govern disputes about their possible satisfaction). If the only thing holding the collective together are shared principles based on what is required for the satisfaction of desire, then there will be intractable disputes about such things. If nothing rules out a priori that such disputes can be settled by appeal to some other principles that the agents already share ("so have the gods eternally decreed...," "thus does impartial reason direct that..."), it is also true that nothing a priori guarantees that such principles will always be there.

## 2:  The Attempt at Being at One with Oneself as Mastery over Others

What is at stake in such confrontations is the realization of such "abstract self-consciousness." Where the collectivity is held together only by some kind of unthinking adherence to some set of principles (or to tradition, a worldview, or the like), when such a challenge is made to it, what must result is a struggle over what is at stake in being so committed to a tradition, a worldview, or the like. Each side demands recognition from the other of its own point of view. For those who defend the tradition or the worldview in which they are at home, the demand is for the challengers to recognize the legitimacy of their take on things. Where there is an incompatibility and, by hypothesis, no way of any further reconciling that incompatibility, then the contest has only a limited set of possible outcomes. As one shows that he is willing to put his life on the line—so that he would prefer death to submission to such a view—each of them is put into the position of having to force the other either to submit or to back off from his claims. The struggle is over who is entitled to set the terms of entitlement.

The self-conscious individual agent, in declining to identify his agency with his desires, finds himself confronted by another agent, who, in choosing this commitment over life itself, throws into question any conception of the self-sufficiency of the good that is based on natural desire. What such a challenge throws into relief is the radical contingency of the agent's choices and principles. Even with, as it were, the best reasons in the world, one can still find oneself confronted by an other who demands recognition and is willing to kill for it, not out of any kind of built-in desire for domination but simply out of the conviction that he is right and so he demands recognition of his rightness. The gap that self-consciousness opens up between the agent and his desires as an organic being shows that at the stage where the argument is carried out at the level of "abstract self-consciousness," there is no position in terms of one's orientation that one simply must take. Nonetheless, however natural any given position might seem at any time to an agent, when the agent is challenged in this way, he must decide how to respond, and this throws into high relief the utter contingency of all such responses. If one of them dies, no recognition has been achieved, and the conclusion of the problem is postponed until another day. If there is only a standoff, nothing has been settled, and the truce remains only a matter of external failure to achieve one's goals—and once again, the final reckoning is only postponed, not overcome. (The aggressing party has been thwarted, just as one can be thwarted by any other natural object, but has not necessarily been shown to have been wrong.) Or one of the parties can choose life over commitment to whatever principle he had, in which he case he capitulates and now serves the other, who becomes the "master." That person chooses to identify himself with a particular desire, namely, the desire not to be killed, and he becomes more "concrete," in Hegel's terms, and the other subject, who abstracts himself even further away from the fear of death itself, becomes the master.

Where there are competing sets of reasons between agents, and one party is willing to stake everything on his own entitlement to his set of principles, the dialectic of mastery and servitude comes into play. Prior to such confrontation, the self-consciousness at stake is, as Hegel puts it, only "sunken" within nature. It has not yet realized its own full nature as that which is always potentially at odds with its nature. It may be very stable in its convictions living in an equally stable social order, but it has not yet established a fully self-conscious appraisal of its reasons *as* reasons, and it cannot do this until such a struggle has occurred.[49] Whereas the animal is at home in its world in that it always acts on principles of its own nature, the human animal as a self-conscious agent institutes a gap between his nature as an agent and his nature as an animal (in at least the minimal sense that he has the capacity to ask himself if any of the motivations of his animal nature deserve to be put into practice, that is, if he should identify with any of his desires).

It is probably important to reiterate Hegel's point to the effect that there is no a priori reason to think that such agents could not establish something like a Hobbesian compact prior to such struggles for recognition, nor is there any a priori reason to think Hobbes was correct or incorrect in holding that all humans are possessed with desires for glory and fear of violent death. These points are, in Hegel's view, simply not relevant to the argument. Whereas such a Hobbesian compact could indeed prove to be very stable and enduring for long periods of time, it can always be undone by anyone or any group for whom the desire for recognition is stronger than the desire for life itself, and, given the gap always present in self-conscious life, there is no a priori reason to think that having such a desire is impossible.

All metaphysically individualist conceptions of agency will either have to project this struggle indefinitely into the future (since, except for contingently happy circumstances of peaceful resolution, there is no way out of it) or have to assume, either sotto voce or more or less explicitly, some kind of Platonist conception of the order of reasons. Although Hegel's own view is both that a common space of reasons must be developed and that the natural dialectic of reasons propels it in the direction of increasing universality, at the outset there is no reason to assume that any such conception is available to those agents.[50]

The space of reasons must be developed out of the structure of desire, and thus the idea of a final end that makes all other choices worthwhile will at first therefore be structured initially around some conception of well-being or happiness—in short, around the idea of some kind of natural or metaphysical fact about human agency that shows what that kind of entity's characteristic function is and therefore what it naturally ought to desire.

Such a conception of a self-sufficient end that is interpreted within that particular framework is going to be compatible with, if not require, some conception of enforced servitude, since the leisure and wealth required for a self-sufficient end of that sort means that in the conditions of finitude, some can flourish only if others do not. (Some can be happy and flourish only if others are not happy and do not flourish.) Particularly in the conditions of the ancient world, so Hegel argues, the "dirty work" the city and household need to have performed will require some to be forced into the service of others, since by and large none will on their own opt for such an arrangement for their own part. Hegel's "master" is thus a shorthand for the person or group who sets the terms of authority—whose particular interests structure the space of reasons that is actually at work in a form of life—so that the satisfaction of their desires is viewed as backed up by something like the will of the gods or the force of reason itself.

The master, by virtue of his domination of the servant, gets more or less to do what he desires, and thus the master, or at least so it seems, is able to be more at one with himself. He seems to be able to translate his desires, whatever they may be, relatively directly into reality through the compliance of the slave. It thus seems that, in his role as master, he need not have his will thwarted by the will of another, even though his will, of course, continues to encounter various natural obstacles.

### 3: Masters, Slaves, and Freedom

Although Hegel is quite clear that he thinks that slavery is never justified, he nonetheless also argues that its lack of justification can only become apparent (and therefore genuinely at work in political life) when there has been both an institutional and conceptual conception of the practice of giving and asking for reasons among "individuals" and not merely among singular subjects. Part of that argument is thus that "the individual," conceived as a locus of basic rights, is itself a social status that must be practically attained, not a metaphysical fact about human agents, and that this practical attainment has a history to it, outside of which it is unintelligible. Once again, it seems that Hegel wants to have it both ways: There is something about agency that requires that it be treated as of infinite worth, but that worth is itself a matter of a socially conferred status that is itself a matter of historical development.[51] How does Hegel think he can make both those claims at the same time?

Although the dialectic of recognition that results in mastery and servitude represents a practically unavoidable stage in human history, it is nonetheless an "untrue manifestation" ("*unwahre Erscheinung*") of the nature of agency (which in terms of Hegel's conception of truth does not mean that it never existed or has never been effective in practical life).[52] What is untrue about it is that since agency involves self-consciousness, the capacity to take a position on the validity of one's experience, the dynamic of agency is that of giving, asking, and demanding reasons for actions and beliefs. Once agents have grasped themselves *as* agents— that is, once they understand what it means in general to be an agent; what their agency is *an sich*, in itself—they must put that conception into practice. As they do so, they find that certain conceptions involve taking what agency means in very determinate ways, at first involving relations of mastery and servitude.

Hegel's own handwritten comments on the section in his 1820 *Philosophy of Right* shows how he was continually seeking to make his position on this a bit clearer even to himself and, most likely even in his own eyes, never really success-fully came to grips with some of the aspects of his view. For example, on the one hand, he writes that it is completely correct to say that slavery is in itself and on its own (*an und für sich*) wrong, but he notes that it is nonetheless a historical phenomenon that belongs to historical times prior to the self-conscious establish-ment of freedom as a principle.[53]

Consistently over his career, his argument was that the full distinction of a rationally justified claim and a merely particular claim is itself something that must be practically worked out over historical time, not something that is a "natural" part of the practice of giving and asking for reasons. We must think that at some distant part of our prehistoric past, the full prying apart of the *an sich*, "in itself" universality of reasons from the particular goals of an individual (or of a tribe or a clan) had not yet been achieved, and thus "might" and "right" had not yet been adequately distinguished. The various relations of mastery and servitude belong to that phase of history, when the practice of giving and asking for reasons had not yet managed to abstract itself fully out of its more immediate and natural context.

There is therefore a "state of nature" in human prehistory that obtains between the combatants in the struggle over mastery and servitude, but it is not the state of nature invoked by the classical proponents of a social contract conception of the state or of governmental legitimacy. Rather, "the state of nature" character-izes not a presocial or prepolitical stage in human development but that stage of human prehistory in which the will is only the "natural will."[54]

Hegel ties this together with the view more or less widely held in his own time that there had to have been such prehistorical groups that were held together only by the force of tradition and custom and who therefore lacked any genuine political unity as unity under anything like the modern concept of law. On his assump-tions, such prehistoric groupings—we can call them "traditional communities or societies" and keep the quotation marks for effect—would thus have also lacked the conceptual tools to think about their own potential freedom. In Hegel's histo-riography, it is only with the Greeks that the concept of freedom as a norm worth actualizing makes its appearance. (His own position on the forced servitude of Africans in modern life is without doubt a disturbing aspect of his own stance on this issue.)[55]

Although Hegel may have found reasons to believe in such a barbaric past in the historiography of his own day—and it is also hard not to notice at work here the overall Enlightenment picture of the gradual displacement of superstitious barbarism by rational reflection—there is no reason for us to take that view of history at anything like face value. However, even if we do set aside Hegel's ver-sions of the human past as being somewhat antiquated, we can nonetheless see that his conceptual point has to do with how we might imagine such a possible community's unity. (Hegel's versions of "Oriental" and African communities make just that conceptual point, but unfortunately, as already noted, his "Orientals" and "Africans" are relatively imaginary communities constructed to make a conceptual point and have nothing to do with real Indian, Chinese, Japanese, or African groups. Alas, it is not a point in Hegel's favor that he completely conflated his imaginary communities with the real ones.)

Greek freedom is, at least in part, being at one with oneself under the conditions that one is aware of responding to reasons as reasons, and it is the slave, not the master, who realizes that there is something he has lost, namely, not merely his own self-sufficiency (taken as happiness or flourishing) but his own freedom as the ability to submit himself to his own law. Whereas the master has not clearly learned to distinguish a desire from a reason for action—that is, distinguish a desire as it is taken to be a good reason for action versus desire as a mere urge demanding fulfillment—the slave has to live with the distinction of desire from reason. Unlike the master, the slave learns to distinguish his own singular "natural" will (the will that conflates desire and reason) from that of another singular will (that of the master). The slave learns that he must act on reasons that do not necessarily fit his desires, and he thus learns that what he lacks precisely is the freedom to act on his own reasons instead of those set by others. Whereas the master is compelled, from his point of view, to take some ultimate desire (or set of desires) as "given" and to view other desires as means to the end of satisfying that particular desire, the slave, as living under the complete authority of the master, is not permitted to have any ultimate desire of his own in terms of which his other desires might be rationally appraised in light of how they contribute to the fulfillment of that desire. For the master, the self-sufficient end is that of happiness. For the slave, the self-sufficient end is that of adhering to the law, and thus peculiarly, only the slave understands what it is to be free.

Ultimately, the master lives an unsatisfying (although not necessarily unhappy) life, whose unsatisfactoriness he nonetheless has difficulty comprehending, whereas the slave lives an unsatisfying life whose unsatisfactoriness is not only comprehensible and whose contradictory nature is always present. The slave must accept the will of the master as authoritative—for the slave system to be genuinely effective, the slave must be held in slavery not only by force but (from the master's point of view, ideally) by his own acceptance of his condition—and yet at the same time, the slave has to realize that the master's will cannot be authoritative. That such a contradiction can continue to exist over hundreds of years does show that it is not a contradiction (at very heart of human mindful agency) and thus ultimately unsustainable.

The master can subsist in his mastery only by having the servant recognize him—confer the status on him—as the master, yet, by the very terms of such recognition, the servant could not possibly have the authority to confer such recognition. Moreover, because the master can get what he desires by virtue of having such servants and "getting what he desires" is an authoritative principle for him, he will be practically (although not a priori) incapable of seeing that his domination is both irrational and yet necessary for his continued happiness.

Only something like a slave revolt or a massive shift of institutional loyalty can end the reign of masters over servants. However, a slave revolt establishes a new topic: freedom. Freedom, that is, is established only by those who have come to be at odds with themselves not merely by having their desires frustrated (which is common to all animals with desires) but by having them frustrated by the wills of others who seek not only to impose their wills completely and authoritatively on them—to treat them like nonrational animals—but also to justify their imposition (to treat them like rational animals). In Hegel's staging of the confrontation between agents that then falls out into a relation between master and slave, the agent who becomes the master does not self-consciously seek freedom—he seeks only the self-sufficiency of himself as an agent and the self-sufficiency of his own norms as the criteria of the desirability of all things that are correctly desired.[56] Mastery fundamentally conflates the normative order with the interests attached to a particular point of view.

Hegel thinks that something like this shift from mastery and servitude to freedom was stirring in ancient Greek and Roman life, and it is in the philosophies of ancient Greece that freedom first comes to be a point of reference. His point about Greek freedom, however, is that although the anguish of slavery was without doubt present among slaves in pre-Greek societies, the institutional and practical conditions for the concept of freedom as self-consciously "being at one with oneself while being at odds with oneself" were not yet worked out. That in turn required the growth of social institutions in which one's own norms existed not merely in a state of relative equilibrium with those of others but where they did so in a situation in which one combined a strong sense of identity with others together with an equally strong sense of one's difference from others.

On Hegel's view, in a "traditional society" with institutions of strong identification with clans and other groups, the practical, institutional structures of the mutual recognition of such difference would be absent. In this (overly idealized) presentation of the human past, the members of such prehistorical societies would have been free in that they were at one with themselves, but their freedom was undeveloped and hence unknown to them, since they had not developed the full gap between their natural lives and their status as self-conscious agents. If we instead take that account of the prehistoric past as a kind of Hegelian thought-experiment—as the creation of a conceptual possibility rather than a genuine piece of historiography—then we can imagine a community in which the selfhood of its members had not been actualized since the ends of life for such people would have to be simply set by mores and traditions and not by any kind of rational deliberation about final ends. Such people could reason effectively about how to realize such given ends, but the ends themselves would have to stand outside the domain of reasoning. Only after the slave revolts of antiquity could there be a reasoning about final ends that was not itself bound to any kind of "given," such as happiness or flourishing.

For there to be such a fully realized freedom, the relation between the master and slave must be transformed into Hegel's conception of a "speculative" identity: Each must come to be self-consciously occupying a position in social space (constituted by relations of mutual recognition) in which one's standing is constituted by that space (or, to put it in the terms Hegel helped to make famous, in which one's "identity" is so constituted), but at the same time, one's stance to one's own interiority (one's own desires, subjective life, wishes, hopes, loves, and so on) is recognized as having an authority on its own.[57] That social space is both inferential and pragmatic: One learns to move about in a social space not merely by making inferences from one meaning to another. One also makes observations, issues entitlements, undertakes responsibilities—which involves making changes in the normative status of others and putting one's own putative normative status, as it were, on view.[58] To occupy a social space is to know one's way around the normative moves permitted, required, stressed, and so forth in that space.

To put it in more Hegelian, dialectical terms: To be such a genuinely free agent, one must be socially recognized as having the authority to do, feel, and believe what is not fully set by the bounds of traditional social authority. The free man or woman, that is, is socially authorized to seek his or her own good, to seek to maintain his or her oneness with themselves by his or her own lights—and to be, in that sense, his or her own law. That kind of freedom is not a metaphysical fact about all the stuff out of which human beings are made, nor is it a claim that humans exercise a special kind of causality different from the causality of the natural world. It is rather that freedom is a social achievement with a very complex history behind it whose realization also requires an equally complex institutional and practical background. As an achievement, it always coexists with the possibility of being undone.

One of the key conditions for the realization of freedom, so Hegel argued, was the arrival of Christianity on the world stage. The idea of God as loving all equally and of everyone's being the same in the eyes of God fundamentally displaced the earlier, more naturalistic conception of final ends as set by nature, custom, or the arbitrary wills of a set of polytheistic gods. Building on the Greek philosophies, the Christian conception of God as the idea of a self-consciousness that is "above" the various other self-conscious communities and not thereby bound to any of their particular identities works to fashion a new conception in which the strong may not do as they please with the weak, however "natural" such a conception might have originally been. This first came about as the slaves of antiquity came to realize that there was a sense in which they remained free and in which they asserted that freedom, despite the obviousness of the situation before them in which they were manifestly in chains.

## 4: The Truth of Mastery and Servitude

Freedom is at first understood in terms of the denial of and escape from slavery.[59] Once the slave understands this and what the opposite of his condition would be, the slave is in a position to develop a positive conception of freedom. The development of the concept of freedom is illustrative of the Hegelian conception of the way in which a concept is developed into its "truth." This Hegelian truth of mastery and servitude is at first that of what Hegel, adopting Kant's own terms, calls "universal self-consciousness."[60] As taking a position in social space, self-consciousness consists in knowing oneself in terms of knowing where one, as an individual, stands in that space, as a set of potentially universal norms. To be self-conscious is to know one's commitments and to know how, within that knowledge of one's commitments, to move around in that social space. Such knowledge about how to orient oneself involves avowing and undertaking commitments that in form are universal (or at least go beyond one's own singular impulses) but also involve knowing who one is as an individual—that is, knowing among other things one's own quirks, one's settled dispositions, one's talents, one's defects, and even perhaps knowing things like which temptations one can easily resist and which present more difficulty and are best avoided—and being able to reason out what is therefore appropriate, required, obligatory, not especially recommended, and so on in light of that kind of self-knowledge.[61] Self-consciousness is thus a unity of the "universal" and the "individual."

"Universal self-consciousness" consists in those norms that make up a social space. It is the space of intersubjectivity, not that of individual self-enclosed monads each reflecting each other's perceptions. This kind of self-knowledge, like the other forms of "consciousness" and "self-consciousness," cannot consist of knowing universalizable rules without any grasp of how those rules (or generalities) are to be put to work in one's actions. To put it in more direct Hegelian terms: The rationality of "the concept" cannot consist in either a one-sided knowledge of general principles or a one-sided knowledge of singularities; there must be better and worse ways of rationally bringing the universal to bear on the particular and vice versa. The "logic" of these terms thus must encompass more than merely tracing out the inferential connections among concepts taken apart from the realization of those concepts.[62] To be rational, that is, should consist not only in being able to move from one concept to another—that would only be to look at the rationality of a concept abstractly and *an sich*, in itself[63]—but also in moving from the concept to the world in a rational manner.[64] In moving from "the concept" to the world in either observation or action, one possibly alters one's own normative status and those of others. It is one thing to be able to move from "duck" to "waterfowl" as a matter of conceptual inclusion. It is another thing to be able to deploy the concept of "duck" in making an observational statement to the effect that there is a duck in the pond over there, and to be able to deploy concepts is to be able to change the normative status of oneself or that of another—as when saying, "there is a duck in the pond" entitles another agent to assert that there is a duck in the pond.[65]

Originally, the agent who becomes the master strives to do just that—alter the normative status of both members of the relation and alter the self-relation of both members so that the other is made not merely to comply with his orders but, more basically, to accept his authority to set the other terms of what entitles whom to what. The function of his acts is thus not merely that of domination by force but of securing acceptance by the other, of altering the self-relation of the other so that he or she takes what the master proposes to be a good reason for belief or action. The truth of the confrontation in the dialectic of mastery and servitude is thus a conception of giving reasons that are claims or assertions not only of individual interest and power but also of others taking up those claims or assertions as having validity.

"Universal self-consciousness," however, is tied to the singularity of the agents and the particularity of the communities they inhabit. Within such communities, each individual agent, in Hegel's terms, "looks as if he is making an appearance in the other" agent ("*als ineinander scheinende*").[66] Each shares a set a commitments, and that sets into motion the realization of such a form of life as establishing practices that move on to the evaluation of such shared commitments in terms of reason itself and not merely in terms of factually shared norms. For example, the distinction between objects and our perspectives on objects shared by all such agents in a form of life is fully realized not merely in trading on shared norms but in subjecting the norms themselves to scrutiny.

The truth, in the Hegelian sense, of universal self-consciousness is that of reason, which runs on the faith that it can discover ultimately what things are— that the whole is ultimately intelligible, even if not right now. The claims of reason introduce more than merely a shared life and history. They introduce something whose dynamic is to throw even deeply shared commitments into question.

Hegel's claim is that "universal self-consciousness" as intersubjectivity requires its actualization in a conception of reason as empowered to make out the intelligibility of things. His basis for this is the view that the kinds of claim-making activities involved in self-conscious life themselves push for a reworking of shared norms (of "universal self-consciousness") into objective norms ("reason"). Such a push comes from what is necessary to work out and resolve the tensions that exist in any series of claim-making activities that rely solely on a conception of norms that are merely shared and which make no further claim to validity than the mere fact that they are shared. Ultimately, the distinctions between subject and object, and that between subjects apprehending each other as subjects and at the same time as objects, are themselves intelligible only in terms of the space of reasons, not merely in terms of what the people of a given way of life happen to think.

To put it more summarily: The subject-object split is itself a moment of the space of reasons. One can build up the space of reasons neither out of the "atoms" of subjectivity nor out of intersubjectivity. One can actualize the commitments made in what seems like a space of traditional norms only by working out a conception of the truth of things, a conception of reason as transcending tradition. It is not that "reason" is presupposed in all such activities of claim making. Rather, it is realized in reflectively carrying out what is necessary to make sense of the claim-making activities themselves.

The truth of mastery and servitude is thus Hegel's reconception of Martin Luther's idea of Christian freedom as a freedom in which the individual Christian is, as Luther puts it, "the free master of all things and subordinate to nobody," while at the same time being "a subservient figure to all things and subordinate to everybody."[67] Each is both master and servant to the other. In Rousseau's and Kant's own secularized transformations of Luther's idea, the moral world is further reconceived as a world in which each agent is both sovereign (as an unconstrained lawgiver) and subject (as unconditionally subject to the law), and both Kant's and Rousseau's versions themselves may be seen as new formulations within individualistic terms of an older Aristotelian idea of constitutional states as those in which all rule and are ruled in turn.[68]

That reason is the actualization of self-consciousness and not its presupposition provides the impulse behind Hegel's historical and social narrations of rationality. Unlike Kant, who thought that there were certain transcendental conditions of self-consciousness—that is, metaphysical commitments that any rational agent had to undertake if he was to be self-conscious at all, even if the authority of those metaphysical commitments was circumscribed within the world as we had to experience it and not the world as it was apart from our experience—Hegel holds that coming to an engagement with reasons *as* reasons is an achievement, not a condition of all experience. To engage with reasons as reasons is ultimately to be engaged with "infinity."[69]

## 5: Objectivity, Intuition, and Representation

In his mature systematic version of his works (his constantly revised *Encyclopedia of the Philosophical Sciences*), Hegel follows the discussion of mastery and servitude with a section on truth in experience. He there makes it clear, as if it were not already so, that he believes in our ordinary judgments as being made true by the objectivity of the objects of judgment.[70] However, with regard to the truths of our own mindful agency, we have the problem that the objects about which we are judging (ourselves) are themselves constructions of mindful agency itself: Our various normative statuses, ranging from "knower" to "postal clerk" are not items found in nonhuman nature but more properly in the structures of recognition that make up human life and history. Nonetheless, the suspicion has always been that whatever else he says, Hegel can have no place for intuition to play the kind of decisive role it plays in Kant and in more empirically oriented conceptions of mind and world.

Intuition (*Anschauung*) is our noninferential relation to objects in the world—noninferential only in the sense that in such contact with objects we make no actual inferences. Intuition in this sense has to be distinguished from "perception" (again taken as Hegel's shorthand for the reflective claim that experience of individual objects in the world offers us reasons for belief and that such perceptual experience makes a failed claim to be "absolute"). "Perception" is only of individual objects, and in its reflections, it showed itself to require a more reflective stance, for which the shorthand was "the understanding" (or intellect, *der Verstand*). Intuition—as the German term, *Anschauung*, implies—has the meaning of being a view on the world, and to have an intuition in this sense is thus (to appropriate another phrase from John McDowell) to have the world in view.[71]

On the Hegelian view, in intuition we do not confront individual objects but a world, a "totality of determinations," which provides us evidence for empirical belief about that world. The world that comes into view in such a way is a world of mutual recognition, a world that, in Wilfrid Sellars's phrase, is "fraught with ought." In Hegel's scheme, the distinction between concepts and intuitions—so crucial to, say, Kant's view—grows out of the actualization of the distinction between intuitions and representations (*Vorstellungen*). An intuition is a discursive apprehension of the world by way of our sensations of that world. Intuitions thus never stop at the singular object, as "perception" took itself to be doing (a crucial distinction Hegel claims to have overlooked in his 1807 *Phenomenology*).[72] To have the world in view in intuition is to strive for a "totality" that intuition on its own cannot achieve. Instead, an intuition requires attention to certain elements in the foreground, for which it must presuppose the world-as-a-whole as a background.[73] Intuition thus gives us a unified, single regard on the world but not that whole world itself, and in intuition, we thereby operate within a unity of subject and object in that we take the world in our intuitive perceptual encounters to be the world as it is—we take ourselves to be aware of the world, not just our sensations of it, although a shift in attention can focus on those sensations themselves rather than the world for which they are the means of knowledge. (On this Hegelian picture, it is a mistake to think that the secondary focus on sensations themselves is thus primary in our intuitive knowledge of the world and that we somehow infer from an immediate knowledge of sensations to the world itself.)

Intuitive knowledge thus operates in the realm in which we let the objects of sense experience set the terms of our beliefs about them.[74] Intuition strives, as it were, for a grasp of the whole, but it can never achieve it. In seeking to actualize the intuitive awareness of the world and awareness of ourselves as occupying a subjective position in that world—to put it to work in our lives—we thus arrive (in Hegel's terms) at representation (*Vorstellung*). In intuition, the world comes into view, but it is in representation that we articulate the difference between our perspective on the world and the world itself.[75] "Representation" is thus a more reflective stance toward things and ourselves.

Another way to put this point would be the following: The distinction between intuition and representation is that between two statuses. For example, that I am seeing a duck in the pond is an observation that I make and attribute to myself. That I see the duck does not entitle anyone else to assert that they see a duck, but that I have seen a duck may entitle others to form the "representation" that there is a duck in the pond.[76] Even though only I am entitled to the claim "I observe (intuit) a duck in the pond," others may be entitled to the more neutral claim based on my expression, "There is a duck in the pond."

To the extent that genuine knowledge goes beyond being agent specific and seeks generality, intuition can thus never be the full realization of claims to knowledge.[77] With the world in view in intuitive knowledge, we do not have full-fledged claims before us, although intuitive knowledge may be in itself, *an sich*, a repository of such claims—at least to the extent that the meaning of these experiences can only be actualized in such explicit claim-making activity. That is, in making a cognitive claim on the basis of intuitive experience, one is not making explicit what is already there in its full form within intuitive experience. One is actualizing the meaning of the experience by rendering it first into representational and then into judgmental form. Such claims emerge only after one has formed a representation of the material presented by intuitive experience.[78] A "representation" in this sense is only a more reflective version of an "intuition"; that is, it involves a shift in the normative status of our experience and not a new kind of experience itself—a shift in the authority of having an observation that does not entitle others to a claim that they, too, have observed the same thing into the authority of issuing a judgment that does (or can) entitle others to make the same judgment. (One can, of course, mistakenly or falsely issue bogus entitlements.)

The move to judgment, to explicit claim-making activity with its different sets of pragmatic authorizations, is thus a move away from intuition and in the direction of pure thought. In intuition, the direction of travel, as it were, is that of a set path. Its constraints are both biological (having to do with the nature of human sensibility) and social (the way in which socialization does and does not affect such sensibility). On the other hand, the direction of "the concept" is that of freely carving out a new path, in which conceptual knowledge begins in sense-experience but gradually actualizes itself more fully in moving away from sense-experience.[79] Or to put it another way, intuitive knowledge follows in the steps of established meanings held in place by existing structures of recognition as constrained by natural states, whereas conceptual knowledge (that of "pure thought") often proposes new paths to take, proposals on how, for example, a word should be used in the future rather than how it has been used in the past (even though such proposals are usually based on usage currently in place).[80] Nonetheless, since concepts are thus prospective in their employment, for conceptual thought, meaning cannot be reduced to use, even though it cannot be established apart from use.[81]

Although the owl of Minerva may fly only at dusk, all de facto use of concepts is in itself, *an sich*, prospective in character. For example, Hegel himself proposes several new uses for words such as *sensation*, *the understanding*, and *reason* and argues that in doing so, we will be better placed to comprehend the place of our own mindful agency in nature. Ultimately, all such proposals for new ways to use old words will have to reflect on itself and what it is doing, and when it does that fully, it becomes philosophy.

*Notes*

1. Whether Hegel is actually repeating Aristotle or is drawing an inference from Aristotle's conception of the voluntary is not itself entirely clear. In discussing Aristotle's own thoughts on the matter, Sarah Broadie, *Ethics with Aristotle* ([New York: Oxford University Press, 1991], xiii, 462 pp., p. 125), notes the ambiguity: "Children (i.e., human beings as yet incapable of such judgment) are voluntary agents, too, and in one place Aristotle says the same of animals (1111 b 8–9).... (It is not clear how nonhuman animals fit into this picture; perhaps Aristotle views their behavior as voluntary in an analogical sense.)" Hegel's own views may share this ambiguity with his inspiration, Aristotle's views.

2. Hegel, *Enzyklopädie der philosophischen Wissenschaften III*, §410; Hegel et al., *Hegel's Philosophy of Mind: Being Part Three of the "Encyclopaedia of the Philosophical Sciences,"* (1830), p. 144: "However, in itself the absolute coming-to-be-free of self-feeling, the soul's untroubled being at one with itself in every particularity of its content is a necessity, for in itself the soul is absolute ideality, that which envelops all its determinatenesses; and it is implied in the concept of soul that it is through the sublation of all the particularities which have become fixed in it that it proves itself to be the unlimited power over them—that it diminishes what is still immediate, existent within it to a mere property, a mere moment, in order to become by way of this absolute negation a free individuality for itself."

3. Hegel, *Wissenschaft der Logik II*, p. 254; Hegel, *Hegel's Science of Logic*, p. 584.

4. It is another matter to go into how Hegel must be thought to understand the finer points of Kant's arguments. Hegel takes Kant to have shown that self-consciousness properly construed is a consciousness of "inner" and "outer" together; indeed, without this form of self-consciousness, there would be no "inner sense" and "outer sense" at all, and he takes himself to have shown that this kind of self-consciousness involves assuming a position in social space. On these issues, see Sally Sedgwick, "Longuenesse on Kant and the Priority of the Capacity to Judge," *Inquiry: An Interdisciplinary Journal of Philosophy*, 43/1 (March 2000), 81–90; Sally Sedgwick, "Hegel's Critique of Kant: An Overview," in *A Companion to Kant*, ed. Graham Bird (Malden, Mass.: Blackwell, 2006).

5. See Paul W. Franks, *All or Nothing: Systematicity, Transcendental Arguments, and Skepticism in German Idealism* (Cambridge, Mass.: Harvard University Press, 2005), viii, 440 pp. Franks argues that the issue of whether the unconditioned is a member of the series or is heterogeneous to the series constituted perhaps the fundamental problem besetting the German idealists after Kant's innovation. However, Franks does not seem to allow that Hegel's own proposal (followed later by the American pragmatists) has to do with the way that something can be self-explicating in the sense of self-correcting and that this way of putting the matter simply avoids the problem of the homogeneity or heterogeneity of one element of the series. That reason is the capacity to achieve the unconditioned is also to be distinguished in Kant's works from reason as a logical or discursive capacity to form mediate inferences and as what Kant calls the "faculty of principles"; see the discussion in Béatrice Longuenesse, *Hegel's Critique of Metaphysics* (Modern European Philosophy; Cambridge: Cambridge University Press, 2007), xxi, 246 pp.

6. See Robert B. Pippin, *Hegel on Self-Consciousness: Desire and Death in Hegel's Phenomenology of Spirit* (Princeton, N.J.: Princeton University Press, 2010), where this idea is worked out in

great detail. I have argued a similar thesis in Pinkard, *Hegel's Phenomenology: The Sociality of Reason*.

7. This language is adopted from Richard Moran, *Authority and Estrangement: An Essay on Self-Knowledge* (Princeton, N.J.: Princeton University Press, 2001), xxxviii, 202 pp., although I think that Hegel's position on self-consciousness is quite different from that of Moran's. For the difference between Moran's position and the German idealist position, see the important discussion in Sebastian Gardner, "Critical Notice of Richard Moran, *Authority and Estrangement: An Essay on Self-Knowledge*," *Philosophical Review*, 113/2 (April 2004), 249–67. On the other hand, a well-argued alternative view that sees a strong similarity between Hegel's and Moran's conception is to be found in Dean Moyar, *Hegel's Conscience* (New York: Oxford University Press, 2010).

8. Hegel, *Enzyklopädie der philosophischen Wissenschaften III*, §410; Hegel et al., *Hegel's Philosophy of Mind: Being Part Three of the "Encyclopaedia of the Philosophical Sciences"* (1830), p. 141: "Habit has been rightly called a second nature—called 'nature' since it is an immediate being of the soul; called a 'second' nature since it is an immediacy posited by the soul, an imagining and thorough training of embodiment, which is appropriate to the determinations both of feeling as such and to the determinations of representation and the will."

9. Hegel, *Enzyklopädie der philosophischen Wissenschaften III*, §359; Hegel et al., *Hegel's Philosophy of Mind: Being Part Three of the "Encyclopaedia of the Philosophical Sciences"* (1830), p. 385.

10. Hegel, *Enzyklopädie der philosophischen Wissenschaften III*, §413; Hegel et al., *The Encyclopaedia Logic, with the Zusätze: Part I of the Encyclopaedia of Philosophical Sciences with the Zusätze*; Hegel et al., *Hegel's Philosophy of Mind: Being Part Three of the "Encyclopaedia of the Philosophical Sciences"* (1830), p. 153: "The I is it itself, and it envelops the object as something sublated in itself, is one side of the relationship and the whole relationship—the light that manifests itself and others."

11. Wittgenstein, *Philosophical Investigations—Philosophische Untersuchungen*, ¶217.

12. Hegel, *Enzyklopädie der philosophischen Wissenschaften III*, §414; Hegel et al., *Hegel's Philosophy of Mind: Being Part Three of the "Encyclopaedia of the Philosophical Sciences"* (1830), p. 155: "The identity of spirit with itself, as it is first posited as the 'I,' is only its abstract, formal ideality." See also Hegel, *Enzyklopädie der philosophischen Wissenschaften III*, §413; Hegel et al., *Hegel's Philosophy of Mind: Being Part Three of the "Encyclopaedia of the Philosophical Sciences"* (1830), p. 154: "The I which is certain of itself is at the beginning still what is subjective, that which is wholly simple, the freedom which is wholly abstract, the completely indeterminate ideality, that is, negativity of all limitation."

13. Ibid., §413; ibid., p. 154: "The 'I' is consequently 'being,' or has 'being' as a moment within itself. When I set this being as an other over against me and at the same time as identical with me, I am knowing, and I have the absolute certainty of my being. This certainty may not (as happens under the aspect of mere representation) be viewed as a kind of property of the 'I,' as a determination in the nature of the 'I.' Rather, it is to be taken as the nature of the 'I.' The 'I' cannot exist without distinguishing itself from itself and remaining at one with itself in these distinctions, that is to say, even without knowing itself, without having or being the certainty of itself. For this reason, certainty comports itself to the 'I' as freedom does to the will. Just as the former constitutes the nature of the 'I,' so the latter constitutes the nature of the will. However, certainty is at first to be compared only to subjective freedom, with free choice (*Willkür*). It is only objective certainty, truth, that corresponds to the genuine freedom of the will."

14. Ibid., §416; ibid., p. 157: "The goal of spirit as consciousness is to make its appearance identical to its essence, to elevate the certainty of itself to truth. The existence which it has in consciousness has therein its finitude in that it is the formal relation to self, mere certainty."

15. The necessity of this kind of contrastive relationship has long been noted by those commenting on the first chapter of Hegel's *Phenomenology*. The article dealing with this in terms of the same kind of concerns at work in contemporary analytical philosophy of language is

Robert Brandom, "Holism and Idealism in Hegel's Phenomenology," in *Tales of the Mighty Dead: Historical Essays in the Metaphysics of Intentionality* (Cambridge, Mass.: Harvard University Press, 2002). On the difficulties of this as an interpretation of Hegel's text, see Redding, *Analytic Philosophy and the Return of Hegelian Thought* (Modern European Philosophy; Cambridge: Cambridge University Press, 2007), x, 252 pp.; and Pippin, "Brandom's Hegel," *European Journal of Philosophy*, 13/3 (December 2005), 381–408.

16.  Hegel, *Enzyklopädie der philosophischen Wissenschaften III*, §418, *Zusatz*; Hegel et al., *Hegel's Philosophy of Mind: Being Part Three of the "Encyclopaedia of the Philosophical Sciences"* (1830), p. 160: "This is distinguished from the other modes of consciousness, not by the fact that in it alone the object comes to me by the senses, but to a greater degree because, at this standpoint, the object, whether an inner or an outer object, has no other thought-determination than, first of all, that of 'being' in general, and secondly, that of being a self-sufficient other over against me, something reflected into itself, an individual confronting me as an individual, of being something immediate."

17.  The importance of the element of "negation as contrast" and how it functions is the core of the account in Robert B. Brandom, "Some Pragmatist Themes in Hegel's Idealism: Negotiation and Administration in Hegel's Account of the Structure and Content of Conceptual Norms," *European Journal of Philosophy*, 7/2 (August 1999), 164–89. This way of looking at the status of sense-certainty as serving both as the basis of a claim and as being fodder for inference is discussed in Pinkard, *Hegel's Phenomenology: The Sociality of Reason*.

18.  One might try to stop the argument at that point and insist instead on some kind of "research program" to determine whether the general conceptual claims about sense-certainty can be reduced (in some viable sense of that protean term) to sense-certainty claims themselves. Hegel's point, however, would be that the larger case he has brought against such a program makes it foolhardy to pursue the project.

19.  Hegel, *Enzyklopädie der philosophischen Wissenschaften III*, §421; Hegel et al., *Hegel's Philosophy of Mind: Being Part Three of the "Encyclopaedia of the Philosophical Sciences"* (1830), p. 162: "the *singular* things of sensuous apperception, which are supposed to be *the ground* of universal experience."

20.  Hegel is relatively clear on this point: Hegel, *Enzyklopädie der philosophischen Wissenschaften III*, §420, *Zusatz*; Hegel et al., *Hegel's Philosophy of Mind: Being Part Three of the "Encyclopaedia of the Philosophical Sciences"* (1830), p. 161: "Although perception starts from observation of sensuous materials, it does not stop short at these, does not confine itself simply to smelling, tasting, seeing, hearing and feeling, but necessarily goes on to relate the sensuous to a universal which is not observable in an immediate manner, to cognize each individual thing as a coherent whole within itself—for example, in 'force,' to comprehend all its manifestations and to seek out the connections and mediations that exist between separate individual things."

21.  Hegel, *Enzyklopädie der philosophischen Wissenschaften III*, §421; Hegel et al., *Hegel's Philosophy of Mind: Being Part Three of the "Encyclopaedia of the Philosophical Sciences"* (1830), p. 162.

22.  See Paul Redding's discussion of this in Redding, *Analytic Philosophy and the Return of Hegelian Thought*. (This should also not be conflated into the Kantian distinction between appearances and things in themselves.)

23.  Hegel, *Enzyklopädie der philosophischen Wissenschaften III*, §422; Hegel et al., *Hegel's Philosophy of Mind: Being Part Three of the "Encyclopaedia of the Philosophical Sciences"* (1830), p. 162: "The next truth of perception is that the object is, to an even greater degree, appearance, and its reflection-into-itself is, on the contrary, something inner existing for itself and is universal. Consciousness of this object is the understanding."

24.  Hegel, *Enzyklopädie der philosophischen Wissenschaften III*, §422 *Zusatz*; Hegel et al., *Hegel's Philosophy of Mind: Being Part Three of the "Encyclopaedia of the Philosophical Sciences"* (1830), p. 163: "The laws are the determinations of the understanding dwelling within the world itself. Therefore, the understanding consciousness (*verständige Bewußtsein*) once again finds its own nature and thus becomes objective to itself."

25. Within this discussion of the "inner" world, Hegel is also concerned with the relations between the older "inherent properties" model of explanation and the more modern "law/event" model of explanation. An exemplary discussion of the philosophical issues at stake, especially those having to do with how Hegel tries to construe how we should speak of causal relations and what that has to do with the older concept of the "inherent properties" of a thing, is to be found in Christopher Yeomans, *Freedom and Reflection: Hegel and the Logic of Agency* (London: Oxford University Press, 2011).

26. Hegel, *Enzyklopädie der philosophischen Wissenschaften III*, §423; Hegel et al., *Hegel's Philosophy of Mind: Being Part Three of the "Encyclopaedia of the Philosophical Sciences"* (1830), p. 164: "As judging, the 'I' has an object, which is not distinguished from it—*itself—self-consciousness.*"

27. See Hegel, *Enzyklopädie der philosophischen Wissenschaften III*, §424 *Zusatz*; Hegel et al., *Hegel's Philosophy of Mind: Being Part Three of the "Encyclopaedia of the Philosophical Sciences"* (1830), p. 165: "...that I have in *one and the same* consciousness *myself* and the *world*, that in the world I re-encounter myself again, and, conversely, in my consciousness have what *is*, what possesses *objectivity.*"

28. Hegel, *Enzyklopädie der philosophischen Wissenschaften III*, §424; Hegel et al., *Hegel's Philosophy of Mind: Being Part Three of the "Encyclopaedia of the Philosophical Sciences"* (1830), p. 165: "The truth of consciousness is self-consciousness and the latter is the ground of the former, so that in existence all consciousness of another object is self-consciousness." This point about self-consciousness not implying a separate reflective act has been long since established in Hegel scholarship, at least as an account of what Hegel means to say. The point is convincingly argued by Robert B. Pippin, *Hegel's Idealism: The Satisfactions of Self-Consciousness* (Cambridge: Cambridge University Press, 1989), xii, 327 pp.

29. Hegel, *Enzyklopädie der philosophischen Wissenschaften III*, §424; Hegel et al., *Hegel's Philosophy of Mind: Being Part Three of the "Encyclopaedia of the Philosophical Sciences"* (1830), p. 165: "In that way, it is without reality (*Realität*), for it itself, which is its own object, is not such an object since no distinction between it and the object is present."

30. Hegel, *Enzyklopädie der philosophischen Wissenschaften III*, §424; Hegel et al., *Hegel's Philosophy of Mind: Being Part Three of the "Encyclopaedia of the Philosophical Sciences"* (1830), p. 165.

31. See Hegel, *Enzyklopädie der philosophischen Wissenschaften III*, §425; Hegel et al., *Hegel's Philosophy of Mind: Being Part Three of the "Encyclopaedia of the Philosophical Sciences"* (1830), p. 166: "This rift between self-consciousness and consciousness forms an inner contradiction of self-consciousness with itself, because the latter is at the same time the stage at first prior to it (consciousness) and as a consequence is the opposite of itself."

32. See Hegel, *Enzyklopädie der philosophischen Wissenschaften III*, §425 *Zusatz*; Hegel et al., *Hegel's Philosophy of Mind: Being Part Three of the "Encyclopaedia of the Philosophical Sciences"* (1830), p. 166: "...abstract self-consciousness...itself still has the form of *something existing*, of an *immediate*, of a being which in spite of, or rather just on account of, its *distinctionless inwardness* is still filled with *externality*. It contains therefore negation not merely *within itself* but also *external to itself* as an *external* object, as a '*not-I*', and it is for just that reason *consciousness.*"

33. Hegel, *Enzyklopädie der philosophischen Wissenschaften III*, §426, *Zusatz*; Hegel et al., *Hegel's Philosophy of Mind: Being Part Three of the "Encyclopaedia of the Philosophical Sciences"* (1830), p. 166: "Self-consciousness in its immediacy is singular and desiring—the contradiction of its abstraction, which is supposed to be objective, that is, immediacy, which has the shape of an external object and is supposed to be subjective."

34. Hegel, *Enzyklopädie der philosophischen Wissenschaften III*, §408; Hegel et al., *Hegel's Philosophy of Mind: Being Part Three of the "Encyclopaedia of the Philosophical Sciences"* (1830), p. 127: "Only when I proceed in this way do I act from the standpoint of *the understanding*, the content with which I am filled receiving in its turn the form of *objectivity*. This objectivity which is the goal of my *theoretical* striving also forms the norm of my *practical* conduct. If, therefore, I want to transfer my aims and interests, i.e. conceptions originating in

*me*, from their *subjectivity* into *objectivity*, then if I am to be intelligent (*verständig*), I must represent the *material*, the reality confronting me in which I intend to actualize this content, as it is in truth. But just as I must have a correct conception of the objectivity confronting me if I am to behave intelligently, so too must I have a correct representation of *myself*, that is to say, a representation which harmonizes with the *totality* of my actual being, with my infinitely determined individuality as distinct from my substantial being."

35. Hegel, *Enzyklopädie der philosophischen Wissenschaften III*, §425 Zusatz; Hegel et al., *Hegel's Philosophy of Mind: Being Part Three of the "Encyclopaedia of the Philosophical Sciences"* (1830), p. 166: "The contradiction outlined here must be resolved, and the way in which this happens is that self-consciousness, which has itself as an object, as consciousness, as 'I,' goes on to develop the simple ideality of the 'I' into a real distinction., and thus by sublating its one-sided subjectivity gives itself objectivity."

36. Hegel, *Enzyklopädie der philosophischen Wissenschaften III*, §425, Zusatz; Hegel et al., *Hegel's Philosophy of Mind: Being Part Three of the "Encyclopaedia of the Philosophical Sciences"* (1830), p. 166: "In order to achieve this goal, self-consciousness must run through three stages of development."

37. This is the interpretation Sebastian Rödl gives of autonomy in his *Self-Consciousness* (Cambridge, Mass.: Harvard University Press, 2007), xi, 207 pp., p. 120: "Being under the laws of reason, I am subject to nothing other than myself in the sense that these laws spring from, and constitute, the nature of that to which I refer *first personally*."

38. Hegel, *Enzyklopädie der philosophischen Wissenschaften III*, §427; Hegel et al., *Hegel's Philosophy of Mind: Being Part Three of the "Encyclopaedia of the Philosophical Sciences"* (1830), p. 168: "Self-consciousness knows itself consequently *in itself* in the object, which in this relation is adequate to the impulse." The *Zusatz* claims: "The self-conscious subject knows itself as *in itself identical* with the external object—knows that this contains the *possibility* of the satisfaction of desire, that the object is thus *adequate to* the desire and thus for just that reason the desire is excited by the object. The relation to the object is to the subject therefore necessary. The subject intuits in the object his *own lack*, his own one-sidedness, sees in the object something that belongs to his own essence and nonetheless is lacking in it."

39. Hegel, *Enzyklopädie der philosophischen Wissenschaften III*, §408; Hegel et al., *Hegel's Philosophy of Mind: Being Part Three of the "Encyclopaedia of the Philosophical Sciences"* (1830), p. 127: "In order to clarify this point, let us remember that when the soul becomes *consciousness*, following on the separation of what in the natural soul exists in an immediate unity, there arises for it the opposition of a subjective thinking and an outer world; two worlds which, indeed, are *in truth* identical with one another (*ordo rerum atque idearum idem est*, says Spinoza), but which, however, to the merely *reflective* consciousness, to *finite* thinking, appear as *essentially distinct* and *independent* of one another."

40. Such a view at least seems to be the upshot of Hegel, *Enzyklopädie der philosophischen Wissenschaften III*, §428, Zusatz; Hegel et al., *Hegel's Philosophy of Mind: Being Part Three of the "Encyclopaedia of the Philosophical Sciences"* (1830), p. 169, where he distinguishes the kind of merely consuming, destructive activity of something like eating food from that of "formative activity"—the terms come from the German, "*bilden*": "The relation of desire to the object is as yet that of utterly self-seeking act of destruction, not a formative activity (*Bildens*). Insofar as self-consciousness does relate itself as a *formative* activity to the object, the latter obtains only the form of subjectivity, a form which acquires an enduring existence in it, but in respect of its matter, the object is preserved. On the other hand, in satisfying its desire, self-consciousness destroys the self-sufficiency of the object, since it does not possess the power to endure the object as something independent. The result is that the form of what is subjective does not attain an enduring existence in the object."

41. This is the point made in the earlier cite to Hegel, *Enzyklopädie der philosophischen Wissenschaften III*, §401, Zusatz; Hegel et al., *Hegel's Philosophy of Mind: Being Part Three of the "Encyclopaedia of the Philosophical Sciences"* (1830), p. 82: "When we speak of the inner determination of the sentient subject, without reference to its corporealization, we are considering only how this subject is *for us*, but not as yet how it is for itself and at

one with itself in its determination (*Bestimmung*, destiny), how it senses (*empfindet*) itself in the latter."

42. Just to make the point clear, Hegel notes in *Enzyklopädie der philosophischen Wissenschaften III*, §444; Hegel et al., *Hegel's Philosophy of Mind: Being Part Three of the "Encyclopaedia of the Philosophical Sciences"* (1830), p. 187, using the same word (*Widerstand*): "...the will...is engaged in a struggle with an external matter that offers resistance, with the excluding singularity of what is actual, and at the same time is confronted by other human wills."

43. Seeing Hegel as a version of some kind of naturalism is not without precedent. See Allen W. Wood, *Hegel's Ethical Thought* (Cambridge: Cambridge University Press, 1990), xxi, 293 pp. However, Wood understands Hegel's naturalism in a slightly different way than is done here. Wood also sees Hegel's project as that showing what expresses our true natures, but where our "natures" are also said to be "historical." In that way, Wood sees Hegel as keeping faith with a somewhat orthodox interpretation of Aristotle as having an idea of what constitutes the set of human needs and what kinds of institutions and practices then best realize that nature. Wood highly qualifies that claim in light of what he calls Hegel's "historicized naturalism" and his "historicized universalism." Wood's account is keenly aware of the kinds of claims Hegel makes about the historical distinctness of certain claims about needs. However, Wood's account wavers on what it would mean to keep faith with such historicism while at the same time holding fast to the universalism his account also professes. In effect, he ends up viewing the historical development of various claims to realize our natures as essentially versions of error-theories—that is, as versions of the claim that this or that institutional setup falsely realized our (inherently universal) natures, even given that Wood explicitly notes that such a historicized conception "does not endorse any general conception of the human good" (p. 34). This may have to do with Wood's well-known and somewhat controversial rejection of the "dialectical" element in Hegel's thought and especially Hegel's *Logic*. Wood's account is rather self-consciously and assertively nondialectical, which is also one of the great strengths of his account. He has given an account of Hegel's position that is free from some of the boundaries set by more traditional historical scholarship, but which in turn has led to a different way of seeing Hegel historically. Although I share much of Wood's emphasis on Hegel's naturalism, I depart from his reading in drawing out the dialectical aspects of his theory and in drawing on the ideas of unity and division rather than on Wood's otherwise admirably developed "philosophical anthropology" (which he attributes to Hegel), which holds that "the fundamental desire that Hegel attributes to self-consciousness is a desire for self-worth or 'self-certainty'" (p. 84). The problems relating to Wood's endorsement of a "universalist historicism" and to his "philosophical anthropology" are drawn out in the review of his book in Robert B. Pippin, "Review of Allen Wood, 'Hegel's Ethical Thought,'" *Zeitschrift für philosophische Forschung*, 47/3 (1993), 489–95.

44. This is the sense in which Hegel speaks of a contradiction between self-consciousness and itself; it is both universal—it stakes a normative claim toward itself—and it is individual, taking its standards from its nature as a desirous organism. Hegel, *Enzyklopädie der philosophischen Wissenschaften III*, §425; Hegel et al., *Hegel's Philosophy of Mind: Being Part Three of the "Encyclopaedia of the Philosophical Sciences"* (1830), pp. 165–67.

45. Hegel, *Phänomenologie des Geistes*, p. 74 (¶80).

46. *The Berlin Phenomenology*, §430, p. 72: "Each is a particular subject, an embodied object. In that way, they appear to me as two against each other, as much as I am distinguished from a tree, a rock, etc.... This embodiment belongs to an 'I,' it is an organic body which now leads a bodily life of an 'I,' and this has vis-à-vis me an absolute self-sufficiency, because it belongs to another 'I.'"

47. As Hegel is cited from one of his lectures in Berlin on the subject: "We have here merely singular self-consciousnesses against each other, each of which could let the other peaceably go his own way, and they could exist with each other according to ideal and idyllic modes, for the desire for domination is an evil impulse, wherever it arises" (*The Berlin Phenomenology*, §431, p. 78). Hegel's reasoning behind this emerges in the *Zusatz* to §429 in the *Encyclopedia* and in §57 of his *Elements of the Philosophy of Right*. He says in

*Enzyklopädie der philosophischen Wissenschaften III*, §429 *Zusatz*; Hegel et al., *Hegel's Philosophy of Mind: Being Part Three of the "Encyclopaedia of the Philosophical Sciences"* (1830): "On the contrary, viewed from its inner aspect, that is, in keeping with its concept, self-consciousness, by way of the sublation of its subjectivity and of the external object, has negated its own immediacy, the standpoint of desire, [and] has posited itself as having the determination of otherness towards itself, has brought this other into compliance with the 'I' (*das Andere mit dem Ich erfüllt*), has made something devoid of self into a free, self-like (*selbstischen*) object, into another 'I.' As a consequence, it therefore confronts its own self as an 'I' distinguished from itself, but in doing so has raised itself above the self-seeking character of merely destructive desire."

48. This is why, in all the lecture notes on the topic, Hegel is cited as stressing that the contradiction is between the "universality" of the agents (i.e., their identity in terms of "abstract" agency) and the naturalness (*natürliche*) of the agents. The agency is said to be abstract in that it is only the conception of natural agency as guided by norms, not the more determinate conception of agency as guided by the norms of this form of life at this time. Thus, in, for example, *Enzyklopädie der philosophischen Wissenschaften III*, §431; Hegel et al., *Hegel's Philosophy of Mind: Being Part Three of the "Encyclopaedia of the Philosophical Sciences"* (1830), p. 171, *Zusatz*: "To overcome this contradiction, it is necessary that the two opposed selves should posit themselves and should recognize themselves in their *existence*, in their *being-for-others*, as what they are in themselves, that is, what they are in accordance with their concept—namely, not merely *natural* but rather *free* beings."

49. Pippin sees the precursor to the confrontation as an inherently "unstable" and "treacherous" set of conditions that provokes the initial conflict. Pippin, *Hegel on Self-Consciousness: Desire and Death in Hegel's Phenomenology of Spirit*. For the more "intersubjectivist" reading of the passages (and the more traditional reading), see Robert R. Williams, *Recognition: Fichte and Hegel on the Other* (SUNY Series in Hegelian Studies; Albany: State University of New York Press, 1992), xviii, 332 pp. Some have seen the struggle for recognition between two agents as merely a metaphor for a more analytical account of the problems of individual self-consciousness, to which Pippin's account persuasively responds. See Pirmin Stekeler-Weithofer, *Philosophie des Selbstbewusstseins: Hegels System als Formanalyse von Wissen und Autonomie* (1. Aufl. edn., Suhrkamp Taschenbuch Wissenschaft; Frankfurt am Main: Suhrkamp, 2005), 447 pp.; and John Henry Mcdowell, *Having the World in View: Essays on Kant, Hegel, and Sellars* (Cambridge, Mass.: Harvard University Press, 2009), ix, 285 pp.

50. See Hegel, *Enzyklopädie der philosophischen Wissenschaften III*, §445 *Zusatz*; Hegel et al., *Hegel's Philosophy of Mind: Being Part Three of the "Encyclopaedia of the Philosophical Sciences"* (1830): "As has already been remarked... *spirit* that is mediated by the negation of *soul* and of *consciousness* has itself, in the first instance, still the form of *immediacy* and consequently the *mere appearance* (*Schein*) of being *external to itself*, of relating itself, exactly like consciousness, to the rational as to something *outside of it*, something merely *found*, not *mediated* by spirit."

51. In his handwritten notes for the lectures on the philosophy of history, Hegel says, "The religiosity and ethicality of a restricted sphere of life (for example, that of a shepherd or peasant) in their concentrated inwardness and limitation to a few simple situations of life, have infinite worth; they are just as valuable as those which accompany a high degree of knowledge and a life with a wide range of relationships and actions. This inner center... remains untouched [and protected from] the noisy clamor of world history." See Hegel, *Vorlesungen über die Philosophie der Weltgeschichte: Berlin 1822/1823*, p. 109; Hegel, *Lectures on the Philosophy of World History: Introduction, Reason in History*, p. 92.

52. Hegel, *Grundlinien der Philosophie des Rechts*, §57; Hegel, *Elements of the Philosophy of Right*, p. 87: "This earlier and false appearance is associated with the spirit which has not yet gone beyond the point of view of its consciousness. The dialectic of the concept and of the as yet only immediate consciousness of freedom gives rise at this stage to the *struggle for recognition* and the relationship of *lordship* and *bondage*."

53. In Hegel, *Grundlinien der Philosophie des Rechts*, §57; Hegel, *Elements of the Philosophy of Right*, pp. 86–88, Hegel has an extended discussion of slavery where he notes that there

seems to be an antinomy at work in it. From the point of view of agency as *Geist*, slavery is absolutely wrong, but from a point of view that has no concept of freedom within itself (but perhaps only happiness), slavery can be justified in various circumstances. The so-called antinomy is not sublated when only one of the sides of the antinomy is asserted as the truth. Hegel's marginal notes on this topic are cited in Hegel, *Grundlinien der Philosophie des Rechts*, pp. 124–26: "Is historical, i.e., belongs in time, in the history prior to freedom— there is history / Is mentioned in relation to slavery, in order to indicate wherein it belongs, how it must be assessed—Slavery is something historical—i.e., it falls within, belongs to a condition prior to right—is relative—The whole condition ought not to be, is no state of absolute right."

54. Hegel, *Enzyklopädie der philosophischen Wissenschaften III*, §432; Hegel et al., *Hegel's Philosophy of Mind: Being Part Three of the "Encyclopaedia of the Philosophical Sciences"* (1830), p. 172: "To prevent any possible misunderstandings with regard to the standpoint just outlined, we must here remark that the fight for recognition pushed to the extreme here indicated can only occur in the *state of nature*, where men exist only as *single* individuals. However, it is distant from civil society and the state because here the recognition for which the combatants fought is already present. For although the state may *originate* in *violence*, it does not rest on it. Violence, in producing the state, has brought into existence only what is justified in and for itself, namely, laws and a constitution. What dominates in the state is the spirit of the people, ethical customs, and laws. There man is recognized and treated as a *rational* being, as *free*, as a person."

55. Hegel's views on the forced servitude of Africans is deeply troubling, and there is simply no way to cast a favorable light on it. Hegel's own views on African culture and slavery were largely uninformed and uniformly hostile, even though he also strongly condemned the very idea of there being any basis for denying human rights on the basis of race. He had unfortunately what could most charitably be characterized as straightforwardly racist views about Africans. There is some evidence that he had some second thoughts on the matter, but they are scanty. For example, he made a note to himself that the rumors that he would regularly read about which had to do with slave conspiracies in the West Indies clearly showed that the African slaves did not merely accept their condition. In his own notes made for himself and his lectures, he says (Hegel, *Grundlinien der Philosophie des Rechts*, §57): "Often in the West Indies the negroes have rebelled, and one still reads every year that in the islands there are conspiracies—however, they become victims of a universal condition—still, they die as free people; the state of the individual conditioned through the universal—the conspiracies themselves [are] a proof of merely partial cast of mind." He even noted in his lectures that "it is in the nature of the case that the slave has an absolute right to free himself" (§66, *Zusatz*). Yet as he made these notes, he also remarked that whereas the slaves could not be blamed for their slavery, the masters also could not be blamed for being slaveholders, since it all rested on the "universal state of things," that is, social conditions, not individual choice. Slavery, he seemed to think in these notes, was something that was a matter of social fact and cultural development, not a feature intrinsic to race, but he held that view while at the same time also holding that African slavery seemed to have something to do with race. Nonetheless, even there his views were at odds with themselves, as we have already noted. In Hegel, *Enzyklopädie der philosophischen Wissenschaften III*, §393; Hegel et al., *Hegel's Philosophy of Mind: Being Part Three of the "Encyclopaedia of the Philosophical Sciences"* (1830), p. 41, he explicitly argues against using any racial criteria for assigning rights: "However, descent affords no ground for granting or denying freedom and dominion to human beings. Man is in himself rational; herein lies the possibility of equal justice for all men and futility of a rigid distinction between races which have rights and those which have none." However, immediately following this passage, Hegel offers up a long discussion of racial difference that, even when put in its best light, can still only be described as deeply disturbing. In Hegel, *Grundlinien der Philosophie des Rechts*, §57, *eigenhändige Bemerkung*, he reverses himself somewhat and goes so far as to say in the *Zusatz* to the paragraph that the slaves are indeed at least partially to blame for their slavery (even though they also share the blame

with their oppressors): "However, that somebody is a slave lies in his own will, just as it lies in the will of a people when they are subjugated. It is thus not merely a wrong on the part of those who make [people] slaves or those who subjugate [others]. Rather, it is a matter of wrong on the part of the slaves and the subjugated themselves." In continuing to remark in these notes that no blame was to be attached for this condition of slavery, he thus both showed himself to be consistent with his overall antimoralistic stance toward things and at the same time (unwittingly) to be utterly and thoroughly morally obtuse about the matter of the enslavement of Africans. To make matters worse, Hegel also holds—for example, in Hegel, *Enzyklopädie der philosophischen Wissenschaften III*, §435 *Zusatz*; Hegel et al., *Hegel's Philosophy of Mind: Being Part Three of the "Encyclopaedia of the Philosophical Sciences"* (1830), p. 175—that all peoples have to undergo a period of tyranny and servitude to another people before they are "ready" for self-government, a passage that sounds like an apology for the Atlantic slave trade. There is no indication in his 1830–1831 lectures on the philosophy of history that he had any change of mind about this.

56. This departs from those who see the master's desire for self-sufficiency precisely as a desire for freedom. However, even Hegel's chapter titles in 1807 undermine that identification, since he there distinguishes the self-sufficiency of self-consciousness (which fails) from the "freedom of self-consciousness" (which as stoicism and skepticism initially fails but sets the stage for a later success). See also Frederick Neuhouser, "Desire, Recognition, and the Relation between Bondsman and Lord," in Kenneth R. Westphal, ed., *The Blackwell Guide to Hegel's Phenomenology of Spirit* (Malden, Mass.: Wiley-Blackwell, 2009), 37–54.

57. See, among other places, Hegel, *Enzyklopädie der philosophischen Wissenschaften III*, §436, *Zusatz*; Hegel et al., *Hegel's Philosophy of Mind: Being Part Three of the "Encyclopaedia of the Philosophical Sciences"* (1830), p. 177: "Here therefore we have the violent disruption of spirit into different selves which are completely free in their existence both in and for themselves and for one another. They are self-sufficient, absolutely obdurate, resistant, and yet at the same time identical with one another and hence not self-sufficient, not impenetrable, but, as it were, fused with one another. The relationship is thoroughly that of a speculative kind, and when it is supposed that the speculative is something remote and inconceivable, one has only to consider the content of this relationship to convince oneself of the baselessness of this opinion. The speculative, that is, the rational and the true, consist in the unity of the concept, that is, of subjectivity and objectivity. This unity is obviously present in the standpoint in question."

58. See Rebecca Kukla and Mark Norris Lance, *"Yo!"and "Lo!": The Pragmatic Topography of the Space of Reasons* (Cambridge, Mass.: Harvard University Press, 2009), xi, 239 pp.

59. On the idea that the concept of freedom emerges out of the experience of slavery in ancient civilizations, see Orlando Patterson, *Freedom* (New York: Basic Books, 1991), v.

60. The phrase comes from §16 of the Kant, *Immanuel Kant's Critique of Pure Reason* (the "B" version of the "Transcendental Deduction").

61. On the contingency and quirkiness of individual self-consciousness, see among other places in Hegel's texts, *Enzyklopädie der philosophischen Wissenschaften III*, §402, *Zusatz*; Hegel et al., *Hegel's Philosophy of Mind: Being Part Three of the "Encyclopaedia of the Philosophical Sciences"* (1830), p. 91: "Because the human soul is an *individual* soul determined on all sides and therefore *limited*, it is also related to a universe determined in accordance with its (the soul's) *individual* standpoint. This world confronting the soul is not something external to it. The totality of relationships in which the individual human soul finds itself, constitutes its actual liveliness and subjectivity and accordingly has grown together with it just as firmly as, to employ an image, the leaves grow with the tree; the leaves, though, distinct from the tree, yet belong to it so essentially that the tree dies if it is repeatedly stripped of them... for without such an individual world, the human soul, as we have said, would have no individuality at all, would not attain to a specifically distinct individuality."

62. Hegel, *Enzyklopädie der philosophischen Wissenschaften III*, §467; Hegel et al., *Hegel's Philosophy of Mind: Being Part Three of the "Encyclopaedia of the Philosophical Sciences"* (1830), p. 226: "What is developed in *logic* are thought, at first as it is *in itself*, and reason, in this

opposition-less element. In *consciousness*, thought likewise comes forth as a stage on the way.... Here reason exists as the truth of opposition, as it has determined itself within spirit itself."

63. Hegel makes this point in *Enzyklopädie der philosophischen Wissenschaften III*, §408; Hegel et al., *Hegel's Philosophy of Mind: Being Part Three of the "Encyclopaedia of the Philosophical Sciences"* (1830), p. 127: "But just as I must have a correct conception of the objectivity confronting me if I am to behave intelligently, so too must I have a correct conception of *myself*, that is to say, a conception which harmonizes with the *totality* of my actual being, with my infinitely determined individuality as distinct from my substantial being."

64. Wilfrid Sellars thought of this not as rational but as part of an a-rational causal story in his doctrine of what he called language-exit rules (which thus couldn't really be "rules" at all). See Wilfrid Sellars, *Science, Perception, and Reality* (International Library of Philosophy and Scientific Method; New York: Humanities Press, 1963), 366 pp. Robert Brandom repeats this version of the Sellarsian account in his conception of reliably differential responsive dispositions in *Making It Explicit: Reasoning, Representing, and Discursive Commitment* (Cambridge, Mass.: Harvard University Press, 1994), xxv, 741 pp.

65. See Kukla and Lance, "Yo!" *and* "Lo!".

66. Hegel, *Enzyklopädie der philosophischen Wissenschaften III*, §437; Hegel et al., *Hegel's Philosophy of Mind: Being Part Three of the "Encyclopaedia of the Philosophical Sciences"* (1830), p. 177.

67. Martin Luther, *Von Der Freiheit Eines Christenmenschen* at www.fordham.edu/halsall/source/luther-freiheit.html.

68. Aristotle, *Politics*, 1317b in Aristotle and Richard Mckeon, *The Basic Works of Aristotle* (New York,: Random House, 1941), xxxix, 1487 pp.[0]: "One principle of liberty is for all to rule and be ruled in turn." In all of his discussion of the truth of mastery and servitude, Hegel is also surely influenced by Luther's translation of a familiar passage in the Bible (King James version), Galatians 3:28: "There is neither Jew nor Greek, there is neither bond nor free, there is neither male nor female: for ye are all one in Christ Jesus." Luther's own translation is worth noting for its terminological analogy to Hegel's vocabulary: "Hier ist kein Jude noch Grieche, hier ist kein Knecht noch Freier, hier ist kein Mann noch Weib; denn ihr seid allzumal einer in Christo Jesu." Luther's conception of Christian freedom fits nicely into the space created by the idea that the free person is both ruler and ruled, sovereign and subject, that plays such a large role in Aristotle, Rousseau, and Kant. For Kant's own statement, see Immanuel Kant, *Grundlegung Zur Metaphysik Der Sitten*, ed. Karl Vorländer (Philosophische Bibliothek, Bd. 41; Hamburg: F. Meiner, 1965), 433. Hegel makes the point quite explicitly in a number of places; see Hegel, *Enzyklopädie der philosophischen Wissenschaften III*, §482; Hegel et al., *Hegel's Philosophy of Mind: Being Part Three of the "Encyclopaedia of the Philosophical Sciences"* (1830), pp. 239–40: "No Idea is so generally recognized as indeterminate, ambiguous, and open to the greatest misunderstandings (and to which it therefore actually is subjected) as the Idea of *freedom*. There is no other Idea with so little awareness of its meaning in common currency. Since free spirit is *actual* spirit, we can see how misunderstandings about it are of tremendous importance in practice. When individuals and nations have once got in their heads the abstract concept of freedom existing for itself, there is nothing like it in its uncontrollable strength, just because it is the very essence of spirit, indeed its very actuality. Whole continents, Africa and the East, have never had this Idea, and are without it still. The Greeks and Romans, Plato and Aristotle, even the Stoics, did not have it. On the contrary, they saw that is only by birth (as, for example, an Athenian or Spartan citizen) that the human person is actually free. It was through Christianity that this Idea came into the world. According to Christianity, the individual *as such* has an *infinite* value as the object and aim of divine love, destined as spirit to live in absolute relationship with God himself and to God's spirit dwelling in him, i.e., man is *in himself* (*an sich*) destined to the highest freedom."

69. Béatrice Longuenesse (*Hegel's Critique of Metaphysics*) claims that this is evidence for Hegel's taking the "point of view of God" on things instead of Kant's "point of view of man." Hegel's

point is, however, that this point of view is unavoidable and that, taken seriously, the "infinite" point of view is required by the "point of view of man" as itself drawing that normative line about itself. This is the crux of the criticism that authors such as Longuenesse have lodged against Hegel, namely, that in holding that there must be a standpoint within thought whereby thought sets its own limits, Hegel adopts the "standpoint of God" instead of the more defensible and modest Kantian "standpoint of man." However, it is precisely Hegel's attempt to fashion a dialectical conception of thought and reality, whereby thought sets its normative limits in terms of demanding that its other serve as that which makes, say, an empirical claim true that leads him to hold that this is not a kind of "superoverview" idea of thought (or a "view from nowhere," in the phrase that Thomas Nagel made famous), but something else that freely acknowledges its own dependence on its other and in doing so, shows that it is itself *freely* establishing that dependence. The difficulties and the tortured twists and turns that an account of such normative line drawing takes is a major part of the subject matter of Hegel's *Science of Logic*, the treatment of which would be another topic entirely and which Longuenesse rightly sees as the heart of her criticism of Hegel.

70. There are many passages one could cite; one is Hegel, *Enzyklopädie der philosophischen Wissenschaften III*, §408; Hegel et al., *Hegel's Philosophy of Mind: Being Part Three of the "Encyclopaedia of the Philosophical Sciences"* (1830), p. 127: "Just as this objectivity is the goal of my theoretical striving, it also forms the norm of my practical conduct."

71. The phrase occurs in, among other places, John Henry McDowell, *Mind and World*. (Cambridge, Mass.: Harvard University Press, 1994), x, 191 pp.

72. Hegel's self-criticism occurs in Hegel, *Enzyklopädie der philosophischen Wissenschaften III*, §418; Hegel et al., *Hegel's Philosophy of Mind: Being Part Three of the "Encyclopaedia of the Philosophical Sciences"* (1830), p. 159: "The spatial and temporality singularities, 'here' and 'now,' as I determined them to be in the *Phenomenology of Spirit* . . . as the object of sensuous consciousness, really belong to intuition." He notes again in §449, *Zusatz*; and p. 199: "Intuition must not be confused with representation proper, to be dealt with later, or with the merely phenomenological consciousness already discussed." In that *Zusatz*, he goes on to say: "In the broadest sense of the word, one could of course give the name of intuition to the immediate or *sensuous consciousness* considered in §418. But if this name is to be taken in its *proper* significance, as rationally it must, then between that consciousness and intuition the essential distinction must be made that the former, in the *unmediated*, *quite abstract* certainty of itself, relates itself to the *immediate* individuality of the object, a *singularity sundered* into a multiplicity of aspects; whereas intuition is consciousness *filled* with the certainty of *reason*, whose object is *rationally* determined and consequently not an individual torn asunder into its various aspects but a *totality*, an *adhesive fullness* of determinations."

73. Hegel, *Enzyklopädie der philosophischen Wissenschaften III*, §448, *Zusatz*; Hegel et al., *Hegel's Philosophy of Mind: Being Part Three of the "Encyclopaedia of the Philosophical Sciences"* (1830), p. 195: "Only by this dual activity of sublating and *restoring* the unity between myself and object do I come to apprehend the content of sensation. This takes place, to begin with, in *attention*. Without this, therefore, no apprehension of the object is possible. Only by attention does spirit become present in the subject-matter. This is not yet knowledge (*Erkenntnis*) of it—for that requires a further development of spirit. Rather, it is as yet only a kind of acquaintance (*Kenntnis*) with the subject-matter."

74. Thus, in Hegel, *Enzyklopädie der philosophischen Wissenschaften III*, §448, *Zusatz*; Hegel et al., *Hegel's Philosophy of Mind: Being Part Three of the "Encyclopaedia of the Philosophical Sciences"* (1830), p. 196: Hegel says about such an act of "paying attention" within perceptual experience: "On the contrary, it demands an effort since a man, if he wants to apprehend a particular object, must make abstraction from everything else, from all the thousand and one things going round in his head, from his other interests, even from his own person. He must suppress his own conceit which would rashly judge the subject-matter before it had a chance to speak for itself, must rigidly absorb himself in the subject-matter, must fix attention on it and let it have its say without obtruding his own reflections."

75. Hegel, *Enzyklopädie der philosophischen Wissenschaften III*, §449 *Zusatz*; Hegel et al., *Hegel's Philosophy of Mind: Being Part Three of the "Encyclopaedia of the Philosophical Sciences"* (1830), p. 199: "First of all, as regards the relation of intuition to *representation*, the former only has this in common with the latter, namely, that in both forms of spirit the object is separate from me and at the same time also my own. But the object's character of being mine is only in itself present in intuition. It is in representation that it first becomes posited. In intuition, the objectivity of the content predominates. It is not until I reflect that it is I who have the intuition that I occupy the standpoint of representation."

76. Mark Lance and Rebecca Kukla (*"Yo!" and "Lo!"*) classify these as "observatives," normative statuses with agent-specific entitlements, to be distinguished from other kinds of normative statuses (such as judgments) that involve agent-neutral input and agent-neutral output.

77. Hegel, *Enzyklopädie der philosophischen Wissenschaften III*, §449 *Zusatz*; Hegel et al., *Hegel's Philosophy of Mind: Being Part Three of the "Encyclopaedia of the Philosophical Sciences"* (1830), p. 200: "*Completed* cognition (*Erkenntnis*) belongs only to the *pure thought of comprehending reason*, and only he who has risen to this thinking possesses a completely determinate, genuine intuition. With him intuition forms only the unalloyed form into which his completely developed cognition concentrates itself again. In immediate intuition, it is true that I have the entire object before me, but not until my cognition, as developed in all its aspects, has returned into the form of simple intuition does the subject-matter confront my spirit as an *systematic* totality *articulated within itself*."

78. Hegel thus rejects the Kantian conception that space and time are subjective forms of intuition. Hegel notes: "Things are in truth themselves spatial and temporal." Hegel, *Enzyklopädie der philosophischen Wissenschaften III*, §448; Hegel et al., *Hegel's Philosophy of Mind: Being Part Three of the "Encyclopaedia of the Philosophical Sciences"* (1830), p. 198.

79. Hegel, *Enzyklopädie der philosophischen Wissenschaften III*, §447, *Zusatz*; Hegel et al., *Hegel's Philosophy of Mind: Being Part Three of the "Encyclopaedia of the Philosophical Sciences"* (1830), p. 194: "All our representations, thoughts and concepts of the external world, of right, of morality, and of the content of religion develop from our sensibility-laden (*empfindenden*) intelligence, just as conversely they are concentrated into the simple form of sensibility (*Empfindung*) after they been fully explicated."

80. Hegel, *Enzyklopädie der philosophischen Wissenschaften III*, §468; Hegel et al., *Hegel's Philosophy of Mind: Being Part Three of the "Encyclopaedia of the Philosophical Sciences"* (1830), p. 227: "Thought, as the free concept, is now in accordance with *content*, also free. Intelligence, knowing itself as what is determining the content, which is likewise its own content, is, determined as existing content, the *will*." Hegel adds in the *Zusatz*: "Pure thinking is, to begin with, an unencumbered conduct sunken into the subject-matter (*Sache*). However, this conduct necessarily also becomes *objective to itself*. Since objective cognition is absolutely *at one with itself* in the object, it must recognize that its determinations are determinations of the *subject-matter*, and that conversely the *objectively* valid, *existing* determinations in the *subject-matter* are *its* determinations."

81. This is the core truth behind Brandom's analogy between the use of case law in common law and Hegel's idea of the historical temporality of our concepts. However, Brandom gives short shrift to the way in which case law must assume the correctness of past usage and fit it into a better narrative. See Ronald Dworkin's discussion of the "chain novel" in Ronald Dworkin, *Law's Empire* (Cambridge, Mass.: Belknap, 1986), xiii, 470 pp. Hegelian sublation resembles the chain novel in one way, but the chain novel conception ignores the ways in which practices simply go dead and require what look like new beginnings. On this prospective character of concept-use in Hegel's thought, see also Redding, *Analytic Philosophy and the Return of Hegelian Thought*.

# PART TWO

PART TWO

# 3

# The Self-Sufficient Good

## A: Actualized Agency: The Sublation of Happiness

Self-conscious life is not naturally at one with itself. As self-conscious life actualizes its originally animal powers, it establishes a distinction between itself and its animal powers. Whatever self-conscious life is at any given point—a perceiver, a theorist, an individual outfitted with this or that set of dispositions—it is capable of attaching the "I think" to that status and submitting it to assessment.

A practical agent is an embodied agent, and such an agent sets himself into motion by inner drives, inclinations, and so on. Like his model, Aristotle, Hegel also holds that for the action to be a voluntary action, the agent must know what he is doing, and his action must not be forced. An action done on the basis of impulse can be thus itself a free, voluntary action if the agent knows what he is doing, the origin of the action lies within him, he is not forced into it, and he is the "master of" or "in control of" his action.[1] Like Aristotle, Hegel also holds that one must distinguish knowing what one is doing from the reason one has for doing it—distinguish, that is, the good for the sake of which the agent acts and the agent's knowledge of what she is doing.

Leaving aside for the moment the issues about the conditions under which one could be said to know the good, Hegel, still following Aristotle, notes that this demands that we ask whether there is any final end for the sake of which all other actions could be deemed worthy of choice. The gap that self-consciousness sets up between the agent and his actions makes it looks like there may well be no resolution to that question. One cannot, after all, rule out a priori the idea that there may be many goods that are each desirable for their own sakes. If so, then one also cannot rule out a priori that those kinds of goods may or may not be consistent with each other. However, even accepting that as a possibility, there is still the possibility that one could have good reason to pursue this good and not some other good. That possibility sets in motion a dynamic that leads one to look for an unconditional good, since reason will demand that one offer some kind of justification for pursuing even some particular good that is desirable for its own sake (given the contingent structure of human, embodied desire), and choosing one good as a means to another looks like it will set into motion the kind of "bad infinity" that Hegel thinks is the root of metaphysical dilemmas. Must there be some ultimate set of goods or goods that stops this regress of goods chosen as means to further goods.[2] If so, then what makes this and not that organization of ends or pursuit of ends more rational than any other set of ends?

Such considerations quite naturally push us to think of happiness as the self-sufficient good that makes our particular choices justified, and the model for construing happiness as such an end is Aristotle's conception of *eudaimonia* (happiness as flourishing and prospering). Hegel takes a "monistic" interpretation of Aristotle's conception of happiness. Happiness is *the* good, the norm, that makes choice of all other goods (even those that on their own are otherwise worthy of choice as ends in themselves) themselves worth choosing in a single life.[3] On that monistic view, happiness is, first, supposed to provide the abstract principle, for example, for choosing among incompatible goods that are each worthy of choice for their own sake. Second, happiness would be the norm that makes one way of life worth choosing over another.[4] If happiness thus fits the bill for being such a monistic good, then the happy person—although he would not necessarily get everything that he desires and almost certainly not everything that is desirable—would be in possession of a norm that tells him what in his various circumstances is worth choosing.

"Happiness" thus seems to stop the infinite series of choosing goods as means to other goods by being itself the final end of such choice. It is chosen only for its own sake, and it functions as some kind of final norm that puts other choice-worthy goods into some kind of meaningful, rational order.

However, happiness cannot satisfactorily perform that role. It is too abstract a criterion to function as such a practice-guiding norm.[5] Unless it piggybacks on other, socially established conceptions of the details of what counts as the "fine" life, it inevitably becomes only a formal conception of coordinating given ends rather than a criterion that can be used to determine them. Hegel holds, rightly, that all such details about the "fine" life—especially once one goes beyond a set of limited and general ideas such as prohibitions against murder and very basic biological goods—can by and large be shown to be historical statuses, not natural facts. If so, then "happiness" as the major part of the first premise of practical reasoning will always be relatively empty.

Instead of happiness, Hegel proposes that a genuinely self-sufficient end would be one in which an agent was "at one with himself." For an agent to be completely at one with himself or herself, however, would mean that there would be a final end that would bring the "inner" and the "outer" into a full harmony with each other.[6] That is, for an agent to be at home with himself or herself, there would be a final end that could be achieved (and would thus not be the object of an infinite yearning) such that the end could be the content of an intention that could be realized in an action and ultimately in a deed. Such a final end would set the standard of success for one's actions. But why would happiness fail to fit the idea of "being at one with oneself"?

An agent's impulses, inclinations, and desires do not order themselves, nor are they ordered by the agent's natural makeup. To be sure, some animals can exercise intelligence and exhibit elements of self-control—they are creatures with subjectivity—but it is the nature of the animal itself, that is, what it is for things to go well for that animal, that determines the principle of correct ordering (which, for animals, ultimately is to reproduce their species even though they have no knowledge that this is the hidden goal of what they do). A species that faces an environment no longer in harmony with itself faces the potentiality of dying out. For agents, on the other hand, the ordering principle must be that of reasoning. What we have reason to do depends on whether we can find any way of ordering our various inclinations, impulses, and desires into a meaningful whole. In putting them into a rational whole, we do not eliminate them or suppress them. We sublate them; that is, as we learn from infancy onward to exercise self-control, we cancel these impulses and inclinations in their status as immediately calling out for their own satisfaction, but we also preserve them—for a human life to go well, it must also make room for these desires, inclinations, and impulses. Whatever the self-sufficient good is, it has to be the nature of human agency itself that is to determine this good.[7] The "nature" of an agent, however, is to be a creature that by virtue of its socialization orders its ends by way of reasons, and thus the ends that express its nature are those that issue from its being a particular, embodied organic rational agent. The order of reasons that it gives itself—beyond the bare formality of there being reasons—is embedded within a world of recognition.

However, at this stage of the development of this idea, it remains open as to whether we should conclude that the good therefore must be monistically conceived (as one good that provides the ordering principle for all other goods and thus sets the standard of success for living well) rather than concluding that there are many, perhaps even incompatible, goods, each of which is desirable for its own sake and not merely as a means to some other good.

One aspect of this is that the agent must form a resolution about which desires or impulses she is to fulfill, and she must be capable of making that resolution stick in the form of an action undertaken to put the resolution into effect. To be able to do that is to have a capacity to refuse an identification of oneself with one's various desires, inclinations, and the like and to form a view as to what resolutions one rationally ought to make. To be in possession of such a capacity is at least a minimal form of freedom in that it indicates that the agent is acting in terms of a law that is her own law and is not given to her outside of her nature as an agent. The monistically conceived good for the agent would thus be, most abstractly conceived, that of the rational good or of the various desires, inclinations, and the like as being set into a rational whole for that agent.

If the rationality of the will is restricted to that of merely ordering other elements, then, so it seems, practical reason can only be formal.[8] As so characterized, the actually free will would have no determinate target at which to aim since its target—itself as an actually free will—is a moving target as it shapes itself in terms of the goals it sets for itself, and that might make it look as if Hegel could only be committed to making something like the claim that if there is a monistic good, it would be the rather empty good of being formally rational (that is, make your practical claims consistent, coherent, and so forth).

On its surface, this conception of the good looks, of course, rather Kantian. The good will would be a will that acts in terms of rational principles that it decides for itself, or to put it differently, the good will would be pure practical reason legislating that its only law is to be its own law, a law that expresses (metaphorically) the "nature" itself of pure practical reason. Kant quite famously argued that at least at this level of characterization, the law could only be formally formulated as a principle of universalization, that is, a law binding on all rational agents. This also left Kant with a sharp line to be drawn between all the particular details of human agents—their specific inclinations, passions, personal commitments, and so on—and the unconditionally binding nature of the law. To rephrase this Kantian point in more Hegelian terms, such a law looks like it forms a comprehensive and intelligible ("infinite") conception of the human good.

Hegel's charge is that such a view about the good is, taken straightforwardly, paradoxical, since it seems to propose that reason sets its own laws in terms of criteria that it sets for itself, and that quickly leads either to an infinite regress of rules necessary to set the rules, and so on, or to the arbitrary establishment of a law that would then be unconditionally binding (which no arbitrarily set law could do). Or even if it is indeed not straightforwardly paradoxical, it still might be taken to express the more humdrum idea that one cannot rationally get behind the laws of reason to find something else from which they could be derived, since deriving them (in any normative sense of that word) would already presuppose that one has always, already accepted the laws of reason itself. (That, too, would be self-contradictory, much in the way that giving an argument against ever giving arguments would also be self-contradictory.) Indeed, something like that view is at work in Kant's view of what he called the "fact of reason" as the idea that we are always, already subject to the normative demands of reason in our first-person practical stances to the world. Without an appeal to reason in the first instance, we cannot, as it were, get the game going at all.[9] Another option might be that its paradoxical nature should be taken to be not paradoxical at all but simply as expression of a clumsy self-contradiction and therefore a kind of negative proof of the necessity of some kind of Platonist (either with a capital P or a small p) conception of reasons as "out there" to be discovered.[10]

Now, the general idea that we get a fuller picture of rational agency as formally bringing some order to its inclinations and impulses and that we then move to a picture of an agent acting in terms of such considerations is hardly a controversial issue. Where Hegel parts company with most of the standard pictures of how to move from the former to the latter lies in his sublation of the Aristotelian conception. The actualized free agent—what Hegel calls the "actually free will" as the will that acts in terms of its own principles in concrete situations—is the "unity of theoretical and practical mindful agency."[11] That is, the actually free agent must know what the self-sufficient final end of life is, and that knowledge must be able to be "translated" into actions undertaken in light of that knowledge. The actually free person is thus like Aristotle's person of virtue: Both operate in terms of a comprehensive conception of the good. For Aristotle, it is like a target at which we aim, whereas for Hegel, the target is always in motion by virtue of our aiming at it. The target is a conception of the good that is concretely changing in light of our employment of the concept itself.

Given Hegel's general conception of conceptual content—that we cannot determine the meaning of a concept without attending to its use and that its meaning is never reducible to its use—one would hardly expect him to conclude otherwise. However, he cannot be expected simply to apply this schema to the material at hand to generate his next move. That would violate his stated approach itself. At this stage of the development of his views, we are entitled to claim only that a mindful agency that knows itself as free must think of its final end as at least compatible with that freedom, such that even if either ordinary happiness or Greek "*eudaimonia*" were to be the final end in terms of which one ordered all the impulses and inclinations, it would still be able to function properly as that final end only if it were determined by our rational natures to be such an end. Only then would agency be true in the Hegelian sense. It would live up to the norm that lies *an sich*, in itself, within the self-conscious grasp of oneself as an agent.

For the truth of agency, more is needed, therefore, than merely knowing the good. If one cannot translate the knowledge of the good into action, then one has only an "abstract" and not an actual conception of the good. What is that "more"? When Hegel addresses that issue, he usually says something rather cryptic, such as telling us that the will's "principle is the will itself" or that this actualization "has its source in the needs, impulses, inclinations, and passions of man."[12] In another place, he notes that "impulse and passion are nothing more than the liveliness of the subject, according to which it exists itself in its purposes and in putting them into practice."[13]

Hegel's own dialectical logic helps to both highlight the problem and obscure it. If the problem is one of logic understood as truth-preserving inference, then if the agent reasons truthfully from some premises about the good and what is required to realize that good (such as "a virtuous person will tell the truth in this situation"), then the next step—actually telling the truth—is an additional step. If this step is blind, the result, say, of mere conditioning, then it also cannot be said to be a step rationally taken. Knowing how to actualize the principle therefore must be an additional way of knowing what to do. This additional kind of knowledge is practical, a kind of "knowing one's way about" and "knowing how to do things" that cannot be reduced to a formalization. However, whereas logic in the ordinary sense is concerned with the relations among concepts (how they stand in the proper inferential relations to each other), on Hegel's understanding of logic, there is also a central concern with the relation between concepts and particulars (or particular actions), and that connection, at least for certain cases, should be understood more in terms of actualizing a concept and not merely succeeding or failing to apply it. Hegel thus apparently does not think that the failure to act correctly must lie simply in some countervailing motivation that overpowers the otherwise rational agent. Rather, it involves a cognitive failure of a particular, practical sort.

This has implications for what would have to be Hegel's conception of weakness of will, a topic he otherwise does not explicitly discuss except in a handwritten reference to Aristotle.[14] Hegel, that is, relies on a more or less Aristotelian conception of weakness of will: A weak-willed agent indeed draws all the right theoretical conclusions but fails to know how to put them into action. The weak-willed agent is thus ignorant but in a very special sense: The agent may not be ignorant of the good "in itself" (*an sich*) but ignorant of the actual good (the good *an und für sich*, "in and for itself"). Hegel's conclusion is not that the weak-willed agent mysteriously fails to exercise some special causal power, perhaps because that power gets overwhelmed by some other power (as a voluntarist conception of freedom of will might have it). Rather, the agent lacks a practical skill (perhaps because he has not been brought up well, perhaps for other reasons). The weak-willed agent thus has a free will in that he fails to act in terms of a principle that is nonetheless both "within him" and "up to him." However, he does not have an actually (*wirkliche*) free will in the stricter Hegelian sense because of his failure in having that kind of practical knowledge, at mastering that particular skill. His inability to translate his will into action is a failure of practical knowledge, of know-how. To put it in more Hegelian language, he therefore does not measure up to his "concept," to the norm of what it would mean in general to be a free agent when that concept is fully actualized.

## B:  The Actually Free Will

To sum up some of the conclusions along the way that has gotten us here: When an individual is truly at one with himself, he achieves a kind of satisfaction in Hegel's special sense of the word. ("Satisfaction," *Befriedigung*, is Hegel's sublated version of the Aristotelian *eudaimonia*, "flourishing.")[15] Satisfaction has to do with carrying out a successful action and, ultimately, with leading a successful life. Ultimately, that at which agents ought to aim is success—the accomplishment of ends worth pursuing—and not happiness, and, in fact, so Hegel also claims, this also functions as the intuitive idea behind many people's conception of what makes a good life.

The agent thus achieves satisfaction when he pursues a life structured by ends that, all in all, are meaningful to that agent—which can be redeemed, which (to put it in the broadest of terms) make sense as a whole to him—and about which the agent has good reason to believe he can be successful at achieving those ends (that is, that the agent has good reason to believe those ends can be actualized). For us moderns, so Hegel claims, the truly successful life is an actually free life, although taken in the abstract, a successful life need not be ethical or moral.[16] Why?

Hegel's promissory note in the 1807 *Phenomenology*—that the truth must be comprehended "not merely as *substance* but also equally as *subject*"[17]—is his shorthand for what he has to say about the actual will. To understand the world as a set of substances is to grasp it as an interacting causal system, and to understand agency in terms of the way in which a substance moves about in the world is to understand the agent in causal terms. However, to comprehend agency fully, one must understand it not only causally ("not merely as *substance*") but also normatively ("also equally as subject").

The animal shows that it takes certain things to be food by eating them, and, of course, if the animal does not take something to be food, it does not eat it.[18] The animal, as Hegel says, is not merely caused to act by conditions external to itself. The animal's goals give a shape to what in its environment solicits a certain behavior and what does not.[19] The wolf is not stimulated to eat by the presence of the grasses that provoke the sheep to eat those same grasses. The wolf is stimulated by the presence of the sheep. (As we have already noted, Hegel takes this to exhibit the special sense of idealism already at work in animal life, and this kind of idealism does not rule out a wide variety of causal explanations.)

Animals display, as already noted, subjectivity: They have inner lives (although in many cases only very meager ones) that seek expression in the world surrounding them. Moreover, as various types of species of animals gain in intelligence, their behavior is in turn shaped by how well they can modify their behavior in light of the ends that are set for them by their own nature.

Likewise, human agents shape their world such that what counts as a condition for action is itself shaped not only by the natural status of humans as self-interpreting animals but by their status as moments in a normative social space. Take the examples of "losing face" or of "not being shown sufficient respect." Now, it is a trivial truth that only a being that has the capacity to suffer from lack of respect can actually suffer from having lack of respect being shown to him, and only a being that can "lose face" can respond to conditions of "losing face." However, each of these examples exhibits the way in which the social world establishes conditions that in turn can cause a certain reaction on the part of subjects and thus offer up a set of possibilities for action that would otherwise not be present in the natural world (if "the natural world" is here understood as "nature deprived of all the norms that are there by virtue of the nature of the species in question"). The conditions that elicit the behavior of human agents are set by the nature of those agents in this highly modified sense: The nature of agents is to create conditions that are not otherwise there in the natural world. Agents respond to matters such as "marriage," "occupation," "voting," "losing face," "Colonel," "paying homage," and so forth, and in doing so, they are responding to "spiritual objects" (as Hegel would prefer to call them) collectively instituted by humans over historical periods in very specific natural conditions.

Where Aristotle's conception of freedom (as the voluntary) goes awry, so Hegel thinks, is that it keeps its analysis of agency at the level of "substance" and therefore at the level of the purely causal explanation of behavior, rather than moving the explanation in the direction of explaining action in terms of "subjectivity." Kant, however, commits the opposite error: He thinks that explanation by "substance" (causal explanation) is so completely at odds with explanation by "subject" that he concludes that if one is to explain how a subject can freely bind herself to norms, one requires a nonstandard view of causality for such agents, that is, a conception of the agent as being capable of initiating a causal sequence without herself being the effect of any prior causal sequence. As it were, Kant thinks that if we are to comprehend the truth "not merely as *substance* but also equally as *subject*," we are required to comprehend two mutually exclusive truths that at first appear to contradict each other, and he thus also thinks that in light of such an impossible situation, only his own transcendental idealism can provide any way to avoid this apparent contradiction. Transcendental idealism must remain committed to its firm and unyielding division between the world known only under the conditions in which we can experience it and the unknowable world that is what it is apart from the conditions under which we can experience it.

The behavior of both human and nonhuman animals is to be explained in terms of the goals that are proper to them and how their behavior is adapted and can be made more adaptable in light of the specific conditions in which they try to achieve their goals. In some animals, there is also a kind of flexibility in adjusting behavior to the achievement of goals that is the mark of intelligence on their part. However, what distinguishes the ordinary animal, even the highly intelligent one, from the human animal is that the animal cannot comprehend its goal as a goal (that is, cannot comprehend its reason as a reason), and thus the ordinary animal is left with less flexibility in adjusting its behavior than is the human animal, who has at least the capacity to entertain his goals as pure possibilities. Indeed, the way in which the animal fixes on its goals and adjusts its behavior accordingly is an exhibition of the lack of full freedom on the part of the animal, even though the animal nonetheless moves itself voluntarily. Thus, as Hegel remarks, we say that in this fixity of means and ends that the animal moves itself by "instinct"—which is not to say that the animal is merely caused to move by conditions external to itself.[20] "Instinct" is simply the name we give to this kind of fixity of purpose specific to the nature of an animal.

The agent confronts her own goals—whether they be organically set goals, such as feeding herself, or socially established goals, such as "getting a promotion"— as possibilities in the sense that even firmly set goals (feeding in light of hunger) can appear to a reflective agent as mere possibilities for the reason that the normative (as possibility) can always be set apart in thought from the nonnormative.[21] If one takes the independence of the normative from the nonnormative to be all there is to the story, then it has to seem that the choosing subject (conceived abstractly) and everything else external to the choosing subject would have to be distinct and separable items. All those other items would have to be either unalterable givens of nature or mere possibilities for the choosing subject, each of which would itself be a fork in the road of future possibilities. The subject would be completely at one with himself only prior to making any choices at all. Any choice would bring in something external to that subject.

The abstraction, however, lies in that very conception itself. Abstractly seen, virtually anything is possible. If one holds fast to the abstract concept of a subject as the unity of experience or as the unified locus to which various entitlements and commitments are ascribed, then it will seem to be the case that the agent must need some criterion to choose among the various external options that are presented to him or her. Moreover, if that criterion is not to be arbitrary, then it must either be internal to the nature of the agent or external to her nature (and thus be imposed on her from the outside). One manifestation of understanding the alternatives in that light is some form of Kantianism, where only reason in general is comprehended as "internal" to the agent—that is, where rationality constitutes the very nature of being an agent at all—and which thus finds itself logically driven to some kind of formalism in its practical philosophy, since giving any more determinate sense to "the rational" would amount to smuggling in content from outside of the rational as such.[22]

However, to understand that the truth is to be comprehended "not merely as *substance* but also equally as *subject*" is not so much to reject that way of understanding the relation between subjectivity (or agency) and animal life (or "substance") as following from the very nature of agency itself. It is to realize that such a conception is abstract and that its realization makes a difference to the abstraction with which we began.

To actualize one's subjectivity is, to state Hegel's conclusion all at once, to act in terms of character. To act fully freely is to act in terms of character as compulsion by rational norms. In this respect, Hegel wishes to bring to fulfillment Kant's conception of agency as constituted by action done in light of reasons but without any claims about metaphysical self-causality. What are the steps Hegel takes to reach that conclusion?

As we have seen, for Hegel, an agent's and an animal's actions are to be explained in terms of the goals or commitments that the agent or animal seeks to realize. The goal thus solicits certain kinds of behavior from the animal, and the more elasticity and adaptability there is in matching the behavior with the goal, the more we say that the animal displays intelligence.[23] Since the key difference between animals and agents (that is, self-interpreting animals) is that the agent can entertain her goals *as* goals (her reasons as reasons), in human agents, "intelligence" goes so far as to be able to distance the agent from all specific goals and to be able to see all of them as mere possibilities, that is, take them in their abstract meaning as not standing in any contradiction with the abstract meaning of subjectivity itself, such that "being a subject" in the abstract does not per se rule in or rule out any (or many) of them.[24]

To get to concrete subjectivity and "second nature," two other aspects must be brought into view.

First, or so it seems, the existing agent must therefore choose among all these goals, and the use of reflective intelligence quite naturally encourages us to accept the ordinary picture of a choosing agent who has before her something like various desires demanding fulfillment and who therefore must freely choose (or employ some criterion of choice) among them. (The picture does not fundamentally change if one substitutes "various goods demanding realization" for "various desires.") For the concrete subject to act, she must be able as "substance" to effect some kind of behavior, that is, exercise the causal powers of her animal nature. That is, as a "substance," she exercises a causality that produces the action, and the causal relation exists between the agent and the action and not between, say, a desire and a piece of behavior.[25] Just as the intelligent animal will undertake its action on the basis of its own nature—on the basis of what Hegel identifies as instinct—the human agent will undertake its action on the basis of her own "nature," which is to be that of a "second nature," that is, an acquired set of dispositions, habits, and the like, and which will be constitutive of a set of basic orientations. The action expresses those dispositions, but it is the agent as characterized by such a set of dispositions that causes herself to act. The agent, taken as a whole, causes herself to act, which means she produces an intention that is then actualized in an action insofar as the action expresses the intention. (As already noted, the action is not a separate "thing" that is caused by the intention.) The agent, guided by the goal, thus adjusts her states (her mental states, somatic states, and so on) so as to put herself into the position of doing the action that makes sense to her.

Although the agent conceived in abstraction from all desires and specific conditions of action has before her an almost infinite set of possibilities, the actual agent always finds herself with a much more limited set. So it seems, "abstract subjectivity" finds itself with a fully indeterminate set of motivations—indeterminate because so universal—which then collapses into a determinate set in any specific situation. What sets the agent into motion cannot then itself be a further intention but must be her own second nature, her acquired set of dispositions and habits. The agent, that is, exercises a certain practical skill at realizing her goal and, to the extent that the action is intelligent, also modifies her goal in light of the means she has chosen and modifies her means in light of the goal she is pursuing.[26]

Second, for a self-conscious being, this second nature can itself become an object of intelligent reflection. Both the ends and the means are subject to intelligent reflection, and to the extent that the agent realizes that, say, a certain end is not worthwhile or needs a great deal of refinement, and the agent has the practical skill to undertake a new set of means for achieving it, then the agent can set to work to modify the second nature she has (although second nature, as itself natural, is of course resistant in varying ways to any immediate modification by the agent). The agent's relation to the goal is that of "deciding" which action to take, not that of a separate activity of having all the elements of willing and action present and then one more act (that of "resolving" to act) being required to set the whole affair into movement (in part because requiring a "resolution" would either require another resolution to resolve oneself, ad infinitum, or would require a uncaused cause to set itself into motion).[27] The nature of an agent is second nature, and thus the agent's nature is never simply given to the agent but is continually being refashioned as it is appropriated as the agent's own nature. As a self-interpreting animal, an agent is an animal that has a different relation to its life. Its life as second nature is an achievement, not something it merely expresses. Its nature is to remake its nature.

The agent herself has the substantial structure she has by virtue of her second nature, or what Hegel identifies as her character. The problem of voluntary behavior as a causal problem is thus the same problem as that of animal motion in general, and that is the problem of how, in Hegel's terms, an individual substance causes certain other events to occur.[28] In this case, the individual animal is a "substance" that causes itself to go into motion: The lion leaps at the gazelle, and the lion is the cause whose effect is its leaping. How the lion does that is, of course, not itself a matter of philosophy but of biophysics.

The great distinguishing features of the self-reflexive nature of human agency thus consist in the ability to make one's own character itself the object of one's willing.[29] Because of other goals or even because of the independence of the normative from the nonnormative, the agent may believe that her own character is faulty or in need of revision. Now, if to grasp one's actions as free is to grasp them as proceeding from rational necessity, that is, to see the activities one undertakes as what would be required by reason (or, to put it very broadly and more colloquially, to see one's actions as "making sense"), then the ideal of a fully free agent would be that of an agent who understands her actions as proceeding from her character and her character as itself consonant with what would be required of a rational agent in those concrete conditions. If to be free is thus to be in possession of a practical skill that enables one to express one's intentions in the actions (or, to the same point in a different way, to actualize one's intentions), then to the extent that the agent cannot understand her dispositions as fully rational, she also cannot understand those actions as free in the full sense, even though they can be voluntary in a more limited sense.

It is in this way that Hegel construes freedom neither in terms of an uncaused causality nor in terms of the more recently popular conception of the free will as standing in a certain type of hierarchy of desires about desires (in which the will is understood to be free not if the agent is the cause of her actions but in terms of whether the agent identifies whatever motivation is doing the work to get her to act with some other motivation or with some other value—or, to put it in the terms of Harry Frankfurt's highly influential characterization of this conception, if the agent's first-order desire matches up with her second-order desire).[30]

Part of the idea behind the hierarchical view has to do with what it would mean to say that the action is "mine," and the idea is that an action can be mine only if I identify myself with it (by seeing it either as conforming to a second-order desire or to some appropriately held, deeper value).[31] From Hegel's standpoint, the hierarchical view would be only another expression of the "abstract" viewpoint in which the agent is seen simply as a locus of commitments and entitlements, and all other matters (motivations, the conditions of action) are therefore understood as "external" to the agent. On that view, the desires are what they are, and the question is only whether I can identify myself with them.

Interestingly, Hegel himself does not speak of "identifying oneself" with any motivation (although he does say things that could, of course, be interpreted as meaning the same thing with different words). Instead, he speaks of the agent's being "in" the action.[32] For the agent to be "in" the action is for the action to be an expression of rational necessity, of what the agent must do in the given conditions in which she is seeking to realize some purpose and for that action to make sense. The agent is fully "in" the action when it both makes sense and involves the person's "second nature" as having to do with her own most important passions and interests, however idiosyncratic they might be.[33] The person is not "in" the action—the status she occupies is not fully habitable—when it expresses the necessity of a "second nature" that cannot make sense to the agent such that the agent does what she thinks she must do, but what she must do is in some deeper sense not intelligible to her. This is a human problem, but, so Hegel thinks, it is also a social and historical problem whose treatment varies depending on the kind of social space available. It turns out to be a big problem in modern states.

As "substance-subject," the agent acts, and being a self-conscious being, the agent is also capable of taking her own character as itself a possible object on which she can direct her action. In taking her character as an object of willing (for example, in trying to acquire new habits or break old ones), she seeks to make the conditions of her willing into the conditions of free willing, to be or to become what Hegel describes as the "free will that wills the free will."[34] In making the will into its own object, the agent—whose habitual behavior results in the establishment of new necessities for herself—establishes a new relation to this necessity. The actually free agent seeks to change the conditions surrounding her action so that what she finds she must do within the given conditions of her activity (both those of her own second nature and the social and natural conditions surrounding her) is something about which she can make some rational sense.

However, even the matter of making one's own character into an object of willing and thus rendering one's second nature more flexible than it would otherwise be is itself a matter of historical and social context. The servant in the original master-servant dialectic, Hegel says, fails to achieve freedom because instead of adopting that kind of flexibility, of making his character an object of willing itself, the servant finds it more rational to resist the domineering tendencies of the master by exercising a kind of stubbornness, an inflexibility about himself, an insistence that nothing can be changed, and so forth. The servant holds onto the ends given to him and refuses to budge from them, defying the master's wish that he might become more flexible (and thus better at his own servitude). The servant, Hegel says, acquires a mind of his own (*eigene Sinn*) only in becoming inflexible (*Eigensinn*).[35] This inflexibility, the refusal to alter the ends or means at issue, is a negative part of one social and historical context, that of ancient slavery. In that context, it was a hindrance to freedom. In the modern world, it plays a somewhat different role.

# C: The Impossibility of Autonomy and the "Idea" of Freedom

In Hegel's technical but nowadays thoroughly unfamiliar vocabulary, such free agency is said to be the "Idea." In its most general form, the "Idea"(in capitals) is the abstract concept taken together with its actualization or, as Hegel puts it, the unity of concept and reality.[36] Although it sounds extremely odd to say that agency is the "Idea"—and it is clear that Hegel himself was also keenly aware that this way of talking, like so many of his other characteristic turns of phrase, did indeed sound a little peculiar to some of his audience[37]—what Hegel wishes to say nonetheless is that, alone among the other objects in the world, agents are self-interpreting. This "Idea is the actuality of humanity, not an Idea that they simply have, but rather an Idea that they are."[38] To be an agent is obviously not to be a disembodied thinker, but it is also not to be a mind that simply applies its subjective conceptions to reality and then changes them when the application fails to work out. It is to be a self-interpreting animal who must work out and develop his concepts in an objective world and who finds that his own concept of himself is changing as it develops that joint conception of "himself and world." As "Idea," an agent works with a conception of his own norms, aspirations, and hopes, together with a conception of the nature of the world and how it contributes to, thwarts, or is indifferent to the realization of those norms. To say that agents "are" the "Idea" is, admittedly, an odd way of putting the point (and a fair case can be made that it is not the most advisable way of putting it), but it is Hegel's shorthand for his thought that agency is best grasped as that of a human organism situating itself in social space.

The "Idea" is thus the unconditioned, the absolute, itself, the joint conception of world and agency together that forms the orientation of the rest of an agent's more commonplace beliefs, choices, and plans. In its full development, it unites within itself the kinds of oppositions that naturally spring up when humans reflect on their own predicament—mind versus nature, body versus soul, norms versus the natural, and so on. When "the Idea" does this successfully, then the tensions that emerge within it are held together instead of coming apart. When those tensions do come apart, the "Idea" is, again in the Hegelian argot, at odds with itself, which means that we are at odds with ourselves, and its shortcomings—that is, our shortcomings—become more and more apparent to the agents who orient themselves in terms of it. As these tensions become more apparent, the form of life structured around that joint picture of world and agency finds that at its conceptual edges, it is starting to cease to make sense to itself.

If freedom is character as rational necessity, the "Idea" of freedom is that of an agent whose character stems from her world and whose world is such that it makes sense to think that what character requires of oneself is ultimately itself redeemable by reasons, that what one does ultimately makes sense. Without the "inner" aspect of understanding the rationality of one's acts, there can be no freedom, and it is not hard to see why someone might be tempted to think that all such freedom is "inner" (especially if what happens in the "outer" world of action seems senseless). This suggests a certain distinctive ideal of freedom: An individual who obeys only the necessities of her own nature and at the same time whose nature is such that it compels her into performing actions that are one and all redeemable. The concept of the ideal with regard to this would be "inner freedom in what is external."[39] This ideal turns out to be more of a fantasy than any kind of real ideal at all.

What would such "ideal" freedom look like? In Homeric poems, a Greek hero gives us a vivid picture about what the concrete shape of that ideal of freedom would be. As if we are switching our field of vision, we can see the concrete aesthetic presentation of such a figure in, say, Homer's poem as a kind of philosophical thought experiment. The hero acts on the basis of "his own law" (his thoughts, passions, and so forth all rolled into one), and, in doing so, he founds a state or the unity of a people. The hero does not simply desire to do what he has a duty to do. (His passions and duties do not simply happen to be the same. He is not a naïve "moral" hero.) What determines what he shall do is simply what he is, and he follows his nature independently of any other desires or duties that might otherwise pull on him in different directions. Now, this picture of what it would be like to be actually free has, of course, a great attractiveness. (Not for nothing has it captured the imaginations of people for much more than 2,500 years.) However, the thought that such a freedom can be actualized is and can only be a part of mythology. As a piece of mythology, it does indeed present us with a way of thinking about ourselves but not as a real project and instead only as a fantasy. Human finitude means that, especially in anything like the political state of affairs, there can be no full way of being at one with oneself, and the ideal itself of realizing that ideal—of our all being self-sufficient Greek heroes—is itself not simply a muddle, not just a daydream, but a rather dangerous fantasy.[40]

The other fantasy is that of a fully "inner" freedom that is metaphysically disengaged from the world around itself. Just as the Greek hero is a myth, the agent as somebody who in all circumstances could blankly do otherwise—that is, could always actualize any one of the abstract possibilities of her action—is also a myth.

For the Hegelian conception of actual freedom, although self-determination is a possibility for agents, there can be no such thing as autonomy in the Kantian sense. Indeed, Hegel himself rarely even uses the word *autonomy*, and he almost always does so only when speaking (usually very critically) of Kant's views. That is, if autonomy is indeed rational necessity interpreted as the independent exercise of a self-causality distinct from all other forms of natural causality, then there is, for Hegel, no such thing. Likewise, if autonomy is complete self-determination of all the principles of action itself, there can be no such thing as autonomy. If autonomy is a metaphysical disengagement from the world, there is no such thing as autonomy. The ideal, that is, of autonomy is a chimera. Autonomy is possible only for mythical Greek heroes, not for human beings in the world.

Self-determination, however, is another matter. An action is self-determined when it is the result of rational necessity in the sense having to do with the agent's character, and it can be a rational necessity only for an agent who is self-conscious (who occupies a place in normative social space). Self-determination is thus not that of having anything like "one's true self as one's rational self" determining one's actions, nor is it that of having one's reasons rather than one's desires determine the action. Self-determination is not autonomy at all.

Moreover, it is only in focusing on abstract subjectivity that one is also led to what Hegel thinks is a perennial philosophical temptation. In thinking about action, it seems quite natural to think that the agent must have had a reason for acting, at least in the sense that the agent had to take something as a justifying principle or ground of his action that was also efficacious in bringing the action about, and if the subject cannot state his principle, that can only mean that, for whatever reason, the agent was inarticulate about his reasons. It therefore seems to fall to the task of something else, such as philosophy, to articulate his principles for him—say, get at the hidden presuppositions of his action—and then to put those principles into a better rational order. The agent, however, need not have any such reasons in mind, at least in anything approaching a reflective sense. In a simple act of free choice—what Hegel calls *Willkür*, that is, "free choice" or "arbitrary choice," as it is variously rendered—there may or may not be reference to a reason. "Should I wear the blue one or the red one?" is a question for which there could be myriad reasons (again, depending on context) but probably is not usually decided for anything like a reason that could be discovered by looking inwardly or in seeking out the presuppositions of the principles that supposedly "had to be there" in action. Instead, they are guided by the agent's overall orientations and the way those orientations themselves are modified in light of the means employed to realize them and the ever-developing "self" in its second nature that is both steering itself and being steered by those orientations. Such orientations themselves are not simply the result of such free choices. They constitute the significance, as we might put it, of the agent's world, which in turn forms the conditions within which the agent always acts.

The actual will is thus that of an agent embedded in a form of life, a "second nature," for whom the conditions of action are themselves made up of his own organic nature, the natural world of which he is a part, and the historical and social practices that form the conditions of his action. He moves around in his world in light of his general orientations and, because of his reflective capacities, can also make his own second nature into an object of the will.

Hegel gives his own highly condensed summary statement of what it would be to fully actualize the norm of free agency: "This unity of the rational will with the individual will, which is the immediate and characteristic element that is the exercise (Betätigung) of the former, constitutes the actuality of freedom."[41] As fully actual freedom, it is a being at one with oneself in activity, where being at one with oneself as a self-conscious rational agent is acknowledged as the final end of life—being at one with oneself as an end in itself, a Selbstzweck, or in the terms in which Hegel quasi-paradoxically puts it, "the abstract expression of the Idea of the will is itself the free will that wills the free will." The free will wills to establish the conditions in which the agent can develop as a fully actual free agent, which includes establishing a character from which the actions may proceed as a matter of normative necessity. Such a conception of the free agent has as its background the conception of one's character as first formed by the circumstances of one's upbringing, along with the conception of reshaping one's environment so that it is more likely to provoke rational rather than irrational actions. The will to change the conditions of action—where the conditions include one's "second nature"— can be either an individual act (a kind of "care of the self") or a collective action to jointly fashion a world in which what we each must do is more rational than it would otherwise be.

The free agent thus acts in terms of a comprehensive conception of life that can be summed up as that of making freedom actual—Hegel's sublation of the Aristotelian comprehensive conception of happiness. It functions as a self-suffi-cient good that both makes various other goods in life worth choosing and lacks nothing in the sense that the successful pursuit of it leaves nothing beyond it itself that a person might reasonably desire or want to will as another final end.[42] In that way, the monistic goal of freedom is supposed to take the place of (or to sublate) the monistic goal of happiness, and as sublating happiness, freedom does not replace or abolish it.[43] Rather, it limits the authority that happiness can claim in an agent's choice of ends.

To be sure, there is a kind of relative freedom, a way in which the competing demands on our minded organic nature are resolved, which can be more or less present in action. Nonetheless, in the natural and social world in which our ideas and intentions are put into practice, we are bounded on all sides. Now, if the ideal is to be a Greek hero, then something like the ideal is unobtainable. We are embodied agents, bound by the limits of our organic nature and always working within a particular, bounded social space. We strive to be at one with ourselves, but as "Idea," we do not attain that ideal, and the only point of rest, as it were, is in acknowledging that the "ideal" is unachievable except as a matter of aesthetic presentation (and, for us moderns, not even that).[44] In Hegel's own language: "For the sake of freedom, the Idea also has ... the hardest opposition within itself; its being at rest consists in the security and certainty with which it eternally creates and eternally overcomes that being at rest and therein brings itself together with itself."[45]

However, if freedom as the "ideal" is unachievable, in what sense can it serve as a final end?

If there is a final end that would be self-sufficient, it would have to meet something like the following kinds of conditions. First, it would have to be a norm by which rational choices among all other ends could be made. Second, it would be self-sufficient in that there would be no other purpose that the agent could rationally desire to have; if it is indeed a final end, then there would be nothing more to pursue than what it itself authorizes. Third, for a life with that as its final end, it would have to provide the actual conditions for there to be confidence in the agent's ability to choose and to actualize her specific ends. (That is part of saying that the end must be actual.)

Organisms are literally, as we saw, ends unto themselves, they are each a *Selbstzweck*, and human organisms, as being each ends unto themselves, also live under the condition of being at odds with themselves. Their nature is to have their nature in question. Self-consciousness establishes a potential distinction of itself from each and every end an agent may elect in that each can entertain the possibility of throwing any of those ends into question in light of other ends.

This requires a form of sociality that animal awareness does not have. (Animals may have sociality, but not that kind.) Self-conscious agents live in a social space in which they are always and already potentially responsive to reasons *as* reasons. This also means that human organisms have within their practical fields the capacity to understand other agents as being, in their own eyes, ends in themselves, although this is not a requirement per se of practical rationality in the abstract. The capacity to see each other as ends in themselves is the result of a historical struggle and of the failure of forms of life based on something else— such as mastery and servitude—to provide a way of life that could ultimately sustain normative allegiance.

As self-interpreting animals, our final end is that of self-knowledge. In the abstract, that is our coming to an understanding of what it is to be an agent (or, more colloquially, what it is to be a human being). In Hegel's own preferred terminology, this would be *Geist*—our own agency, individually and collectively, as self-interpreting organisms—coming to a full self-consciousness. This end would be not only a final end—it would be the last link in a chain of other ends—but also a self-sufficient end in the sense that an agent with this good before her would be able to develop a structure and arrangement of other ends that, when chosen each for their own sake (as ends in themselves), would actualize a good life. Such an end lends intelligibility to the other ends chosen in light of it, and as an intelligible, self-sufficient end, it need not rationally motivate us to choose anything else beyond itself—we do not need that end and then yet also need something else to be at one with ourselves.

Fully actualized self-consciousness—humanity's coming to understand itself as self-interpreting animals—could emerge only as this kind of final end after the logic of consciousness and self-consciousness had historically worked itself out. The dialectic of mastery and servitude is supposed to show how self-consciousness cannot be self-sufficient when each agent understands himself "monadically," since the logic of that kind of individualism leads it to set as its aim individual self-sufficiency—such as the self-sufficiency of the master setting all the terms of entitlement for himself and the servants—and such individual self-sufficiency can be attained only by denying the self-sufficiency or the possibility of self-sufficiency to others. (In an odd way, for Hegel, Aristotle was right in drawing the conclusion that the wealth and leisure attendant on that kind of self-sufficient flourishing probably required a servant class. He was wrong in thinking that such a mode of flourishing was a rational, final end.) The very failure of mastery to culminate in being at one with oneself provokes both masters and slaves to understand themselves and their world differently, namely, to be concerned instead with the realization of freedom as the only mode in which such being at one with oneself can be achieved. The failure experienced by the master is rooted, as it were, in his conception of *Beisichselbstsein*, being a "self" at one with oneself, as really being *Bei-sich-eins-sein*, that is, being at one with oneself as a "one," a monadic subject or a self-enclosed totality. The servant, who is completely at odds with himself, ultimately has a more workable conception of the self, since the servant simply cannot conceive of himself as a "one" disconnected from the rest. The master's self-conception, that is, is ultimately a failed conception of having a *self*, which always involves having being recognized as such a self.[46] Despite its ultimate failure, however, it has, for perhaps obvious psychological reasons, remained an attractive ideal for centuries.

## D: Being at One with Oneself as a Self-Sufficient Final End

Now, on the one hand, the claim that the final and self-sufficient end of life is actualized self-consciousness might seem, when stated in that way, to be barely plausible. How could any determinate end—say, choosing between going to the grocery store to pick up some extra things and staying home and making do with what one has—be chosen on that basis of that as a final end?

The finality and self-sufficiency of such an end, however, does not depend on its being linked to other less final ends in just that way. On Hegel's conception, other ends are not a means to that end, nor is that end inclusive of all those ends—that is, it is not an end that within itself includes all the things one might rationally desire—nor are other ends approximations to it.[47] Rather, it is the sublation of those other ends. It takes them up as circumscribing their authority. Those other ends, on the other hand, are to be understood in light of the functions they serve within certain spheres. The ends of social life, for example, are to be understood in terms of the role they play in the social space of the moral life, of a shared ethos of what is fitting and best for family life, civil society, and political life, and various practical deliberations all begin with the goods involved in those other ends as first premises of practical reason. Thus, one might start with something like "Marriage is best when..." and reason to a conclusion that takes into account one's own circumstances and one's own individuality to reach any practical conclusion. However, if one were to ask why the premise "Marriage is best when..." is justified, one would have to look at the purpose or function marriage and its commitments play in a social order and note how it fits together with other functions in that way of life as modes of human self-understanding, that is, ways of articulating in more concrete terms the requirements of a successful human life. In that sense, each of these other goods is a way of orienting oneself in the natural and social world, a way of charting a course of human life over time that articulates what is worth pursuing and what is not and which takes as its frame the finitude of human life and various facts about it (aging, maturation, disease, predictability and lack of predictability, and so forth—the grasp of which are required to actualize the more abstract concepts of the good).

Ultimately, reflection on all the other modes of reflection on what it is to lead a good human life is itself the final end, but not, as we just said, in the sense that other goods are thereby subservient to it, nor they are only means to it, nor are they mere approximations to it (they are very different), nor is the final end inclusive of all the other ends. This final end sublates all the others in that it recognizes itself as the direction in which such reflection on human life is heading, even though none of the other modes of reflection is necessarily aiming at it. It is, as it were, the purpose but not the target. Moreover, as the sublation of the other ends, it does not entirely displace their authority within their own spheres—as if it were the wildly implausible claim that, for example, all political discussion that is not explicitly oriented to some overtly expressed conception of human self-comprehension is somehow therefore deficient as a political discussion—but it does serve to provide a more focused view on what in effect has been going on in those other ways of living. Finally, as "Idea," as the unity of the abstract meaning and its realization, this final end is not a goal that is to be achieved. It is itself an achievement that consists in an activity of coming to grips both with the kind of absorption in life that is bound up with life itself and with the self-dissociating that comes with self-consciousness. The goal of coming to grips with that tension in self-conscious life and the activity itself of coming to grips with the tension and remaining at one with oneself within the tension are not a means to freedom. It is freedom itself.

The final end of life is thus understanding what it is to be a good human being, and that final end itself is divided into various spheres (what it is to be a good parent, a good friend, a good citizen, and so forth), which it sublates. As such, when the conditions for such genuine reflection on what it is to be such a reflective being are present—when the proper conditions are in place for *Geist's* reflection on what it is to be *geistig*—then such reflection is the only place where we are genuinely at one with ourselves and thus free. As the culmination of "absolute spirit," the sphere of practices whose raison d'être is to provide that kind of reflection, philosophy is thus the final end of life.

It is important to note that the final end of life as philosophy is not that of being a philosophy *professor*. Hegel's point is, rather, Aristotelian (or at least follows the Aristotelianism of the end of the *Nicomachean Ethics*) in one obvious way: The final end is for Hegel, as it was for Aristotle, something like contemplation, and, as it is for Aristotle, it is characterized by Hegel as divine. However, as noted, Hegel's final end is not a target at which the other goods aim, nor is it something for which they are only approximations, nor does it mean that philosophy brings out the presuppositions behind everybody else's thoughts. Rather, it is the end toward which the logic of all such self-reflection eventually pushes—in a way analogous to the manner in which an extended argument can, by the force of its own logic, drive toward a conclusion for which none of the people making the argument actually intentionally aimed. It also does not follow that people who practice this kind of reflection (philosophers) are better people (not only does it not follow but also it is most likely not even true), nor that they are as a rule in any way happier people. They are merely the people who do that kind of thing better than others do it. That they do that kind of thing better than others also does not mean that others are always doing deficient versions of what they do (as if the artisan, the statesman, and the natural scientist were all doing some kind of deficient philosophy that the philosopher did better). Philosophy is the conceptual contemplation of what it means to be a *geistig*, minded agent, and thinking about what it means to be human is something toward which all agents are pushed by the logic of being an agent. What it means to be a human is not a question that only professors ask with the appropriate seriousness.

That idea has two parts to it. One part is trivial: On the whole, philosophers do better at philosophy than nonphilosophers. However, the other part is more substantive. It is that philosophy should take its basic purpose to be a reflection on *Geistigkeit*, on what it means to be minded. It, of course, also does not follow a priori that philosophy professors do this better than other philosophers, even though de facto, for bureaucratic and time-scheduling reasons, it may turn out that at any given time some philosophy professors are better at doing important aspects of philosophy than others. Still, it was certainly not always true that professors were the best philosophers, as people as varied as Moses Mendelssohn,

Benedict Spinoza, David Hume, and John Stuart Mill demonstrated by their own example. It is, after all, possible that it is not true even now, and even if it is, it need not be true in the future.[48]

## Notes

1. For the different ways in which Aristotle uses these criteria to delineate the domain of the voluntary, see Susan Sauvé Meyer, "Aristotle on the Voluntary," in Richard Kraut, ed., *The Blackwell Guide to Aristotle's Nicomachean Ethics* (Malden, Mass.: Blackwell, 2006), 137–58; and Sarah Broadie, *Ethics with Aristotle* (New York: Oxford University Press, 1991), xiii, 462 pp.

2. Aristotle, of course, argues that there must be one final good that stops the regress, and it is a matter of great dispute about the interpretation of Aristotle as to whether that good should be seen as inclusive—as containing all the lesser goods within itself—or as a noninclusive final good. There seems to me to be convincing arguments against the interpretations that argue for the "inclusive view" to be found in Richard Kraut, *Aristotle on the Human Good* (Princeton, N.J.: Princeton University Press, 1989), viii, 379 pp.; Richard Kraut, *Aristotle: Political Philosophy* (Founders of Modern Political and Social Thought; Oxford: Oxford University Press, 2002), xii, 520 pp.; Gabriel Richardson Lear, *Happy Lives and the Highest Good: An Essay on Aristotle's Nicomachean Ethics* (Princeton, N.J.: Princeton University Press, 2004), viii, 238 pp.; and Broadie, *Ethics with Aristotle*.

3. See in Lear, *Happy Lives and the Highest Good*, "Chapter 3: The Self-Sufficiency of Happiness."

4. Hegel, *Enzyklopädie der philosophischen Wissenschaften III*, §479; Hegel et al., *Hegel's Philosophy of Mind: Being Part Three of the "Encyclopaedia of the Philosophical Sciences"* (1830), p. 238: "…since happiness has affirmative content solely in the impulses, decision lies within them, and it is subjective feeling and 'individual pleasure' that must be the deciding factors as to wherein happiness is to be situated (*setze*, posited)." In his handwritten notes to §20 of *Grundlinien der Philosophie des Rechts*, Hegel notes in this regard: "The *whole* of satisfaction. Universal end—*happiness*—but without content within itself, indeterminate—for actually [it] is a singular, *pleasant* sensation, satisfaction of a *singular* impulse—not that of the universal—a universal that remains universal within its determinateness."

5. Hegel, *Enzyklopädie der philosophischen Wissenschaften III*, §480; Hegel et al., *Hegel's Philosophy of Mind: Being Part Three of the "Encyclopaedia of the Philosophical Sciences"* (1830), p. 238: "Happiness is the abstract *universality* of the content which is merely represented and which is merely *supposed* to exist."

6. Ibid., §473; ibid., p. 234: "If the will, i.e., the unity existing in and for itself of universality and determinateness, is to be satisfied, i.e., is to be *for itself*, then the adequacy of its inner determination and its existence are supposed to be posited through the will."

7. Ibid., §480; ibid., p. 238: "However, the truth of *particular* determinateness (which *is* just as much as it is *sublated*) and of *abstract singularity*, of arbitrary free choice (which, in happiness, equally gives itself a purpose as much as it does not give itself a purpose) is the *universal* determinateness of the will in itself, i.e., its self-determination itself, freedom."

8. Ibid., §482; ibid., p. 239: "The Idea as abstract is once again only existent in the *immediate* will. It is the aspect of the *existence* of reason, of the singular will as knowledge of that determination which constitutes its content and purpose, and of which it, the will, is only formal activity."

9. See Terry P. Pinkard, *German Philosophy, 1760–1860: The Legacy of Idealism* (Cambridge: Cambridge University Press, 2002), x, 382 pp. Paul Franks notes that this *Faktum* is something fashioned, not a fact in any ordinary brute sense, and it is, on Franks's reading, one of the crucial keys to the rest of the development of German idealism. See Franks, *All or Nothing: Systematicity, Transcendental Arguments, and Skepticism in German Idealism* (Cambridge, Mass.: Harvard University Press, 2005), viii, 440 pp. Robert Pippin takes Kant's

own statement of it to be clearly metaphorical and not paradoxical, although he then says that the metaphor is so deeply puzzling that it looks for all the world like a paradox. See Pippin, *Hegel's Practical Philosophy: Rational Agency as Ethical Life* (Cambridge: Cambridge University Press, 2008), pp. 70–71, 105. On Pippin's view, the puzzling aspect is overcome only by switching away from Kant's to Hegel's position (which seems to amount to admitting that for Kant there really is no nonparadoxical way of unpacking the metaphor since it is only by moving to Hegel's position that one avoids the appearance of insoluble paradox).

10. Charles E. Larmore, *Les Pratiques Du Moi* (Ethique et Philosophie Morale; Paris: Presses universitaires de France, 2004), 264 pp. John McDowell also seems to hold some version of this view in *Having the World in View: Essays on Kant, Hegel, and Sellars* (Cambridge, Mass.: Harvard University Press, 2009), ix, 285 pp.

11. Hegel, *Enzyklopädie der philosophischen Wissenschaften III*, §481; Hegel et al., *Hegel's Philosophy of Mind: Being Part Three of the "Encyclopaedia of the Philosophical Sciences"* (1830), p. 238: "The actually free will is the unity of theoretical and practical spirit."

12. "A second moment is necessary before it can attain reality—that of actuation or realization; and its principle is the will, the activity of mankind in the world at large. It is only by means of this activity that the determinations existing in themselves (*an sich*) are realized." See Hegel, *Vorlesungen über die Philosophie der Weltgeschichte: Berlin 1822/1823*, pp. 81–82; Hegel, *Lectures on the Philosophy of World History: Introduction, Reason in History*, pp. 69–70.

13. Hegel, *Enzyklopädie der philosophischen Wissenschaften III*, §475; Hegel et al., *Hegel's Philosophy of Mind: Being Part Three of the "Encyclopaedia of the Philosophical Sciences"* (1830), p. 236: "However, impulse and passion are nothing else than the liveliness of the subject. It is in accordance with them that the subject is in his purposes and their being put into practice."

14. His one full discussion of weakness of the will is in his handwritten notes to his own *Philosophy of Right*. See Hegel, *Grundlinien der Philosophie des Rechts*, §140; Hegel, *Elements of the Philosophy of Right*, p. 171: "[Pascal] likewise cites the opinion of Aristotle (*Nicomachean Ethics* III.2 [1110b27]), who distinguishes between acting οὐκ εἰδώς and acting ἀγνοῶν; in the former case of ignorance, the person concerned acts *involuntarily* (this ignorance relates to *external circumstances*; see §117 above), and he cannot be held responsible for his action. But of the latter instance, Aristotle says: 'All wicked men fail to recognize what they should do and refrain from doing, and it is this very defect (ἁμαρτία) which makes people unjust and in general evil. Ignorance of the choice between good and evil does not mean that an action is involuntary (i.e. that the agent cannot be held responsible for it), *but only that it is bad.*' Aristotle, of course, had a deeper insight into the connection between cognition and volition than has become usual in that superficial philosophy which teaches that *emotion and inspiration, not cognition*, are the true principles of ethical action."

15. In his lectures on the history of philosophy, Hegel identified *eudaimonia* as "the energy of the (complete) life willed for its own sake, according to the (complete) virtue existing in and for itself." See Hegel, *Vorlesungen über die Geschichte der Philosophie II*, p. 222.

16. A satisfying life need not be a moral or an ethical life. Hegel, *Vorlesungen über die Philosophie der Weltgeschichte: Berlin 1822/1823*, p. 102; Hegel, *Lectures on the Philosophy of World History: Introduction, Reason in History*, p. 86: "We must further note that, in fulfilling their grand designs as necessitated by the universal spirit, such world-historical individuals not only attained personal satisfaction but also acquired new external characteristics in the process." The link between satisfaction and moral or ethical value is itself a social, historical link, not an a priori link. The more interesting question for Hegel is thus which forms of life are such that satisfaction is also ethical, where the norms to which we hold each other are such that one cannot lead a successful life that embodies various goods that are compatible with ethical goods. Thus, where the social world is seen as corrupt or inherently violent, true virtue will seem to be impossible or a matter of self-deception. This forms part of Hegel's interpretation of Shakespeare's tragedies. See Benjamin Rutter, *Hegel on the Modern Arts* (Cambridge: Cambridge University Press, 2011).

17. Hegel, *Phänomenologie des Geistes*, p. 23 (¶17)

18. The example of animals and food has been put to use by Robert Brandom in *Making It Explicit: Reasoning, Representing, and Discursive Commitment* (Cambridge, Mass.: Harvard University Press, 1994), p. 86.

19. See the remarkable discussion in Christopher Yeomans, *Freedom and Reflection: Hegel and the Logic of Agency* (London: Oxford University Press, 2011).

20. Hegel, *Enzyklopädie der philosophischen Wissenschaften II*, §360; Hegel and Miller, *Hegel's Philosophy of Nature: Being Part Two of the Encyclopedia of the Philosophical Sciences (1830), Translated from Nicolin and Pöggeler's Edition (1959), and from the Zusätze in Michelet's Text (1847)*, p. 388: "The mystery thought to occasion the difficulty in understanding instinct is simply this, that an end can be grasped only as the inner *concept*, so that explanations and relationships stemming from the mere understanding soon reveal their inadequacy in regard to instinct. The basic determination of the living being seized on by *Aristotle*, that it must be conceived as acting purposively, has in recent times been almost forgotten until *Kant*, in his own way, revived this concept in his doctrine of *inner* purposiveness, in which the living being is to be treated as *its own end (Selbstzweck)*. The difficulty here comes mainly from representing the purposive relation as *external*, and from the prevalent opinion that an end exists *only* in *consciousness*. Instinct is purposive activity acting unconsciously."

21. This is, I take it, what is at stake in what Hegel says in §5 of *Grundlinien der Philosophie des Rechts*; *Elements of the Philosophy of Right*, p. 35: "The will contains (a) the element of *pure indeterminacy* or of the 'I's pure reflection into itself, in which every limitation, every content, whether present immediately through nature, through needs, desires, and drives, or given and determined in some other way, is dissolved; this is the limitless infinity of *absolute abstraction* or *universality*, the pure thinking of oneself."

22. The logic of Kant's push to formalism is elegantly made by Sally Sedgwick, "Reason and History: Kant versus Hegel," *Proceedings of the American Philosophical Association* 84/2 (November 2010), 45–59. (See also Yeomans, *Freedom and Reflection*; and Klaus E. Brinkmann, *Idealism without Limits: Hegel and the Problem of Objectivity* (New York: Springer, 2010.)

23. Hegel himself seems to want to restrict the word *intelligence* to its application to adult self-conscious agents and to deny it to children and animals. See, for example, §246, Hegel, *Enzyklopädie der philosophischen Wissenschaften II*; Hegel and Miller, *Hegel's Philosophy of Nature: Being Part Two of the Encyclopedia of the Philosophical Sciences (1830), Translated from Nicolin and Pöggeler's Edition (1959), and from the Zusätze in Michelet's Text (1847)*, p. 9: "This unity of intelligence and intuition, of the inwardness of spirit and its relation to externality, must be not the beginning but the goal, not an immediate, but a unity that is produced. A natural unity of thought and intuition is that of the child and the animal, and this can at the most be called feeling, not mindedness (*Geistigkeit*). But man must have eaten of the tree of the knowledge of good and evil and must have gone through the labor and activity of thought in order to become what he is, having overcome this separation between himself and nature."

24. This is one way of taking the often discussed §§5–6 of Hegel's *Philosophy of Right*. In §6, he notes that it is only in "particularizing" itself that the subject "steps into existence in general." See Hegel, *Grundlinien der Philosophie des Rechts*; *Elements of the Philosophy of Right*, p. 39.

25. Although in action, the causal relation lies between the agent and the action, this does not mean that the agent as a substance cannot be analyzed further into various causal subsystems. Animal life is perfectly capable of biophysical explanation, but explanation of the operations of organic animal life requires us to account for animal behavior in light of goals that the animal seeks.

26. If one focuses on the simplest actions (turning on a light switch, reaching and grasping an object), this aspect of the relation between means and ends can be easily overlooked. This point about the relation between means and ends is made central to the Hegelian account in Yeomans, *Freedom and Reflection*.

27. Moreover, it is striking that rather than appealing to something like Kant's conception of autonomous willing (of what, anachronistically speaking, we can call the Kantian picture of

agent-causation) to explain how it is that reasons can move us, Hegel himself prefers the Aristotelian expression "unmoved mover" to characterize the relation between the agent, as an individual substance, to the action. For example: "No truly ethical existence is possible until individuals have become fully conscious of their ends. They must have knowledge of the unmoved mover, as Aristotle calls it, of the unmoved motive force by which all individuals are activated. For this force to become effective, the subject must have developed to a condition of free individuality in which it is fully conscious of the eternally unmoved mover, and each individual must be free and self-sufficient in his own right." See Hegel, *Vorlesungen über die Philosophie der Weltgeschichte: Berlin 1822/1823*, p. 91; Hegel, *Lectures on the Philosophy of World History: Introduction, Reason in History*, p. 77. The distinction between the executive function of "deciding" and that of the extra causal push of "resolving" is discussed by Hegel in §12, *Grundlinien der Philosophie des Rechts*; Hegel, *Elements of the Philosophy of Right*, p. 46.

28. See the critical discussion by Sebastian Gardner, "The Present Situation of Philosophy: The Limits of Naturalism and the Interest of German Idealism," in Espen Hammer, ed., *German Idealism: Contemporary Perspectives* (London: Routledge, 2007). The idea of the agent as "substance/subject" is intended to respond to some of those criticisms. I am also indebted to Christopher Yeomans for his own discussion of the issue in *Freedom and Reflection*.

29. That one makes one's own character (one's second nature) into an object of willing is part of what Hegel intends to highlight by arguing that the proper concept of freedom emerges out of the concept of "reciprocal interaction" in nature, not as a defiance of causality in nature. See Hegel, *Wissenschaft der Logik II*, p. 251; Hegel, *Hegel's Science of Logic*, p. 583: "The *unity* of substance is its relation of *necessity*. However, this unity is only an *inner necessity*. In *positing itself* through the moment of absolute negativity, it becomes *manifested* or *posited identity*, and thereby the *freedom* which is the identity of the concept. The concept, the totality resulting from the relation of reciprocity, is the unity of *both substances* of the reciprocal relation. However, in this unity they now belong to freedom, for they no longer possess their identity as something blind, that is to say, as something merely *inner*. Rather, the substances now have essentially the determination of *seeming-to-be* (*Schein*), that is, of being moments of reflection, whereby each is no less immediately united with its other or its positedness, and each contains its positedness *within itself*, and consequently in its other is posited as simply and solely identical with itself."

30. Harry G. Frankfurt, *The Importance of What We Care About: Philosophical Essays* (Cambridge: Cambridge University Press, 1988), x, 190 pp.

31. See also the criticism of hierarchical views of one's "identification" with the action in Yeomans, *Freedom and Reflection*.

32. Thus, Hegel, *Enzyklopädie der philosophischen Wissenschaften III*, §475; Hegel et al., *Hegel's Philosophy of Mind: Being Part Three of the "Encyclopaedia of the Philosophical Sciences"* (1830), pp. 236–37: "An action is the subject's purpose, and likewise it is his activity which puts this purpose into practice. Only through this—that in this way the subject also is in the least self-interested action, i.e., through his interest—is there an action at all.... The ethical concerns the content, which is as such the *universal*, something inactive, which has its activation in the subject. This—that it is immanent therein—is the interest and, as making a claim on the whole effective subjectivity, is the passion."

33. See Pippin, *Hegel's Practical Philosophy*. Pippin straightforwardly attributes a kind of hierarchical conception to Hegel, where "freedom" means that the agent can "identify" with the actions (which for Pippin means to see them as justified), even though he also quite clearly rejects some of the other versions of this account as suitable for understanding Hegel's position: "In such a self-relation I do not transcend or negate the content of what I find myself inclined to do, but find a way of identifying with a determinate content (or passion, inclination) among my options" (p. 39). In the book, he also seemed to suggest that this kind of account excludes all causal accounts, but he has since clarified his position on that issue and claims it does not exclude causal accounts. See Robert B. Pippin, "Hegel on Political

Philosophy and Political Actuality," *Inquiry: An Interdisciplinary Journal of Philosophy*, 53/5 (October 2010), 401–16.

34. Hegel, *Grundlinien der Philosophie des Rechts*, §27; Hegel, *Elements of the Philosophy of Right*, p. 57: "...the abstract concept of the Idea of the will is in general the free will that wills the free will."

35. Hegel, *Phänomenologie des Geistes*, p. 155 (¶196): "His having a mind of his own is then merely *stubbornness*, a freedom that remains bogged down within the bounds of servility."

36. Hegel speaks of the "Idea" both as the unity of concept and objectivity (*Objektivität*) and as the unity of concept and reality (*Realität*), and he seems to take the two to be equivalent. See Hegel, *Enzyklopädie der philosophischen Wissenschaften II* (8), §213; Hegel et al., *The Encyclopaedia Logic, with the Zusätze: Part I of the Encyclopaedia of Philosophical Sciences with the Zusätze*, p. 286; and Hegel, *Enzyklopädie der philosophischen Wissenschaften III*, §437; Hegel et al., *Hegel's Philosophy of Mind: Being Part Three of the "Encyclopaedia of the Philosophical Sciences"* (1830), p 177: "Reason as the *Idea* appears here in the determination that the opposition of concept and reality itself, whose unity it is, here has the more precise form of the concept existing for itself, of consciousness and the present object externally standing over and against it." In his lectures (for example, those on philosophy of art in 1826), he says: "Idea means only the unity of the concept and reality, of the generally realized concept" See Hegel, *Philosophie der Kunst oder Ästhetik: Nach Hegel, Im Sommer 1826; Mitschrift Friedrich Carl Hermann Victor von Kehler* (Jena-Sophia: Studien Und Editionen Zum Deutschen Idealismus Und Zur Frühromantik. Abteilung I, Editionen; München: Fink, 2004), p. 34.

37. For another one of his phrases expressing the "speculative identity" of thought and being (that, according Hegel's post-Spinozist view of things, they are both moments of a whole), he says: "Those who understand nothing of philosophy clasp their hands to their heads when they hear the proposition: *Thought* is *being*." But then he immediately adds, "Nonetheless, the presupposition of the unity of thought and being lies at the basis of all our actions. We make this presupposition as rational, thinking creatures." See Hegel, *Enzyklopädie der philosophischen Wissenschaften III*, §465; Hegel et al., *Hegel's Philosophy of Mind: Being Part Three of the "Encyclopaedia of the Philosophical Sciences"* (1830), p. 224.

38. Hegel, *Enzyklopädie der philosophischen Wissenschaften III*, §482; Hegel et al., *Hegel's Philosophy of Mind: Being Part Three of the "Encyclopaedia of the Philosophical Sciences"* (1830): "This Idea itself is as such the actuality of people, not something they *have* but something they *are*."

39. Hegel, *Aesthetics: Lectures on Fine Art*, p. 170; Hegel, *Vorlesungen über die Ästhetik I*, p. 224.

40. "The ideal artistic figures [of the hero] are transferred to the age of myths...in the world of today, with its civilized, legal, moral, and political conditions, we see that nowadays the scope for ideal configuration is only of a very limited kind. For the regions in which free scope is left for the independence of particular decisions are small in number and range....It would be inappropriate to set up, for our time too, ideal figures, e.g. of judges or monarchs." See Hegel, *Vorlesungen über die Ästhetik I*, p. 253; Hegel, *Aesthetics: Lectures on Fine Art*, pp. 189, 193.

41. Hegel, *Enzyklopädie der philosophischen Wissenschaften III*, §485; Hegel et al., *Hegel's Philosophy of Mind: Being Part Three of the "Encyclopaedia of the Philosophical Sciences"* (1830): "This unity of the rational will with the singular will, which is the immediate and characteristic element for the activation of the rational will, constitutes the simple actuality of freedom."

42. See Lear, *Happy Lives and the Highest Good*, pp. 59, 63. This characterization of the final good draws on her discussion of Aristotle's conception of it.

43. In his lectures on the history of philosophy, Hegel attributes this idea of the final end as including its realization to Aristotle, even though he rejects the Aristotelian principle of happiness being that final end: "In the practical field, Aristotle determines the highest good as happiness—the good itself not as an abstract Idea but rather in such a way that the moment of actualization is essentially within it." See Hegel, *Vorlesungen über die Geschichte der Philosophie II*, p. 222.

44. On the impossibility of art's fully achieving the kind of reconciliation it seeks, see Benjamin Rutter, *Hegel on the Modern Arts* (Cambridge: Cambridge University Press, 2011).

45. Hegel, *Wissenschaft der Logik II*, p. 468; Hegel, *Hegel's Science of Logic*, p. 759: "By virtue of the freedom which the concept attains in the Idea, the Idea possesses within itself also the hardest opposition. Its rest consists in the security and certainty with which it eternally creates and eternally overcomes that opposition in coming together with itself."

46. My thanks to Thomas Kuhrana for help on this point.

47. Gabriel Richardson Lear (*Happy Lives and the Highest Good*) argues that Aristotle takes happiness to be an approximation to divine contemplation. I myself once argued that for Hegel, the absolute for humans should be understood as an approximation of the genuine absolute, but I have since become convinced that this cannot be the basic sense of the Hegelian conception. For that misguided interpretation, see Terry P. Pinkard, *Hegel's Dialectic: The Explanation of Possibility* (Philadelphia: Temple University Press, 1988), xi, 236 pp. That book also made the crucial mistake of thinking of Hegel as overly concerned with the Kantian conception of the conditions of the possibility of thought and experience. Hegel is far more concerned with the conditions under which thoughts can be actualized than with how they are possible.

48. It is probably worth noting that in one obvious sense, this conclusion runs at odds with Hegel's own program of turning philosophy into a *Wissenschaft*, that is, into the kind of specialized discipline that can be pursued only by university professors. On Hegel's conceptions of the relation of the philosophy to the nature of the university, see Pinkard, *Hegel: A Biography* (Cambridge: Cambridge University Press, 2000).

# 4

# Inner Lives and Public Orientation

## A:  Failure in Forms of Life

Our capacity to be at one with ourselves is therefore itself in the practical sphere intrinsically bounded and never fully "infinite," even though different practical spheres can be more or less conducive to such freedom. The metaphysical dilemmas about agency find, in a way, a practical solution: "Now man's physical needs, as well as his knowing and willing, do indeed get a satisfaction in the world and do resolve in a free way the opposition of subjective and objective, of inner freedom and externally existent necessity."[1] However, in the modern world especially, where the dependency of each on the other has become so complex, the finitude of all of our purposes results in each of us being, in Hegel's word, only a "fragment."[2] In that world, for each of us to be "infinitely" at one with ourselves in the practical world would require us to be a position to actualize all of our commitments, and that is impossible. The inescapable contingencies of the natural and social world is one obvious way in which one's commitments can all fail. Likewise, weakness of will as a failure to acquire a certain kind of skill (i.e., a lack of practical knowledge) is another. One could obviously extend the list.

There is, however, yet another way in which a self-interpreting animal can get it wrong about herself, which has to do with failures internal to the collective form of life itself in which one lives. Hegel's form of sublated Aristotelianism holds that part of the freedom of an action consists in it being "up to the agent" to do or not do the action and that the kind of theoretical and, just as important, the practical knowledge required for this has to do with the agent's psychological makeup, which itself cannot be something entirely "up to" the agent (on pain of a badly infinite regress—if one were responsible for the actions one takes in light of one's character, one would then be responsible for the character, and thus for the character that chooses the character, and so on).

For Aristotle, that regress about what is "up to one" must ultimately terminate in facts about how one was raised, since that would also determine whether one could then truly or more adequately perceive the good. The regress, that is, has to end at one's upbringing, at a form of life and educative formation.

To an important extent, Hegel agrees with the way Aristotle understands the matter.[3] However, Hegel draws only a quasi-Aristotelian conclusion from this. It might seem that inquiries into action push one back into inquiries into character, and inquiries into character push one back into inquiries into the goodness of the community that creates these characters, and that is where the argument stops— or, more likely, where a new argument begins, since one now needs some standard by which to judge the goodness of entire communities. From that point, it then seems as if, very roughly, the choice is between the idea of a community living up to its own ideals and a community living up to "the" ideal, and when that step is taken, a rather familiar dialectic gets underway about whether the standards are internal to the community itself, which seems to beg the question entirely, or transcendent to the community, which itself raises a host of other worries.

Hegel's own commitments push him into saying that since all such standards are historical and social in nature—one always reasons from within a social space—the standards must therefore be internal to the community, and left at that, it, too, seems to beg the question. Hegel's proposal is that this all too familiar way of looking at matters can best be comprehended if we both take this Aristotelian idea of "how people are raised" as the last word and also take seriously Kant's own idea about the will metaphorically giving itself its own law. If we do so, or so goes Hegel's view, we will end up with something neither orthodoxly Aristotelian nor orthodoxly Kantian but something better: Hegelian.

For Kant, the will may fail if it does not conform to a law that it has given itself, not if it fails to express an objective and independent fact about the good. The agent (or in the Kantian metaphor, "the will") authorizes itself to act only on those maxims that are always and at the same time universal, and thus when it fails to give itself a universal law, it fails internally, that is, in terms of its own standards, not in terms of its measuring up to, say, a timeless and independent order of things. Now although for Kantians, the will must measure up to the eternal standards of reason itself, these are nonetheless the standards of the will itself, not standards that the agent intuits as existing in a timeless realm independent of all willing.

Although Hegel thought that Kant's versions of what it meant for a maxim to contradict itself were unsatisfactory, there is another sense in which Hegel actually absorbs Kant's idea and then looks at what it would mean to fail at giving oneself a maxim in light of the conditions under which agents exist within structures of mutual recognition. That is, the failure may not lie merely in having a self-contradictory maxim or in failing to will the means to the end, but rather in having one's maxim be either directly contradictory within the conditions of mutual recognition—within the conditions of both holding oneself and holding others to that maxim—or, more important, be such that the tensions involved in holding oneself and others to that maxim are such that it becomes impossible within the conditions of human life to maintain any kind of proper affective connection to the maxim.[4] In terms of a form of life itself, the contradiction is thus not, as it were, in the statement of the individual maxim itself but in the way each agent must, in taking certain things to be absolute, hold himself and others to a certain conception of what it is to be an agent, both in the abstract and in the concrete cases. In such cases, the tensions imposed on the agents who hold themselves and others to those norms is such that it undermines the affective relation agents can have to those norms. The contradiction is thus not between maxims that are self-defeating in a formal manner but within the kind of unity with their affective, embodied lives that agents must live in that form of life if they are to count in their own eyes and in the eyes of others as successful. When that unity is shattered, agents gradually lose the motivation to continue being the kind of people they have become, or they become progressively more alienated from themselves and others.

The good life is a successful life, and a successful life is one in which one is "at one with oneself," that is, in which one's projects make sense to oneself, in which it is rational to think that these projects (large and small) can be actualized, and in which one actually realizes those projects. To the extent that a form of life is as a whole fully or deeply at odds with itself, the people operating within it are faced with what must seem like the impossibility of a successful life. They cannot achieve what it is that they take to be necessary to achieve. When a successful life is ruled out, the legitimacy of that form of life begins to fade in the eyes of those living in it. Such a loss of allegiance is not necessarily a matter of abstractly logical necessity but as feature of the psyches of humans.

A form of life can therefore fail to achieve practical truth not because it does not match up with some set of facts (say, about human nature) but because, in Hegel's language, it cannot match up with its concept, and, to stick with Hegelian language, failure to match up with its own concept in turn alters the concept with which it has failed to match up.

Hegel does not therefore have a theory of how human nature matches up with social life in better or worse ways. Rather, he has a theory of how humans collectively hold themselves to certain goals that turn out to be "untrue" because they impose what seem to be impossible commitments on themselves. Such commitments express something false, not because the commitments fail to fit the independently established moral facts but because they fail to present a workable form of life.

Now, that might suggest that Hegel is rejecting, say, a sober Aristotelian reflection on what institutional structures best fit certain key facts about human flourishing and substituting instead a kind of less than sober a priori theory about which forms of life are best. If indeed he were doing that, he would be violating his own strictures. The kinds of ends that humans take up, and therefore the kinds that fail, are not independent of the facts of human life. They are sublations of those facts, that is, ways in which the authority accorded to certain facts is circumscribed by another authority. It is a fact that in human life, people age, and many of them become old. How much authority, for example, should be vested in such people simply because they are old is an issue that goes to the heart of where the ground-level commitments of a form of life lie and thus what kinds of reasons people may demand and what kinds they can legitimately give. As we have already seen, it is part of Hegel's story about modern life that it is required to vest enormous authority in the natural sciences vis-à-vis what we may be said to know about nature, and it is also required to invest an enormous amount of authority in the "inner life." One does not ignore the facts, but as one might put it, one needs a conception on a different level about who and what speaks with what authority about the facts.

Indeed, one of the facts Hegel acknowledges is that however contradictory a form of life may be, and however much of an impact that way of being untrue may have on the lives of its participants, people can live with those contradictions and whatever anguish they bring with them for centuries. If anything, that seems to be a fact about human psyches. However, for Hegel, the more interesting question has to do with when such contradictions become so compelling that we must acknowledge them and thus when the anguish in living within those contradictions becomes too much. At that point, the lives in a form of life become uninhabitable.

## B: The Phenomenology of a Form of Life

If having the regress of "it being up to the agent" stop with facts about how one is raised in that form of life, and if by hypothesis the social space of that form of life bears within itself deeply contradictory commitments, then agents raised within that form of life will never be able to achieve any kind of oneness with themselves unless they could, impossibly enough, jump out of their form of life itself. Unfortunately, the idea that one could unbundle oneself of all of one's commitments and then heroically shift oneself over to a new set of commitments is a task as mythical as the actions undertaken by the more overtly mythical Greek heroes. (That it is mythical, of course, does not prevent it from presenting an attractive picture for people alienated from their own form of life.)

To the extent that we can understand the ground-level commitments of a form of life as aiming at truth and some sets of commitments as being better suited to that aim by virtue of their having come to be required in light of the dissatisfactions produced by the use and logic of their predecessors, we can get a rough-and-ready sense of how to sketch a direction in historical time. That would be to look at the collective efforts at comprehending our highest interests (in the "unconditioned") analogously to the way in which physicists look at "true" as opposed to merely "apparent" motion—or, to use the physicists' own term, in light of a phenomenology. Hegel's own phenomenology is a theory of the true movement of forms of life whose failure is such that a different form of life that has within itself a historical sense must understand itself in light of how it understands the failures of its predecessors. The "true motion" of human mindful agency in history is that of having a direction without a purpose in mind. It presents us with something like what Kant called "purposiveness without a purpose," a direction that is nonetheless not consciously guided by anybody or anything in a particular direction.

Now, there is a way of viewing this kind of approach to history that is not really part of Hegel's core conception, even though the view is suggested by the presentation Hegel himself makes. This is the view that history consists in a number of concrete shapes—those of a people or nation—lining up, as it were, for Hegelian inspection and to be put into their proper order. Each "people" then succeeds another as something called "spirit" leaps from one place to another. Thus, one gets China and India being replaced by Egypt on the world stage, only to have Egypt replaced by Greece, Greece by Rome, Rome by European Christianity, and finally the avant-garde of European Christianity (northern Europe, the "Germanic," although not exclusively *deutsche* Europeans) hogging the stage at the end and taking its bow. Sublation in history is, on this view, replacement: Greece replaces Egypt as the scene of the action, Rome replaces Greece, and so on.

In his very popular lectures on the philosophy of history, Hegel certainly left his (mostly very young) audience with more or less that impression. However, that picture also belies his own procedure. What the phenomenology of history worries about are the internal tensions of forms of life and how the norms that generate those tensions are circumscribed by another context asserting its own normative authority. It is the move to a different context that is crucial, not the wholesale replacement of one shape by another. Roman rule circumscribes the authority of the Greek way of life, and it does this not simply by conquering it but by also supplying a legitimation strategy that underwrites its claim to circumscribe it. Moreover, there is no a priori method of any sort that would allow one to sort out in advance of the facts how this was to proceed (as if one imagines one could have had such a manual and thereby given the Romans a fairly detailed list of instructions for replacing Greek rule with Roman power).

Hegel's story of progressivism in history is therefore not that of the slightly comical picture of "spirit" leaping from one place to another on the globe in order to realize itself better but rather a story of how procedures of reasoning were realized in different ways such that there was a kind of progress in the sciences and in ethical matters that did not amount to just a change of venue. It is a path-dependent progressive development that moves in many contingent ways, but what makes the path rational, where it is rational at all, is that later circumscriptions of authority can lay their claim to legitimacy on the difficulties internal to the area they were circumscribing. In such a phenomenology, moreover, it is not everything along the path that can be handled this way. Only the articulations of the "absolute" count as part of that story. That is, what a phenomenology in this sense lays claim to studying is not, say, why this and not that was a better way to engineer a bridge or a build a dome on a public building, but why such and such laid claim to being the unconditioned, the basic end point of reasoning in general for a form of life. The Hegelian idealist proposal is that only such a view of the development of what constitutes the unconditioned is the proper subject matter of philosophical history.

This is also not a theory of any kind of metaphysical causality in history that supersedes or transcends normal causality, although there are indeed passages in Hegel's popular lectures on the philosophy of history that suggest that "reason" or "spirit" itself is always standing behind the curtain and manipulating the actors on stage to play out their roles in the way required by the script. "Reason" in the abstract is not a cause in that sense. What is bound up with being a rational agent is that one becomes an organism for whom the issue of making something better becomes itself an issue, and the very idea of progress is part of what it is to be a rational agent. This does not guarantee or in some causal way ensure that progress—getting better at any kind of practice—will be made, but inherent in the idea of there being a history of the kind of animals whose lives are carried out in social space is that they at least have the idea of getting better at marking some things: better at technology, better at taking care of the vulnerable, and better at understanding that to which they are committed. This, of course, does not mean that all claims of getting better at something really do mark progress, nor that all change is progressive. Hegel was as aware as anyone else that we are really quite good at fooling ourselves about that.

## C:  Greek Tensions, Greek Harmony

In his 1807 *Phenomenology*, Hegel titled the sections on ancient Greece "The True Spirit." This form of life is "true" in that it presents us with a view of what our agency would look like if we were both self-conscious (and hence at odds with ourselves in some sense) and yet at the same time and in some appropriately deeper sense also at one with ourselves and our world. Or again to put the point more in the form of a slogan: In such a form of life, we would live in harmony with ourselves and the world even amid the deepest tensions. Now, although Hegel titles this "the true spirit," its "truth" is that it lived in a contradiction with itself that constantly threatened to make that form of life fully unintelligible to itself. It therefore also constantly faced the threat that it could not be sustained, either in actuality or in theory. In the end, the Greek *polis* proved to be too small to defend itself, and it eventually succumbed to the demands of empire (first to those of Greek empires themselves and later to those of the Roman Empire). Its ideal of harmony proved to be more of a dream than a reality. Most remarkably, the Greeks themselves, at least on Hegel's view, had a relatively clear conception of its dreamlike quality.

Now, judged by later standards of historical accuracy, Hegel's portrayal of Greek life is, to say the least, idealized. However, his use of the model of the Greek *polis* as an example of "true" spirit illustrates what he takes to be a conception that lies at the heart of what it is to be a self-conscious animal. The animal as animal is completely absorbed in its tasks. Although some animals may form beliefs and may even deliberate in some form about their behaviors, the animal nonetheless never has to ask itself if it is a good thing to be an animal of that type, nor what a good type would be, nor whether it would be good to have more rather than fewer of its kind. For the self-conscious animal, on the other hand, who may also be completely absorbed in its activities, it is still always an open matter as to whether it is to entertain its activities as possibilities. The ideal, as it were, built into self-conscious life is the ideal of a unity, or even a harmony, between self-consciousness and absorption, that of being fully engaged in an activity while at the same time being aware of doing it right, of fully attending to the normative proprieties of the activity.[5] (Examples are easy to line up: the dancer who feels happiest in the public performance of the dance; the scientist fully focused on her work; the reader in rapt absorption with the text; the artisan fully absorbed in his craft.) What a conception of "true" spirit would show us therefore would be the conditions under which the union of self-consciousness with such absorption could be achieved not in isolated individual cases but as a condition of the form of life itself. The *polis* in its idealized form presented a compelling picture of what such a way of life would concretely look like.

Hegel's view of the ancient Greek *polis* plays a remarkably similar role to that of the state of nature in Rousseau's *Social Contract*, and his criticisms of it obviously draw on Rousseau's criticisms of contemporary life. The life of the ancient Greek *polis* (like Rousseau's state of nature) offers us an idealized picture of what life would be like before some kind of corrupting element has set in, and, given the now ineliminable fact of such corruption, it then asks whether the kind of freedom that formerly existed could be reactualized in modern conditions without somehow having to either re-create the state of nature or resurrect the vanished life of the ancients. For both Rousseau and Hegel, the so-called corrupting element is, of course, "individualism," although each of them takes "individualism" and what is corrupting about it in different senses. Each takes it that it is imaginable that there could be a harmony between individual freedom and the practical requirements of social and political life. However, Hegel at least takes it that such a harmony as the (idealized) Greeks made for themselves nonetheless cannot be an actuality "for us." Moreover, so it turns out, it could not have been possible in the long run even for the (idealized) Greeks who once had it. The failure of the Greek *polis* to sustain itself also shows that what Rousseau conceived as corrupting in fact marked both a kind of progress and an irretrievable loss and thus illustrates the limits of just how intelligible (or, in Hegel's sense, "infinite") political life can be.

Hegel puts the Greek model to use to highlight his own antiutopian thoughts about the possibilities of political life, which in his own context, played off the fact that he was surrounded by a host of others at the same time who not only (as he did) conflated the idealized *polis* with the real *polis* but also drew rather different conclusions from it about what life together in society should be like. Hegel's sketch of Greek life was such that if he were successful in the sketch, he would have shown that even in its most idealized conditions, it could not be a possibility for us, and the idea of either restoring it or employing its ground-level ideals for any modern project was not merely hopeless but most likely a dangerous enterprise as well. His criticism pivots on what turned out to be one of the most appealing metaphors of the Romantic period in which he lived, namely, that of all "life" (social, political, and so on) as "organic" in nature or at least as ideally "organic."

What would such a perfectly harmonious state of affairs look like? First of all, the social order would have to be divided into positions or social "stations" that carried various social responsibilities with them. Thus, there would have to be social positions that effectively dealt with issues of raising and distributing food, sanitary conditions, raising children, dealing with those who flout social rules, defense of the community against external enemies, judges to oversee the law, and more.

Second, in such an idealized community, each such position would be filled by the person who is by nature best suited to fill it.

Such a community as a whole would, in its very nature, be "organic" in two senses: First, if each person (each "organ") occupying his or her own special position in the social order were to do his or her job correctly, then the whole would spontaneously harmonize with itself, and, second, this organic structure would not be the result of anybody's having designed it. It simply is what it is, and its "organs" (the various offices) are by nature adapted to secure it.

Several features of such a social order stand out. First, all agents would find themselves embedded within a set of absolute ethical prescriptions in the form of unconditional duties to do such and such. These prescriptions would form the first principles of their practical reasoning, such as "It is best that warriors do..." or "It is best that wives do...." The unconditional authority of the "whole" is thus transmitted to each agent in the form of an unconditional duty. Each therefore has an absolute reason to do what is required of him or her according to their respective stations. (The unconditionality of the duties follow from their being "organic" requirements.)

Second, that in fact certain people occupy these positions could not be construed as merely conventional (at least in the long run). It cannot be that if a particular position is necessary for the "organism" to function well, the fulfillment of that function could turn out to be only a matter of luck. Thus, if there is indeed a natural function in the polity, then there must by nature be something (or someone) there to perform it.

Third, since there will be widely shared conceptions of what counts in the public world as carrying out the requirements of one's position, the "inner" and the "outer" for each agent will in most situations be fully congruent. Although there will always be bad luck in that some will fail to carry out their duties or will commit blunders in some unforeseeable way, this cannot be because there is any intrinsic discrepancy between forming an intention and knowing what to do. In such an organic community, people have absolute duties, and in principle, they know exactly what counts as carrying them out, and they know that in carrying them out in that way, they will be recognized by others as having correctly done what they were required to do.

For this to function as an ideal, the people who inhabit these positions and offices in social life have to do so self-consciously. Even though they would be fully absorbed in the working out of their positions, they would have to do so with a sense that the laws that govern the workings of the "organs" themselves both exhibit justice and have the force of positive law. If one "organ" has more resources directed to it, it is because it needs it, not because of some arbitrary division of goods.

The ideal society is thus not a "traditional society" that is unreflectively at one with itself. In Hegel's idealized presentation, the ancient Greek *polis* was fully conscious of its own organic nature, such that the *polis* as a collectivity realized that the laws holding their polity together were neither simply traditional laws nor laws of nature but the products of self-conscious acts of legislation. A "traditional" society simply proceeds by the laws it assumes are there for all time. Greek society, in being conscious of its own nature, realized that it had to construct the laws by which the "organism" regulated itself. Although the first principles of practical reason were, for these Greeks, given by nature—at least in the sense that they were fixed for all time—the legislation necessary to put them effectively into practice was not. Legislation required intelligence and reflection on the best way to actualize those first principles, even if the first principles themselves were not a matter of choice or reflection.[6]

Such a community thus seems to provide a practicable way for freedom (as the unity of self-consciousness and absorption) to be realized. Each member of the community finds himself or herself equipped with a more or less determinate orientation in life. The artisan has his orientation, the warrior has his own, the wife and mother has her own, and so forth. Each can be fully absorbed in his or her status, while at the same time fully aware that many of those statuses are the products of human-made legislation, not nonhuman nature.

In such a system, the only appropriate constitution—taken not as a written document but as the widely shared set of common commitments that underlie the political community—would be democratic.[7] The citizens of the community (free adult males) have as their office the interest of the community at large. In deliberating on and enacting legislation, each citizen in turn acts in terms of a law that is "his own," and each citizen is thus free.

For Hegel, therefore, it was important that he contrast this sense of the freedom of the Greek *polis* with (an imagined) "oriental" despotism. Despotism is the condition in which the individual has to act in terms of a law that is not his own—where only "one," the ruler, is free—whereas in Greek life, the citizens ("some") are free in that they act in terms of a law that is jointly authored in light of commitments they share. Such a form of life, of course, presumes that some commitments are simply given and that the interest of the political community—the state, in Hegel's terminology—functions as a given first principle in the lives of the citizens, as something that is of unconditional importance to them.[8] They, as its self-conscious organs, must take that general or "universal" interest as their own interest, since as self-conscious "organs," they could not imagine themselves having a life of any genuine worth outside of that political community. Outside of their political community, they would think of themselves, to use Aristotle's own image, like that of a hand cut off from the body. Or as Aristotle also said, only a god or beast could live such a life severed from societal association. Hegel thus approvingly cites Montesquieu's dictum that the foundation of democracy must be that of virtue, since the practice of democracy supposes that each individual both can and will put the interests of the community before his own, while at the same time holding fast in his inner life to a commitment that each citizen, himself and others, be free.[9]

For Hegel, the final end of life is that of being at one with oneself in a fully self-conscious manner that can be actual only if there is a political unity in which each follows his own law—which must include his own particular idiosyncrasies—in working out the shared commitments he has with others. In a "traditional community," the unity is already present as custom and ethos and functions as a background that simply requires articulation for it to be effective. In a democracy, the only background consists in the shared commitments that enable individuals to deliberate on their policies and fashion new commitments. To the extent that these are genuine commitments, they form the basis on which individuals participate with their full set of interests, along with all their idiosyncratic allegiances. When the community decides what is to be done, it is not by articulating something that is already there (as it is done in the "traditional community") but by producing something new as a result of discussion and deliberation.

Moreover, the laws that form the background of this kind of deliberation must themselves be both equal and just since without that element of justice, the individual citizens could not be fully present in and fully engaged with those deliberative actions. As Hegel notes in his lectures, only in such a democratic form of life can the individual lead a life in term of his own law, one that brings together all the aspects of his own subjective talents, idiosyncrasies, and rational character or, in his words,

> The main thing in democracy is that the citizen's character be sculptural (*plastisch*) and of a piece. He must be present at the main negotiations; he must take part in the decision-making as such, not merely through his own vote but in the push and pull of affairs; the passions and interests of the whole man are concentrated therein and that warmth is present throughout the entire decision.[10]

In the equality of the *polis*, the individual can participate fully without sacrificing his individuality since, from his own point of view, he would be participating on the basis of a common commitment to the end of securing what is best for the *polis* under the conditions of such equality.

For this reason, inequality of property among the citizens was not allowed to develop to extremes, Hegel notes, and thus,

> next to this freedom and within this freedom each and all inequality of character and talent, every differentiation of individuality could be asserted and exerted in the most free-wheeling way, and in those circumstances, one could find the richest encouragement for the development of such individuality.[11]

Since each could get the others to follow his lead only by means of persuading others to follow that lead, it followed that "the insight, to which all were supposed to be committed, had itself to be produced by warming up individuals by means of oratory (*Rede*)."[12] Thus, in having no other means by which to bring others to one's point of view except for rhetorical suasion, individuals were compelled to follow only that to which their own particular reflective dispositions inclined them to follow, and that was workable only to the extent that the set of shared commitments sent roots deeply enough into the dispositions of each individual so that each participant's subjective point of view was left open to the arguments of others. In that form of second nature, not merely were individuals thereby empowered to put their own particular talents into play, "they had a calling to do so," and an individual who is so called "can only make himself felt when he knows how to satisfy the point of view as well as the passions of a cultured people."[13]

Ultimately, the inner life expressed itself truly in the public realm. The role of the heart, of good intentions and the like, had to take the form of public reasons for them to have any force—"*geltend machen*," in Hegel's ordinary German, which also means to carry any "validity" with them.

Given what Hegel has to say about Greek democracy, one might well think—if one knew nothing else about him—that in his own day he would thus have been a passionate democrat. However, despite his account of the warmth of Greek democracy, Hegel nonetheless rejected democracy for his own time, arguing instead for a representative government based on a constitutional monarchy in which the affairs of state and the matter of legislation were to be handled by a select group of university-trained experts. (Like Rousseau, Hegel equated democracy with Greek democracy per se and not with any form of representative government.)

Yet he also held that the only time in which people actually had before them a distinctly articulated, practical conception of what would count as a full realization of the final end of human life (being at one with themselves) was there in the ancient Greek form of direct democracy. Why?

## D:  Empire and the Inner Life

Hegel had some clearly stated objections to importing Greek democratic ideals into a modern state of affairs. The Greek *polis*, as already mentioned, was simply too small to defend itself, and it eventually had to give way to empire. However, for Hegel, its failure lay deeper in what it took to be finally authoritative for itself—it lay in its conception of the "absolute," the "unconditioned."

The Greek democratic way of life rested its conception of the political community (the "state") on its being like (or almost identical with) an organism. If the political community is indeed something like an organism, then its basic order cannot be thrown into question, any more than—to stretch the analogy—the liver can demand that the pineal gland give an account of its role and reason for being. However, what grounds are there for believing that the political community is any kind of organic unity at all? Is there anything outside of a belief that the divine, necessary, and unchangeable order of things—nature or the gods (or both)— arranges things in that way?

This set of assumptions that underlies the way the political community must think of itself as being like an organism indicates why Hegel thought that such a form of life was itself so fragile that its continued existence was always in question. If nothing else, such a community requires a mixture of reflection and of prere- flective, unargued starting points for that reflection. This is an already volatile mixture, since once the practice of reflecting on such norms took root and established itself, there is no intrinsic reason for such reflection not to extend beyond reflection on the norms themselves to reflection on the rules of criticism for such norms. Once that kind of reflection is successfully put into motion, it has no natural stopping point. Its own movement leads it to throw into question the shared commitments necessary for such a democratic way of life based on individual virtue.

It is also striking that the genuine realization of the "true spirit" could express itself only in a fully democratic polity. If indeed freedom is living in terms of one's own law, and that law is supposed to be redeemable in terms of its rationality—it is the law that makes sense to oneself—then the only way for such freedom to be fully realized is for all the agents in question to deliberate together, on the basis of shared commitments, as to what they are required to do to actualize those commit- ments. Like Rousseau, Hegel also thought that although this embodied the "true spirit"—a form of life in which people were most fully at one with themselves in the unity of self-consciousness and absorption—it was also actualizable only in small communities.[14] To the extent that the smallness of the *polis* made it impos- sible to defend itself, the full realization of freedom that was possible only within it was thus not sustainable over the long run. The failure of the *polis* to defend itself meant that the course of events required it to be replaced by something larger— Hegel speaks of empire (*Reich*)—that unlike the *polis* could indeed sustain itself but at the cost of giving up that kind of collective realization of freedom.[15]

How successful does Hegel judge this form of life to be? On his own reckoning, this—the only genuine actualization of "the true spirit" in history—lasted at best only sixty years.[16] The failure of the *polis* to sustain itself had several causes. The necessity of its smallness was one of them, but, like many others, Hegel notes how the Greek city-states still managed to defend themselves rather spectacularly a few times, most notably in the war with the Persians. However, once the various assemblies of different *polis* had defeated their enemies, they turned against each other. What was at work in that self-destruction?

The answer to that lay in the second reason for its demise, namely, that the kind of reflection and demand for public reason giving that was the lifeblood of that kind of democracy was also its undoing. The Greeks interpreted their political life in organic terms, and that meant that the final ends of life had to be "given" by the nature of the political "organism." However, once those final ends were subjected to reflection about the best way to actualize them, there inevitably followed a kind of questioning about the rationality of the principles or ends themselves, and the very idea that something had to be taken as authoritative even though it could not be given a rational redemption could not long survive the kind of critical attitude that Greek life had thus set into motion.

In particular, the breakdown of two of the ideas that seem to underlie Aristotle's thought, namely, both that nature determines that there are certain functions in society that must be carried out and that nature thus also determines that there are people who are by nature well fitted to those functions, also set into motion the development of a kind of individualism that such a form of life could not itself sustain.[17]

Third (and related to the second point), for such an organic view of political life to be sustainable, it must also include within itself the conception, to put it most generally, that nature itself somehow fits our aspirations and that the world responds to our hopes and ambitions. (This is, of course, also at the basis of a good bit of religious belief.) Otherwise, there is no reason to believe that a political life will spontaneously organize itself into the various spheres that it does or that the duties associated with the different spheres are unconditional. For the Greek form of life to work, it thus had to mix a view about the ultimate unintelligibility of the world—its being strange, mysterious, and subject to unintelligible divine will— and a view that nonetheless had it cooperating with human aspirations such that the spontaneously produced harmony required was not a daydream. Even if its tragedies taught it that any human harmony with the world at large was a matter of luck, its political life supposed that things were otherwise. Ultimately, to come to terms with that problem, it had to become philosophical.

The Greek form of life justified itself in terms of its beauty (as the spontaneous harmony among its actors). In doing so, it did not, in its presentation of its key ideas to itself, expound them first in philosophical form but in terms of art— most notably, epic and tragic drama—bound up with a religious view of the world.[18] The philosophical form it then took was provoked by what it had seen in its art, and this new form also brought new ideas into the picture. In justifying itself in terms of beauty, the Greek form of life thus had no trouble with the idea that there are certain final ends that orient individual agents in terms of their own particularities, that those ends are necessary because they are natural, and that the result is a spontaneous harmony of different stations and personal outlooks.

Hegel reads Sophocles' tragedy *Antigone* as a kind of aesthetic reflection on the tragic character of such a form of life. A young woman, Antigone, is faced with two unconditional requirements: that of performing the proper burial rites for her dead brother and that of obeying Creon—her uncle, a man, and the ruler of Thebes, who has banned these rites for her brother. She cannot do both and is thus forced into taking a position on what she must do. However, as a Greek and particularly as a woman, she is also unconditionally forbidden from making up her own mind about what is ultimately required of her. Thus, from some aspect, whatever she does is wrong, and she cannot opt out by doing nothing at all. The very act of taking a position on such an issue of unconditional final ends is in effect making herself into the law that chooses laws, that is, in effect making herself autonomous, and it is for doing so that the chorus condemns her. Although Creon and Antigone are at odds about who is in the right (and each has a claim to it), Antigone is the true heroine of the play that bears her name. Both Antigone and Creon are each in their own way provoked into fanatical action by the contradictory character of the other. However, in having his authority to rule challenged, Creon, in fanatically holding to his authority, becomes merely a tyrant. On the other hand, when Antigone is forbidden to give her brother the burial rites that she takes to be her unconditional duty to perform, she becomes slightly fanatical about her duty to perform those rites, and it is her insistence on her acting in terms of her own law—the duty of a sister to a brother and *her* self-chosen duty— that makes her into the heroine of the action, since in choosing her own law as trumping that of Creon's, she in effect also makes herself the judge of what counts as the unconditional law binding her. However, at that point, because Antigone still lacks any real principle for judging, her particular temperament has to take the place of such a principle. Nonetheless, her status at the end of the play is what is crucial. Creon unthinkingly becomes a tyrant; Antigone self-consciously becomes something like a free subject.

The play *Antigone* aesthetically presents to the Greek audience the contradiction between the necessity of taking some laws or final ends as given and the necessity of having to take nothing as given (since Antigone's own decision to put her own law above Creon's law can be justified only by a law higher than either one). The harmony demanded by Antigone between herself and the world only shows how deeply that harmony cannot be taken as a natural harmony. This kind of antinomy presented in tragic form itself thus provokes a new kind of reflection, that of philosophy, which, having found that the unconditional final ends with which somebody like Antigone found herself presented were in fact contradictory, now seeks the unconditioned not in the givens of nature or social life but in what reflective reason can find out for itself.

This not only throws open the issue as to whether the final ends that were taken to be given now must be open to the kind of debate and public questioning formerly reserved for matters of common purpose but also ultimately disenchants the nature that was supposed to be at the basis of the "organic" unity of political life, which itself rapidly leads, as Hegel puts it in his 1807 *Phenomenology*, to the "depopulation of heaven."[19] The two gods of the *polis* that Hegel mentions, Athena and Eros—each of which offers an aesthetic comprehension of the union of reason and passion within human existence—are now displaced into myth.[20] Reason, so it seems, is now on its own.[21]

In the place of a teleologically and divinely ordered nature, what appears on the scene is at first a newly formed art of arguing itself—"sophistry"—namely, an attempt to understand in real terms what it takes to bring others over to one's own side of the argument once the shared and unargued commitments of the organic view of the world are no longer in full force. Where the background of shared commitments to a common good and a sense of virtue, of contributing to the common good, and of the belief that the parts somehow spontaneously and organically harmonized was in force, there was no need for a fixed standpoint on things, and whatever was the standpoint that emerged, it came out of discussion and deliberation. However, the very idea that unfettered communication without any prior commitment to something like the common good or, especially, to the ideal of truth can lead to a life that is satisfying for the citizenry was thrown into question—or so Hegel thought—by the ongoing decline of the *polis* as the sophists assumed their pride of place in it.

The alternative was, of course, Socratic. If final ends were not to be fixed by nature (or, very generally, by the divine structure of the cosmos), then they had to be fixed by reason itself. However, Socratic reflection both on these ends themselves and then on the very nature of the rational powers used to establish them was itself the expression of what *Antigone* had already dramatically presented: Within the accepted order of final ends, the individual was compelled into a position that forced him or her to choose among ends in terms of some kind of standard not (at least on the surface) already contained in those ends themselves.

Whereas the sophists simply wanted to win the argument, the Socratic ideal emerged as the commitment to a conception of truth that puts limits on what could count as legitimate persuasion. Hegel draws another, far more controversial conclusion from this: In making that kind of commitment, Socrates actually invented something new—namely, "morality" as distinct from "ethics" (*Moralität* in distinction from *Sittlichkeit*, a distinction to be examined later).[22] Now, for Hegel, the pre-Socratic Greek form of life already had, to be sure, a conception of freedom as the ability of an agent to form intentions, make decisions, act on those decisions, and both take and receive responsibility.[23] However, in "morality," there is something new joined to that conception of freedom: We are supposed to abstract ourselves as much as possible from out of the shared commitments that we already have and seek to perform only those actions (or to form only those intentions) whose authority we can vouch for with our own powers of insight, which under the influence of Socrates increasingly became identified with our rational powers.

In its wake, that brought about a move to a conception of individual subjectivity as having a kind of authority it could not have had before. What becomes authoritative now is the "individual" as the bearer of responsibilities who must think through issues for himself, and the "individual" whose inner life, with its complex emotional undertow, now acquires a new authority on its own. As Hegel phrases it, what is now authoritative is subjectivity conceived as the "principle of inwardness, of the absolute independence of thought within itself"[24]—freeing itself not merely from its dependence on what is traditional but even from what comes about through the oratorical feats of the assembled *polis*. To a world shaped in the wake of the Socratic turn, the result is almost platitudinous: Persuasion within the limits set by a shared commitment to the common good is to be altered and reformulated—sublated, *aufgehoben*—into rational persuasion structured by a shared commitment to reason itself, and the focus of thought thus shifts both to "what, if anything, does reason require of us in general?" and "why should we care?"

Not unsurprisingly, given everything else he says, Hegel even claims that this Socratic principle of "individuality" forms the "principle of modern life" itself, where increasingly the individual is socially credited as having an authority based on the way he sees things.[25] The move away from the freedom of the *polis* and the keen focus on oratorical suasion practiced by the sophists had to provoke a set of sweeping artistic, religious, and institutional changes. Perhaps overstating his own case a bit, Hegel even claims that all subsequent European history has the Socratic principle at the basis of whatever else it takes to be authoritative for itself.[26]

After the Socratic intervention; the tragedies of Aeschylus, Sophocles, and Euripides; the comedies of Aristophanes; and finally the collapse of the *polis* itself, the groundwork had been socially and historically laid for the appeal to one's own private conscience. For rational, publicly stated reasons, the individual has become socially authorized to act in light of reasons that he need not state publicly.

However, once heaven has been depopulated, nature has been disenchanted, and individual inwardness has been given this kind of unprecedented authority, there is also no longer, on Hegel's view, any possibility for democracy. The *polis* could sustain democracy (for a brief while) only because of its small size, but in any much larger context, appeal to the common good among such divided individuals could only be "abstract" and, as such, open to the worst seductions that clever orators—the successors to the Sophists—can spin out for such a populace.

Once the fully organic model of political life is jettisoned, then the difference of interests among the citizens becomes fully established. The idea of a common

good in the sense of any shared commitments that structure practical deliberation becomes thinner and thinner (or more "abstract"). On the Hegelian account,
as what we now call pluralism appeared in the ancient world and then made itself
felt more and more in the development of European culture, politics became the
arena merely of power and the exercise of power rather than the arena of deliberation among free citizens. In Hegel's own phenomenology of this idea—an account
of its "true motion" in history—spirit is then said to gradually "empty" itself and
to "relinquish itself" of any reliance on the idea that in the very concept of our
agency, there are any final ends necessarily built into it. (The term Hegel employs
to describe this development is *Entäußerung*, the term Luther used to translate
the idea of God's "emptying" himself to become human.)[27] Political life—the
"state"—becomes purely an instrument of power, and basic differences among
subjects (not citizens) of the state becomes a background fact of life.

The issue therefore facing "us moderns" is whether we can create the warmth
of Greek democracy within the conditions of such radical differences of interests
that pervade the real world in which the concepts of matters like self-rule are to
be realized. Hegel took this to imply that although we can achieve the highest
degree of being at one with ourselves only in a democracy, we cannot hope to put
ourselves in that position again.[28] We instead require a more rational order—one
that has a place for Socrates in it—but we cannot have a more beautiful or an
equally free order.[29]

In place of the older realization of freedom, Hegel instead proposes a kind of
technocratic state with a representative form of government run by bureaucrats
who graduate from the right universities, all of which is headed up by a figure-
head monarch who merely listens to his ministers and dots the *i*'s on documents,
and where the institutions of representation in the government are not, he
insists, necessarily democratically accountable to those they represent. In some
ways, Hegel's proposal resembles the kinds of proposals for bureaucratic democracy run by technocratic elites that have been an object of serious discussion
throughout the twentieth century but without the fig leaf of democracy attached
to it. Why, though, would he think there was any warmth to that arrangement?
Or did he?

### Notes

1. Hegel, *Vorlesungen über die Ästhetik I*, p. 136; Hegel, *Aesthetics: Lectures on Fine Art*, p. 98:
   "Now man's physical needs, as well as his knowing and willing, do indeed get a satisfaction
   in the world and do dissolve in a free way the antithesis of subjective and objective, of inner
   freedom and externally existent necessity."
2. Hegel, *Vorlesungen Über Die Philosophie Der Kunst (1826)*, ed. Annemarie Gehtmann-Siefert
   (Frankfurt a. M.: Felix Meiner, 2003), p. 77: "The entire finitude of ends is here. Many individuals contribute to any whole of event and action. In accordance with their own individual
   activities, those individuals appear as fragments."
3. See Hegel, *Grundlinien der Philosophie des Rechts*, §153; Hegel, *Elements of the Philosophy of
   Right*, p. 196: "The right of individuals to their subjective determination to freedom is fulfilled in so far as they belong to ethical actuality; for their certainty of their own freedom has

its truth in such objectivity, and it is in the ethical realm that they actually possess their own essence and their inner universality.... When a father asked him for advice about the best way of educating his son in ethical matters, a Pythagorean replied: 'Make him the citizen of a state with good laws.'"

4. Hegel's own proposal for this kind of internal failure of the will thus differs in a crucial way from the distinction first elucidated by Onora O'Neill in Kant's own thought when Kant speaks of the difference between "contradictions in conception" and "contradictions in the will." On O'Neill's view, "contradictions in will" concern practical contradictions in willing certain objects and failing to will the means to realize that willing. However, Hegel's view has more to do with the kinds of impossible requirements that certain forms of recognition place on agents jointly holding those commitments. See Onora O'Neill, *Acting on Principle: An Essay on Kantian Ethics* (New York: Columbia University Press, 1975), x, 155 pp.

5. The use of the terms *self-consciousness* and *absorption* is indebted both to Michael Fried's work in the history of art, *Absorption and Theatricality: Painting and Beholder in the Age of Diderot* (Berkeley: University of California Press, 1980), xvii, 249 pp., and to Robert Pippin's commentary on it, "Authenticity in Painting: Remarks on Michael Fried's Art History," *Critical Inquiry*, 31/Spring (2005), 575–98.

6. Thus, Hegel, *Vorlesungen über die Philosophie der Geschichte*, ed. Eva Moldenhauer and Karl Markus Michel, 20 vols. (Theorie-Werkausgabe, 12; Frankfurt a. M.: Suhrkamp, 1969), p. 307; Hegel, *The Philosophy of History* (New York: Dover, 1956), p. 251. Hegel notes, "The democratic state is not patriarchal and does not rest on uneducated trust. Rather, it belongs to laws as well as the consciousness of both their rightful and ethical foundations and their positive status. At the time of the kings, there was as yet no political life in Hellas, and only slight traces of legislation."

7. Ibid., p. 306; ibid., p. 250: "Only the democratic constitution was appropriate to this spirit and this state." See also ibid., p. 308; ibid., p. 252: "Here the *democratic* constitution is the only possible constitution: the citizens (*Bürger*) are not yet aware of themselves as particulars and thus not aware of themselves as possibly evil; the objective will is unbroken in them."

8. Ibid., p. 309; ibid., p. 253: "The state as an abstraction, which for our intellects is what is essential, was unknown to them. Rather, to them, the [chief] purpose was the living father-land: This Athens, this Sparta, this temple, this altar, this mode of living together, this circle of fellow citizens, these ethical mores and habits. To the Greeks, the fatherland was a necessity without they could not live."

9. Ibid., p. 307; Hegel, ibid., p. 251: "The chief moment in democracy is that of an ethical cast of mind. 'Virtue is the foundation of democracy,' said Montesquieu. This remark is equally important as it is true with regards to the idea that one usually has about democracy."

10. Ibid., p. 312; ibid., p. 255: "In democracy, the main point is that the character of the citizen (*Bürger*) be sculptural (*plastisch*), all of a piece. He must be present at the main public hearings; he must take part in the decision as such, not merely with his vote but in the press of being emotionally moved and emotionally moving others, since the passion and interest of the whole man is absorbed in it, and the warmth attendant to the decision is also present." In *Die Philosophie der Geschichte: Vorlesungsmitschrift Heimann (Winter 1830/1831)*, ed. Klaus Vieweg (Munich: Fink Verlag, 2005), p. 125, Hegel also notes that "the democratic [constitution] is what was suited for the Greek spirit, for living, self-sufficient individuality. In that city, each could be present with his whole particularity in order to actively co-contribute."

11. Hegel, *Vorlesungen über die Philosophie der Geschichte*, 12, p. 318; Hegel, *The Philosophy of History*, p. 260.

12. Ibid., p. 312; ibid., p. 255: "The insight which all were supposed to avow had to be produced through the stirring of individuals by means of *oratory*."

13. Ibid., p. 317; ibid., p. 260: "...it not only allows individuals, to put their talents to use, it summons them to do so. At the same time, the individual can only assert himself when he knows how to satisfy opinion, as well as the passions and lightheartedness of a cultivated people."

14. Ibid., pp. 311–12; ibid., p. 255: "It must be noted that such democratic constitutions are only possible in small states that cannot be much bigger than a city. The entire Athenian state was unified in one city.... Only in such cities, can the interests of all be equal, whereas in large empires different interests which conflict with each other are to be found. Living together in a city, in the circumstances in which one is seen daily, makes a common culture and a living democracy possible."

15. Ibid., p. 312; ibid., pp. 255–56: "In large empires, one can ask around, gather votes in all communities and count the results, as happened in the French convention. However, this is a dead life (*Wesen*), and the world has then already fallen asunder into world in name only (*Papierwelt*)."

16. Ibid., p. 323; ibid., p. 265: "The most beautiful blossoming of Greek life lasted approximately 60 years, from the Median wars of 492 BC until the Peloponnesian wars at 431 BC."

17. Bernard Williams argues that this was not in fact the Greek view at all. On his view, the Greek attitude was, for example, that slavery was socially necessary but not for all that just. It was simply a piece of bad luck that one was a slave, and that form of injustice was simply the way the world worked. Aristotle, to his credit, saw that social necessity did not make it just, but, very much not to his credit, argued that there were nonetheless natural slaves for whom it was not merely terrible luck that they were slaves but who were also suited for the position. See Williams, *Shame and Necessity* (Sather Classical Lectures; Berkeley: University of California Press, 1993), xii, 254 pp.

18. Hegel, *Vorlesungen über die Philosophie der Geschichte*, 12, p. 308; Hegel, *The Philosophy of History*, p. 252: "As in beauty, the element of nature, in the sensuous of nature, is present. Also in this ethical life, laws exist in the form of a natural necessity. The Greeks remain on the middle ground of *beauty* and have not yet attained the higher standpoint of truth. Since customary mores and habit is the form in which the right is willed and carried out, that form is rigid and does not yet have within itself the enemy, that is, immediacy, reflection and subjectivity of will. The interests of the community may thus remain entrusted to the will and resolve of the citizens, and this must be the basis of the Greek constitution—for no principle is yet present, which can strive against such ethical life willing itself and hinder its actualization."

19. Hegel, *Phänomenologie des Geistes*, p. 540 (¶741).

20. Hegel, *Die Philosophie der Geschichte: Vorlesungsmitschrift Heimann (Winter 1830/1831)*, p. 124: "Athena is the city of Athens, to whose battlements she belonged, as the muse (*Genius*) that they knew as their own. Eros is an object which is a god. However, Eros is also their own feeling, something human, because that feeling represented the spiritual essentiality in its particularity." The reference to Eros is missing from Karl Hegel's (Hegel's son) editing of the *Philosophy of History*, even though it is in the manuscript he was using. Perhaps there was some discomfort for him in his father's mention of Eros. That is not an issue that will be decided here.

21. The idea that an ongoing tragic occurrence at the heart of the one full achievement of freedom—Greek democracy—colors all of Hegel's philosophy of history is made by Christoph Menke, *Tragödie Im Sittlichen: Gerechtigkeit Und Freiheit Nach Hegel* (Frankfurt am Main: Suhrkamp, 1996), 334 pp.; Menke updates the consequences of this line of thought in *Reflections of Equality* (Cultural Memory in the Present; Stanford, Calif.: Stanford University Press, 2006), xii, 226 pp.

22. Hegel, *Vorlesungen über die Philosophie der Geschichte*, 12, p. 329; Hegel, *The Philosophy of History*, p. 269: "Socrates is famous as a moral teacher. To a greater degree, he is the *discoverer* of morality."

23. In this way, Hegel would be in agreement with Bernard Williams's rather trenchant dismissal of those who think that the Greeks had no concept of the "moral" life or that their concept of freedom was too undeveloped to really count as freedom. See his discussion of the relative emptiness of "metaphysical freedom" in *Shame and Necessity*, p. 152.

24. Hegel, *Vorlesungen über die Philosophie der Geschichte*, 12, p. 328; Hegel, *The Philosophy of History*, p. 269: "the principle of inwardness, of the absolute independence of thought within itself."

25. Hegel, *Vorlesungen über die Geschichte der Philosophie I*, 18, p. 404: "Thought is interpreted as the principle, so that it at first has a subjective appearance. Thought is subjective activity. It therefore comes on the scene in an era of subjective reflection, a positing of the absolute as subject. The principle of modern times begins in this period—with the dissolution of Greece in the Peloponnesian wars."

26. Ibid., p. 515.

27. Philippians 2:7: "...sondern entäußerte sich selbst und nahm Knechtsgestalt an, ward gleich wie ein andrer Mensch und an Gebärden als ein Mensch erfunden."

28. On the relation between Hegel and democratic theory (and in particular on the relation between Hegel's conceptions of democracy and the conceptions offered by Aristotle, Montesquieu, and Tocqueville), see especially the indispensable discussion in Jean-François Kervégan, *L'Effectif et le Rationnel: Hegel et L'Esprit Objectif* (Bibliothèque d'Histoire de la Philosophie Temps Modernes; Paris: J. Vrin, 2007), 407.

29. As he puts it in his lectures, "The democratic political shape of the Greek state is beautiful, not deep, as the modern time demands." See Hegel, *Die Philosophie der Geschichte: Vorlesungsmitschrift Heimann (Winter 1830/1831)*, p. 126.

# 5

# Public Reasons, Private Reasons

## A: Enlightenment and Individualism

When Hegel published his *Phenomenology* in 1807, he tended to think that the decisive historical gap was that between the life of the ancient Greeks and the life of Europeans during and after the Enlightenment. Thus, in his 1807 book, both Rome and the medieval period were given only a few pages of discussion. As it were, it seemed that whereas the Greeks had gone from their actualized life of freedom to a stage of philosophical and scientific enlightenment that then undermined that actualized freedom, modern Europeans were in the process of moving from the Enlightenment to a stage of actualized freedom (as signaled most significantly by the French Revolution and Kant's philosophy).[1] The directions were different. The Greeks had a free life with a deeply embedded polytheistic religion, but this religious life could not withstand the force of the kind of acidic reflection put into play by Socrates, Plato, and Aristotle. For Europeans, on the other hand, the authority of the Christianity that had knit them together for 1,800 years was beginning to unravel under the pressure of their own Enlightenment, but this was laying the ground for the actualization of their own freedom. Hegel's rather audacious idea was that this meant that for the first time in 1,800 years, Europeans were now close to authentically understanding the Greek experience without the distortions overlaid on it by the Christian sublation of the ancient world. What was still at issue was whether the thoroughgoing criticism (at least within the French Enlightenment) of all forms of religion and tradition would lead to nihilism, as some German critics of the Enlightenment (such as Jacobi) warned, or whether it would precipitate a new stage of actualized freedom.[2]

In its culmination in Kant's philosophy, so Hegel thought, the Enlightenment took a decisive turn. The idea that pure reason unfettered from any dependence on experience could discern the ultimate nature of the world now had to be taken as an irretrievable thing of the past. That in turn ruled out the continuation of traditional metaphysics and any simple retrieval of the Greek idea of the ultimate intelligibility of the world. Likewise, Kant's idea that "pure practical reason" could, unfettered from any dependence on human passions and desires, provide an unconditional, genuinely action-guiding set of commands had also—or so ran

Hegel's controversial thesis—proven to be unworkable in its Kantian form. Although in its critiques of all appeals to tradition, nature, or revelation as having any basis in reason, the Enlightenment had broken down the resistance to anything other than an appeal to self-legislation itself, it still had little within it with which to respond to the problems bound up in any such appeal to self-legislation (namely, its seemingly empty or paradoxical or flatly self-contradictory character). The Enlightenment had put the link between reason and self-legislation on the theoretical agenda, and the French Revolution had put the problem of freedom as "*liberté*" squarely on the political agenda. How was this new agenda to be actualized in the life of the people?

To carry out part of this project, Hegel proposed that what we needed was a philosophical explication of the *Grundlinien*, or baselines, of a philosophy of the normative—of *Recht*—in general. Such an explication would look at how what functioned as "the" normative within modern life—morality, the legal regime, the proprieties of everyday life, and the ways religion lays claim on society and the state—could be understood to be expressions of an aspiration to the absolute, the unconditioned, that is, an aspiration for life to be rationally intelligible and not to consist in mere assertions that we simply had to accept and that could not be open to question or whose authority was simply attributed to a mystery.

On the basis of the kind of philosophical history that he developed at length in his 1807 *Phenomenology*, Hegel took himself to have shown that the unargued premise of modern life has to be that of freedom, and the basic questions about it—including the crucial philosophical issue of what exactly freedom is and whether it is even intelligible to speak of human freedom—have to do with whether it can indeed be actualized. This turned on the Socratic invention of morality—in effect, the invention of "the individual." Now, although the "individual" had proven to be the element of corruption in the ancient Greek social order, in the modern social order, the "individual" seems to be the core unit, its most important achievement.

To be an "individual" is to be taken by oneself and others to be a self-originating source of claims against others and against the political order as a whole. This self-originating status of "individual" is a social status sustained in a structure in which agents recognize each other as entitled to that status and in which agents take this entitlement to be an unargued premise of the social order. How, then, can agents sustain a kind of mutual recognition of a status that looks as if it asserts itself as not being dependent on any kind of recognition as a status at all?

Taken merely as a self-originating source of claims, "the individual" is (in Hegel's sense) only "abstract." As a bedrock status of "the right" in general, such individuals are said to have rights, and thinking about which rights they might have quickly falls out into something like the basic Lockean triad of rights to life, liberty, and property (as the kind of claims an individual can typically make against the characteristic types of injuries that can be visited on him by something like royal authority). This is so not because such agents already are in a metaphysical sense Lockean individuals, but because historically they have come to occupy the social status of something like Lockean individuals. As general statements of the unconditional claims "individuals" can make against each other and against state authority, such inalienable rights are "abstract"—their actualization is not given in the mere statement of what such unconditional claims are.

If their status is indeed taken to be unconditional and thus to require nothing else for themselves, then it quickly becomes a barely habitable status in that it envelops all those who attempt to inhabit it within a nest of contradictions and stresses. There are the various familiar conceptual dilemmas about such rights, such as "Are rights relative to social purposes, the commands of a sovereign, or the social acceptance of some general rules, or do rights have a status independent of all of those?" There are the obvious puzzles about how to balance such rights, such as "Does life trump liberty?" Now, it is central to Hegel's dialectical conception that it is a chimera to think that any of those dilemmas could be definitively resolved within a philosophical-metaphysical theory by pure reason alone. However, if the balance between them cannot be rationally struck in that way, then their actualization in practical life will prove problematic in the way that living out a contradiction always proves problematic. If nothing else, individuals who think of themselves as only Lockean rights bearers (and nothing else) will have to develop delicate psychological skills to navigate through the contradictions with which they live.

Given the finitude of human life, violations of rights—either by accident or intent—will be a constant feature of that life. Possession of rights to something like property thus will require us to adjudicate claims when something such as either property acquisition or property transfer goes wrong (or when there is damage to another's property), and for such adjudication between competing rights or assertion of rights to count to the same degree as a realization of freedom as does the status of "rights-bearer" itself, there must be accessible reasons for judging one way as opposed to another—reasons that, if they are to have the same universal status as those of rights themselves, cannot therefore be those merely of a tribe or a clan or a nation. Without the exercise of that kind of universalistic reason giving, any such adjudication would instead turn out to be merely an exercise of individual (or clannish or royal) power or interest. Thus, we are required by the logic of the classical Lockean rights themselves as they are to be put into practice to seek, in Hegel's words, "a justice...freed from subjective interest and subjective shape and from the contingency of power."[3]

A contractarian solution to this is ruled out, since if indeed the very rights at issue are to grasped as themselves moments of a form of life, then they cannot be used to justify that form of life. Thus, if "property" is taken to be a basic right, and if there is no way of adjudicating disputes over property, then the right itself will remain "abstract" and not "concrete." It will be, in Hegel's sense, a right with no actuality and therefore a status that will be uninhabitable. Indeed, without the proper authority to adjudicate disputes about property, the very distinction between "mine" and "thine" in regard to property would itself be only an abstract, unactualized possibility.

If there can be no a priori (i.e., traditional philosophical) resolution of these disputes, then the solution to some of the various antinomies of "abstract right" must be practical, not theoretical. There must be an institutional setup that makes these unavoidable tensions livable and rational to hold. A balance between competing unconditional rights must be struck, even though there can be no a priori reason to strike it one way as opposed to another. Rights require recognition both of their unconditional status and of their relative status within a distinct way of life. That makes them necessary and deeply problematic.

Only the "moral point of view"—the standpoint Socrates invented—can promise to carry out such an adjudication since it commits us both to doing the right thing because it is the right thing, even in those cases where it goes against our own interests, and to doing the right thing from a standpoint that transcends any particular point of view. "Morality" is required if abstract right is to be actual and not remain merely "abstract."

## B: Morality and Private Reasons

While the turn to "morality" is (for us moderns) to be justified by its being necessary for the actualization of "abstract rights," morality itself, of course, emerged long before any such conception of rights had been developed. However, the Socratic invention of morality also brought in its wake what Hegel called "the inward turn" in individual life—an *in-sich-gehen*, in Hegel's invented terminology.[4] Although neither Socrates nor anybody else invented inwardness, the Socratic insistence on the individual's distancing himself from all of his socially given requirements and, most important, on appealing only to his own insight into the rationality of things bestowed a new authority to this inwardness. Ultimately, the only orientation left for such a will would have to come from "the free will that wills the free will."[5]

"Morality" is an actualization of "the individual." It supposes that the "individual rational agent" has within himself or herself the necessary resources to make moral judgments and put them into practice. Such individuals may depend on each other in a variety of empirical ways, and some of these dependencies may go as deeply as any organic fact can go. Nonetheless, the "moral point of view" is that of something at least like, if not identical with, Kant's "kingdom of ends," in which each agent is both sovereign as lawmaker and subject to the commands of a moral law whose validity and binding power transcend his own individuality. In Kantian terms, the moral agent becomes an actual moral agent in the process of thinking himself as belonging to such an idealized community of moral agents.

As a limited (finite) expression of the unconditional demands of practical reason—and thus as a finite expression of the absolute—"morality" generates

conflicting conceptions of itself. Detached from being embedded in a larger practical life, it runs into the same kind of regresses and conflicts that all such purely
conceptual dilemmas about the unconditioned encounter.

For example, there are the inevitable disputes about the relation between
intention and "deed" and how to assign responsibility. Our settled beliefs about
these cases will, given the antinomies that "morality" develops, push us in different directions.[6] The abstract concept of "morality in itself," detached from life,
cannot answer that question. Likewise, there are the inevitable and morally irresolvable moral dilemmas that arise in the wake of the moral point of view. One set
has to do with cases of agent regret, that is, cases where something is not one's
fault, but we still nonetheless say there is something "wrong-making" about it.
The other set has to do with what Hegel calls "lifeboat" cases, about who (if anybody) is to be thrown overboard, whether active intervention is morally more rep-
rehensible than passive acquiescence, and so forth. (These days, such cases involve
items more technologically advanced from Hegel's own day, such as trolley cars
running on tracks that can be switched.)

The moral point of view also generates competing absolute conceptions about
whether and to what extent the consequences of action play a crucial role, no role,
or a mixed role in the appraisal of the moral quality of an action. Likewise, the
ideal community of moral agents (where each is both sovereign and subject) seems
to require that we construe the rational as the formal requirement to act only on
a universalizable rule and that acting on such a rule is equivalent to treating all
such beings who can themselves act on such a rule as entitled to respect. Yet it also
requires us to do the good, and if what is rationally required for us is to bring
about the most good, and if what is good for humans is happiness, then everyone
has an obligation to promote happiness, not necessarily to respect the capacity to
act on a rule.

Nonetheless, although the problems of moral philosophy remain irresolvable as
conceptual problems, the "moral point of view" itself is necessary for a social order
for which, in its own self-understanding, "the right of a subject's particularity to
find satisfaction ... is the pivotal and focal point in the difference between *antiquity*
and the *modern* age."[7] All of the familiar puzzle cases in, say, contemporary moral
theory that involve putting one's own interests ahead of moral interests—such as
tales of painters forsaking their families for the pursuit of a glamorous commitment to art or of ordinary people refusing to be moral saints—will necessarily
continue to pop up, and all attempts to put the house of purely moral theory in
order will one and all fail, since the centrality of the practices in modern life that
sustain these puzzle cases are unlikely to go away under the pressure of any revi-
sionary moral theory. That moral theory continually finds itself in a standoff between versions of, for example, self-interest and moral impartiality is rooted in the
inward turn that propelled the Socratic invention of morality in the first place.

Reason cannot rest content with such contradictions, and it thus pushes itself
to the idea that there simply must be some basic, overarching good that resolves

these contradictions and would both motivate us as individuals to achieve it and also be impartially justifiable.

This conceptual push to find a such resolution, in fact, has its practical counterpart in the historical development of the authority of appeals to individual conscience. "Conscience" signifies the right of the individual agent "to recognize nothing that I do not perceive as rational," a right whose content is, of course, left completely open if left simply at that.[8]

However, the actualization of such an idea merely repeats the older antinomies in another form. On the one hand, true conscience is responsive to reasons *as* reasons. On the other hand, to the extent that the "right of conscience" is really put into practice, no individual can be compelled to follow the dictates of anything that he cannot, by his own powers of insight, understand as rational. "Conscience" thus requires that at the same time the individual both must be and cannot be the court of last resort in these matters.

One of the major points Hegel makes about the moral point of view is that when put into practice—as its concept becomes actualized—it begins, under the pressure of reflection, to look self-defeating. It demands of individuals that they place themselves outside all contexts, it demands that they submit to the rules of reason, and it demands that they submit to no rules for which their own conscience has not vouchsafed while also holding that conscience cannot determine those rules. However, as essential to modern practice, it also looks as if it must by its own measures alone rescue itself from this threat.

Given those tensions at work within its practice, in its actualization "morality" thus continually threatens to transform itself within modern circumstances into either a form of moralistic preciousness or into a fierce judgmental moralism. In the 1807 *Phenomenology*, Hegel treated both possibilities as a confrontation between what he called, following the parlance of his own time, "beautiful souls."[9] Whereas Kant had seen the problem of morality as lying in the possibility of a contradiction in one's conception of the action to be performed or in one's will (as failing to will the means to a necessary end), Hegel proposed that looking at the way in which beautiful souls must confront each other puts a similar kind of logical pressure on individuals who, although not engaged in outright self-contradiction, must nonetheless contradict the key conception held in common by each other as each seeks to inhabit the status of a "moral individual."

The confrontation is between two agents who have each reached the point where each takes for granted that reason's only grasp of the unconditioned consists in the demands of practical reason to be bound by the unconditional duty to act in terms of an unconditional moral command. To the extent that this leads to something like an appeal to conscience as a final refuge—both the last unquestionable excuse and the basic duty above all others—it leads in practice to a focus on one's inner purity and a kind of "inner" wholeness. That is, each commits himself to submitting all of his maxims to the unyielding demands of something like the categorical imperative—a commitment that is, of course, potentially at odds with the other contingent features of one's life (one's needs, desires, personal commitments, and the contingency of the world in which such actions are realized).

The problem with this idea of purity of heart is that, like all such finite conceptions of the absolute, it lends itself to multiple and incompatible solutions and to different ways of living out its metaphysics. Hegel stages his confrontation between two such embodiments of the unconditional ideal of purity of heart. Both agents are worried about the connection between purity of heart and action. Each is painfully aware that not all actions result as intended, especially when interpreted by others. Each is convinced that a sharp line can be drawn between the purity of intention and the impurity of action, even though each is concerned about how the impurity of action (its deleterious consequences) can cast doubt on whether the intentions were as clean as they were claimed to be.

One agent becomes convinced that purity of heart is to be maintained by holding onto the purity of his motive as preserved throughout his actions, despite the contingency of their realization. For such an agent, although he may, of course, do wrong or fail to adequately test his motives by appeal to the categorical imperative, the purity of his willingness to submit all of his maxims to the moral law cannot, he claims, be doubted. In his own eyes, he is always a moral hero.

The other agent takes the purity of his motive to lie in his capacity for moral judgment and not in moral action itself. Although the second agent will also act and may do wrong for a variety of contingent reasons, it is the purity of his capacity for judgment that is supposed remain unimpaired, and, highly aware of how the contingency of the world interferes with the performance of a purely intended action, the second agent tends to be more than reticent about acting since it always threatens to sully the otherwise unblemished purity of his inwardness.

Both agents take their inwardness to be pure and unsullied and affirm their willingness to submit all their acts to the categorical imperative. Both realize that acting in the world, in all its finitude, inevitably compromises the unconditionality, the "infinity," of the moral law. Nonetheless, one agent acts and takes the beauty of his soul to be preserved throughout his action (whatever public meaning the action turns out to have) by virtue of his inward conviction to test all his maxims by the categorical imperative. The other agent does not act and instead takes the beauty of his soul to be evidenced by his very refusal to sully himself with the impurity of the world. One acts, knows his actions may go wrong, but stands by his claim to purity; the other is glacially slow to act, quick to condemn, but also stands by the purity of his soul. From the standpoint of each of them, the other looks like a hypocrite. From the judgmental agent's point of view, the one who acts seems like a hypocrite, since if he were really pure, he would, of course, not act at all. From the standpoint of the compromised, acting agent, the judgmental agent seems like a hypocrite since he claims an inward purity but never actually does anything that would be evidence of it.

Ultimately, as each comes to see himself in the other, to see that the other holds the same commitment as himself and is entitled to the same negative judgment, each is led to avow that, in Kant's terms, each is radically evil. That is, each comes to understand that he cannot easily pry apart the contingency of his own situated perspective (and thus his own individuality, or "self-love") and his own acquiescence to the demand for a unconditional justification of his actions. The mutual acknowledgment of radical evil is the prelude to forgiveness and reconciliation with the knowledge that what seemed like an insurmountable moral and metaphysical division can in fact achieve a practical resolution. The contradiction between the opposing ways in which one can inhabit the status of a "moral individual" is thus made livable by the practice of such forgiveness, but it does not go away.

Now, in making this kind of claim, Hegel is proposing neither a new moral philosophy nor a new and different theory of rights. Rather, he is arguing that none of the key disputes about the basic concepts in moral theory can ever be definitively solved in the sense that there can be a decisive argument in favor of one side of one of the many antinomies that make their appearance in the history of moral philosophy. The resolution of these kinds of problems in "morality" is practical in that different practical contexts circumscribe the authority of other contexts and thus manage to calm the threat that such conceptual dilemmas at first seem to present to reason itself. If indeed "morality" actually calms the threat that the antinomies of "abstract right" pose but does not make those antinomies go away, then likewise "morality" also does not subsume "abstract right" into itself, as if the problems of "abstract right" were all to be transformed into problems of moral philosophy. Nor is Hegel claiming that the problems of moral philosophy are, since irresolvable metaphysically, not real problems but only simulated or counterfeit problems. They are the real problems of morality as a practice.

This quite naturally puts great strains on the practices of moral judgment. In any other areas of life than those in which such problems about the unconditioned appear, it is difficult to count oneself as rational if one self-consciously sustains incompatible commitments. However, what reflection—which can emerge in any area of life—reveals is that many of our most basic commitments, such as to the practice of "morality" itself, involve living within just these kinds of incompatibilities. That Hegel often describes this as involving some kind of pain or suffering is thus not surprising. To be threatened with a contradiction at the heart of one's understanding of one's world is to be threatened with a loss of meaning, and such a threat generally prompts either further reflection (such as transpires in art, religion, or philosophy) or, perhaps more often, a renewed effort to suppress such reflection so that life can go on as before.

## C: Ethical Life and Public Reasons

The wider practice of "morality"—as involving universally valid reasons, good intentions, and an appeal to conscience—both presupposes and significantly underwrites the conception of individualism that emerged out of the tensions engendered within the nonindividualist forms of life of antiquity and also, more or less, those of medieval Europe. (The so-called Socratic invention of "morality" was never actualized as a smooth and unbroken process.) However, if "the individual" as a self-originating source of claims is itself a social, normative status, then we can each be individuals only if others are also (recognized as and held to be) individuals, and that is possible only by collectively holding each other to the status of "moral agency."[10] However, individualism cannot be sustained by the practice of "morality" alone. It also requires the complicated social goods of "ethical life," *Sittlichkeit*, for us to be successful "individuals."[11]

In addition to whatever other problems morality faces when its many internal tensions come to the surface in reflection, it also has trouble offering any kind of determinate orientation in life. Because its claims must appeal to "any rational agent," morality is inherently thin in its content and cannot be terribly specific about how its concepts are to be realized in practice. In particular, all the issues about how to apply the basic concepts of morality only bring out how ultimately the "principle/application" model of meaning—rather than Hegel's own conception of an "abstract meaning" being changed in its "concrete realization," that is, as the concept is put to use in life—slides toward complete arbitrariness when it is actually put to work in anything (such as the moral life) that claims the status of the unconditioned. In short, a life in which the good was completely identical with the "moral good" would, in addition to harboring the tensions already mentioned, be dangerously thin and always caught between what would seem to be conflicting duties without there being any clear way to manage the inevitable moral conflicts that arise in trying to apply such a thinned-out set of principles that are inherently at odds with themselves. The unrealizability of such a life would mean that lives lived only in terms of "rights" and "morality" would in the long run have trouble sustaining themselves.[12]

To that end, Hegel argues that for the moral life to work—to be "actual," *wirklich*, efficacious—such a way of life must be embedded in a scheme of "ethical life" (*Sittlichkeit*). The "ethical good," Hegel says, is the "living good," as opposed to the "abstract good" of morality.[13] It consists in the social goods that orient and make effective—that is, make real, actualize—the kind of individualism that "morality" presupposes. It forms the orientations for a whole life, not just parts of it.[14]

The "ethical good" is, in Hegel's terms, the "Idea" (*Idee*) of freedom itself. However, that must itself be qualified. In his lectures on the philosophy of history, Hegel claims that "the first principle of the Idea in this form is the Idea itself as an abstract entity, and the second is that of human passion. These two are warp and weft in the fabric of world history. The Idea as such is the reality, and the passions are the arms which serve it."[15] In this sense of "Idea," it is, at it were, a kind of picture of certain key social facts about practices and institutions—facts about what a form of life actually values and how what it does value is sustained in mutual acts of recognition—and how those social facts function as very determinate goods that motivate people. It forms, that is, a set of social facts whose apprehension commits agents within a historically determinate form of life to certain patterns of action, expectation, feeling, and so on—it becomes a "second nature" for them. As such, it forms, in Hegel's terminology, the "substance" of the lives of the agents, which has "subjectivity" for its "infinite form," that is, which forms a set of unconditional demands on an individual, which because of the agent's education within the terms of that form of life, also manifest themselves as goods, as things that both actually matter and are supposed to matter.[16] Within such a form of life, such goods function as the first principles of practical reasoning, being embedded statements of the form "Such and such is best for people."

Hegel's reliance on such shared ethical mores to complete his practical philosophy is yet another controversial aspect of his overall views. For a long time in Anglophone philosophy, Hegel's view about ethical life was more or less identified with Bertrand Russell's quip to the effect that in Hegel's philosophy "freedom" meant only the freedom to obey the police. Although that view has long since been shown to be far off the mark, it remains a matter of controversy as to what exactly Hegel is in fact claiming. One way of interpreting his claim is to see him as arguing that to be moral, we must interpret the rules of morality in terms of whatever it is that our given society factually takes to be required of us.[17] In addition to the fact that this would have Hegel asserting the fully implausible view that we have unconditional duties to abide by the de facto mores of our time and place, it clearly has trouble fitting into Hegel's view that we should not be looking for an "application" model at all (and that we should instead focus on his "realization of the concept" model).[18] If nothing else, it ignores Hegel's repeated statements about the finitude of such goods and the need to submit them to rational criticism. A similar communitarian interpretation would have it that Hegel is recommending these goods simply because they happen to be our goods and thus express the essence of who we are as members of this particular community.[19] As our goods, they are supposed to have some objective validity that goes beyond our merely having them. However, that runs up against Hegel's own repeated invectives against treating a particular community's goods as rational simply because they are the goods of one's own community. "Being de facto one's own," however near and dear it might be, does not on its own add up to an unconditional imperative of reason itself.

As "actual rationality" (as existing rational mores and ethos), the final ends of ethical life are also supposed to provide more determinate orientations than the moral life can provide on its own. Although the moral life demands that agents step outside all the social mores in which they live and justify their motives and actions in terms that any rational agent (not just an agent living within any particular set of mores) could accept, ethical reasons make more limited cognitive demands on agents, demanding of them only that they act in light of reasons that are in effect, already at work in their given social arrangements.

To the extent that there is an "ethical life," there exists a concatenation of basic practices and institutions that carry within them orientations for rights-bearing, moral agents when they reflectively attempt to make sense of the course of a life from birth to aging and death. Unlike Kant's postulation of a future state in which virtue would be rewarded with happiness, Hegel instead claimed that within some existing practices, there can be a rational expectation that a life carried out with an orientation to those goods-as-social-facts would itself be a successful (although not necessarily happy) life. It would be life of *Befriedigung*, satisfaction, success in living a good life. Although such a social world may lack the warmth of Greek direct democracy, it nonetheless has a kind of fragile nobility that Greek life lacked: It is a world in which faith in the organic unity of the people and the whole cannot be present and in which whatever unity there is must instead be held in place by each thinking of himself or herself as both sovereign and subject of the whole. It is, that is, a world where the "concept"—reason itself—and not the "organic" per se is authoritative.

*Notes*

1. On Hegel's early Kantianism and the way he originally saw it as related to the revolution, see Pinkard, *Hegel: A Biography* (Cambridge: Cambridge University Press, 2000), xx, 780 pp.
2. I discuss Jacobi's worries and his use of the term *nihilism* in Pinkard, *German Philosophy, 1760–1860: The Legacy of Idealism* (Cambridge: Cambridge University Press, 2002), x, 382 pp. I have given a fuller treatment of the *Phenomenology*'s use of history in Pinkard, *Hegel's Phenomenology: The Sociality of Reason* (Cambridge: Cambridge University Press, 1994), vii, 451 pp. For a shorter, perhaps more digestible version, see Terry P. Pinkard, "Hegel's *Phenomenology* and *Logic*: An Overview," in Karl Ameriks, ed., *The Cambridge Companion to German Idealism* (Cambridge: Cambridge University Press, 2000), 161–79.
3. Hegel, *Grundlinien der Philosophie des Rechts*, §103; Hegel, *Elements of the Philosophy of Right*, p. 131.
4. In the lectures on the philosophy of history, he compares Socrates to Luther in this respect: "Spirit's inward turn begins [Socrates-Luther]"; see Hegel, *Vorlesungen über die Philosophie der Geschichte*, p. 418; Hegel, *The Philosophy of History*, p. 340.
5. Hegel, *Grundlinien der Philosophie des Rechts*, §27; Hegel, *Elements of the Philosophy of Right*, p. 57.
6. Ibid., §117; ibid., p. 144.
7. Ibid., §124; ibid., pp. 151–52.
8. Ibid., §132; ibid., pp. 158–61.
9. The phrase "beautiful soul" is not Hegel's creation. It was a commonplace in eighteenth-century aesthetics and moral thought. See Robert Edward Norton, *The Beautiful Soul: Aesthetic Morality in the Eighteenth Century* (Ithaca, N.Y.: Cornell University Press, 1995), xi, 314 pp.
10. See Kervégan's account, where he speaks of the "institution" of individuality, in *L'effectif et le Rationnel: Hegel et L'Esprit Objectif* (Bibliothèque d'Histoire de la Philosophie Temps Modernes; Paris: J. Vrin, 2007), pp. 371–75.
11. The German term *Sittlichkeit* could also be easily rendered as "morality" (but then how would one translate "*Moralität*"?) or simply as "ethics" (but then how would one distinguish "ethics" from "morality"?). The root of the term, *Sitte*, has to do with the ethos and mores of a way of life, with an emphasis on the more "moral" aspects of ethos and mores. Thus, "moresness" or "ethosness" might be literal translations, but it is painfully obvious why they would be bad choices. The French version of *Sittlichkeit* as "*éthicité*" seems like a good choice.

12. The move from "Morality" to *Sittlichkeit* is thus not a move whose justification is that without it, the whole system would not thereby include all the valuable things we think it is supposed to include (that it needs to be expanded, for example, to include our other intuitions). Even Allen Wood, who otherwise shares the idea that Hegel is looking for the conditions under which certain conceptions can be realized, sometimes falls into talking that way, as when he says: "If the moral standpoint is limited to considering nothing but the rights and welfare of individuals, then it might not able to deal with the value we accord to social institutions, and that might prevent it from giving an adequate doctrine of duties." See Wood, *Hegel's Ethical Thought* (Cambridge: Cambridge University Press, 1990), p. 172.

13. See Hegel, *Grundlinien der Philosophie des Rechts*, §142; Hegel, *Elements of the Philosophy of Right*, p. 189.

14. This is Hegel's reworking of the Aristotelian truism that "But we must add 'in a complete life.' For one swallow does not make a summer, nor does one day; and so too one day, or a short time, does not make a man blessed and happy." See Aristotle, *The Nicomachean Ethics*, trans. W. D. Urmson, J. O. Ross, and J. L. Ackrill (The World's Classics; New York: Oxford University Press, 1998), p. 14.

15. Hegel, *Grundlinien der Philosophie des Rechts*; Hegel, *Elements of the Philosophy of Right*, p. 71.

16. Ibid., §144; ibid., p. 189.

17. See Sabina Lovibond, *Realism and Imagination in Ethics* (Minneapolis: University of Minnesota Press, 1983), 238 pp.

18. Hegel, *Grundlinien der Philosophie des Rechts*, §10; Hegel, *Elements of the Philosophy of Right*, p. 44: "the understanding...takes the relationship of freedom to what it wills...merely as its *application* to a given material, an application which does not belong to the essence of freedom itself."

19. See Paul Franco, *Hegel's Philosophy of Freedom* (New Haven, Conn.: Yale University Press, 1999), xviii, 391 pp.

# 6

# The Inhabitability of Modern Life

## A: Alienation

One of the longer sections of the *Phenomenology* was titled "Spirit in Its Alienation," and Hegel is often credited, fairly or unfairly, with having introduced the concept of alienation into the mainstream of philosophical thought. What does it mean to be alienated?

One of the difficulties in the very concept of alienation is that of its diffuseness. It is notoriously hard to pin down, although its experiential aspects seem very real. However, at least minimally put, to be alienated is to see what is one's own as somehow not one's own. Now, this experience of alienation is relatively familiar. One might have feelings, even strong ones, that one wants to disavow, or actions one undertook might seem or come to seem not really one's own; one's employment can seem to be "other" than oneself, or one can find oneself still committed to something—a spouse, an office, a job, a project—for which one oddly no longer feels any commitment. In short, alienation is one way of being at odds with oneself. Alienation is not simply oppression or being coerced or feeling social pressure. It is a state where one seems to be in contradiction with oneself.

Alienation would thus seem to be a prime case of unfreedom or at least a hindrance to freedom in not being at one with oneself. In Hegel's sense, alienation is the state of being committed and not committed at the same time. It is the experience of having the commitment imposed on oneself while not having undertaken it, but nonetheless it remains a commitment.[1] Another way in which alienation manifests itself is as felt commitment coupled with purposelessness. (The distinction between the alienated and nonalienated state thus does not exactly track the Kantian distinction between autonomy and heteronomy.)[2]

To live in alienation is to live in a status that one cannot fully inhabit. There are obviously many ways of being in contradiction with oneself that do not involve alienation but are simply states of confusion or unawareness of the contradiction, and one way to exit from a contradiction is to opt for one or the other side of it or to reformulate matters so that the contradiction is no longer present. Alienation supposes that one cannot do that because the state of alienation, as distinct from a state of confusion about, for example, what one ought to believe has to do with a commitment that is basic to one's other commitments but also does not seem to be true (or at least in the right way).

For Hegel, another striking case of alienation has to do with a basic norm that has gone dead but whose normative force is still felt. One is alienated from something about which one is supposed to care, whose normative pull remains partially there, but whose grip on oneself has broken down. In the cases where one is alienated from a norm, one is still bound to the form of life that justifies it as essential to (or is at least playing an important function in) that form of life. Alienation threatens the very idea of a successful life since it involves a kind of self-consciousness about one's internal contradictions.

A particular set of commitments can go dead in that it no longer seems to have any purpose, even while the form of life itself continues. The one-sided marriage arrangements of, say, the Victorians have come to be seen by enormous numbers of the contemporary populace as flat-out incompatible with the actualization of a collectively democratic and free life, and a considerable body of novels and films put on display what it is like to be in such a marriage when its norms have gone dead for at least one of the participants. From the personal side (the "aspect of subjectivity"), the experience of alienation has the agent feeling himself or herself committed to something (a job, a marriage) whose purpose now seems absent or murky at best.

More radically—and these cases interest Hegel himself the most—the whole form of life itself can go dead in that what it takes as fundamentally authoritative for itself (as expressed in its reflections within the practices of its art, religion, and philosophy) can no longer sustain allegiance because of the incompatible entitlements and commitments such a way of life puts on its members. However, since people cannot simply shed their forms of life, participants in such a form of life— a way of "going on with things"—gradually come to feel alienated from it. (Hegel himself seemed to think that the collapse of antiquity and the shift to a Christian culture was the paradigm instance of an entire form of life going dead yet living on, but that is another issue.)[3]

## 1: Diderot's Dilemma

As we can rephrase it, in alienation, one remains committed to a norm but can no longer inhabit it. Hegel's two paradigms of alienation have to do with, first, the way in which people were said to be alienated from God and how Christianity supposedly dealt with that alienation, and, second, with the alienating structure of the ancien régime in Europe prior to its collapse, first in France and then rapidly across Europe itself. The latter had to do with the establishment of the European state system and the fact that in such a system, where power and interest were the prime factors, small states were always in danger of being swallowed by larger, more aggressive states, and in which, at any time, there were always plenty of recent historical examples of how real that danger was. Because of this, monarchs needed power, and for that they needed money. Seen from that standpoint, monarchs seeking to stabilize their rule could only see the various privileges of the ancient estates and other historically entitled groups as irrational blockages in a system that, in the eyes of the monarchs and their retinues, needed to be centralized in their own courts. The more or less successful absolutizing tendencies of the French monarchs were the paradigm for the direction in which the logic of the European state system was headed.

As the life of the medieval and early modern world—with its multifarious estates and their assorted historically based privileges—gave way to the early modern world of absolutizing monarchs, the old privileges dissolved under the pressure of the new state system and its need for power and money, and the basic social divisions were reduced at least in theory to those of the monarchy, the ecclesiasticals, the nobility, and commoners or, for all practical purposes, to the social power of royals and nobility versus commoners.

In that constellation, an explicit rationale emerged for the legitimate exercise of state power. Only those of royal descent and the aristocracy had the necessary capacities for "virtue" (honor and self-sacrifice) that marked them as fit for exercising or carrying out state power. Commoners, including the wealthy bourgeois of the newly rich towns, were assumed to be too immersed in self-interest to be capable of such virtues. However, since the absolutizing monarchs needed wealth to pursue their ambitions, and since increasingly that wealth was to be found in the newer fortunes of the wealthy bourgeoisie, the carrot that the monarchs held out for the loyalty and cooperation of these newly wealthy people was that of ennobling them. They increasingly became known as the nobility of the robe (having earned their titles by rising within the legal system, often as judges and magistrates, or by amassing fortunes through clever investment, often in the slave trade), and they were viewed, at least initially, as suspect by the older nobility, who, imagining themselves to have secured entitlement to their aristocratic titles by the military heroics of their ancestors, thought of themselves as the nobility of the sword.

With the rise in prominence of the nobility of the robe, the more ancient idea that nature, as it were, designs functions and then creates the right people to fill those functions became even more discredited, since it was now becoming abundantly clear that the nobility of the robe got to where they did on the basis of recognition and power. In the world where the hierarchies in social power and status were assumed to be fixed by something like the natural order, there was a relatively stable set of orienting goods for each hierarchy. However, in a social world based purely on recognition and power, there could be no more orienting goods than those involved in maintaining one's status via recognition of that status from others. Each had to become recognized by somebody who had the status to recognize them, and someone could have that status only by in turn being recognized by someone themselves of high enough status. The logic led to the monarch as the "sovereign," as the individual who sets the rules by which

others must live and who is the ultimate source of all other recognition. In principle, the sovereign has the authority to recognize and requires no recognition
from others to have that authority. That is, of course, a conception always tottering on the edge of complete incoherence.

Where that is the case, what has been a "practice" with its associated goods
becomes instead a game, and in games, the point is to keep scores or tallies on
each other to see who, if anybody, is ahead in the game. Now to the extent that
one buys into the game as the price of being a concrete agent at all—of participating in social life as opposed to being merely caught in its net—the only orienting good will have to be that of securing recognition from others and bestowing
recognition only when that is a means of securing recognition for oneself. Since
life must be led forward, and some kind of orientation is needed, the only "goods"
that will take root will be those that are established by those with the power and
status to bestow recognition.

This is a recipe for alienation: To the extent that one buys into playing the game
(and there are a variety of psychological and social reasons why that would hard to
resist, including the absence of appealing alternatives), one is committed to goods
to which one is not really committed. To be committed to a good because it is recognized by powerful others to be a good is in effect to be noninstrumentally committed to something for instrumental reasons, which can work in some situations,
but in those situations where the agent is reflectively aware of this, its logic leads
in the direction of self-undermining doubt.[4]

The culmination of the ancien régime is to be found, so Hegel claimed, in the
main character of Denis Diderot's short piece, *Rameau's Nephew*. In the piece, a
narrator (perhaps Diderot himself, perhaps not) tells of his encounters with a
musician (the nephew of the famous composer Rameau) who quite self-consciously
has no deeper commitments than to bow to the commitments of those more powerful than him, that is, to bend his will to what the market demands of him, to
flatter those who need flattering, and to say whatever it takes to get ahead in this
world. The nephew in effect tells his audience that he will be whomever they need
him to be, and he does this spontaneously, without inhibition or apology. In the
last analysis, it is, after all, who he really is, which is to be just that kind of
character. Moreover, he seems satisfied with his results—he is, after all, very successful—and he certainly does not seem to be unhappy in any way (even though
perhaps some would quibble about whether he is "flourishing").[5] Nor is there
anything inconsistent in the nephew's attitude: "Do what it takes," even if doing
it involves doing different things at different times, and "do what it takes" without
in any way being an "immoral" individual.

The nephew presents us with the figure of somebody who is completely at one
with himself in being at odds with himself, that is, an alienated character who
fully accepts his alienation as a fact of his life and affirms it as the logical result
of a form of life of which he feels a part. He thus accepts the contingency of his
way of being at one with himself. He himself is comfortable with switching

personalities, but he knows others are not nearly so relaxed about doing so as he is. (He is, we might say, even tolerant of these other points of view.) If Hegel's point about Greek democracy was that "the main thing... is that the citizen's character be sculptural (*plastisch*) and of a piece,"[6] then the nephew cannot be the model citizen of any new kind of Greek democracy. The nephew is certainly not "of a piece," and, as for the dimensions of his character, he would no doubt himself say that he appears "flat" when he needs to be and more "sculptural" when that is what is required.

Hegel was not alone in his time in seeing the ancien régime as having effectively brought this kind of alienation to its highest point. It did not escape notice that the artificial life and courtly pomp of the ancien régime were rather oddly combined with the regime's self-conscious pretense that the nobility were really by nature or by God suited for the extraordinary privileges they enjoyed. Part of Hegel's own understanding about the dynamics of modern life was that it was the very emptiness of the ancien régime itself that brought in its wake the actuality of a new order based on final ends whose ultimate authority did not rest on their being given by nature or God but on being redeemable by reason itself. The modern world, that is, was the sublation of the Greek organic model of social life into a form of unity whose ends were set by what was required to make sense of individual lives within a rationally organized political life, not in terms of any metaphysically organic nature.

To be sure, Hegel continued to use the metaphor of the organic to describe what he saw as the structure of the new social order (and thus helped to fuel the ongoing controversy about the status of Hegel's own alleged "organicism").[7] However, the kind of "organic" unity that is possible in modern life is that of "the concept," not that of a natural-divine order in whose arrangement there are simply given ends and social offices ordained to actualize those ends. In saying that it is "the concept," Hegel means to indicate the way in which the ultimate justification for the use of other certain key concepts (such as "family," "civil society," "state," and "morality") makes reference to the role those concepts play in a form of life. Whereas in (Hegel's view of) the Greek model, it is the divine order of the world— a metaphysically "organic" conception—that sets our final ends, in the modern world, it is the complex of demands that come with what it is to be a rational agent that is the "whole" within which such ends are to be set. In political and social terms, an agent can be at one with himself only in terms that now make sense to him in such a pluralist and secular political world. The final ends of life, that is, cannot be taken as given but must "make sense" and not merely be elements of a given fate.[8]

It is this sense in which it is now "the concept" and not mere "nature" that sets our ends, and this sense is deeply historical, a result of who "we" have collectively come to be. Part of Hegel's view about the impossibility of "democracy" in the modern world had to do with his idea that any kind of democracy rests on the "organic" idea that the social organism establishes various functions for each person, and that to each function, it assigns a person suited for it. Such an meta-physically organic view is to be sublated by a more conceptually organic view—which in turn does not really merit the title "organic" at all—except for the way in which such a conceptual view is also a holistic view and in that sense alone is anal-ogous to an organism. In modern society and political life, the "right of particu-larity" has too much of an impact, and there is no good sense in which the "individual," now equipped with his newfound authority over his own conscience, has to think of himself as automatically fitting, or even being obligated to fit, into his "organically" preordained slot.

The character of Rameau's nephew seems to think that alienation is the only real alternative in such a world. He represents a case for why living like that may be the only way to be true to oneself as such a divided creature in the modern world. The nephew does not disguise his chameleon nature, nor does he lie to him-self about who he is. (His authenticity about who he is remains compatible with his sincerity about it.) Indeed, he seems to argue that in his own case, his psy-chology is no more disjointed than that of any other normal run-of-the-course person. Thus, that fact that he is purely a creature of what the market for music demands of him is neither at odds with human nature in general nor with his own proclivities. He is, after all, not pretending to be somebody he is not. He *is* what he does for his patrons. The nephew's claim is that, however shocking his own stance may be to the more tender sentiments of his interlocutor, it is nonetheless a true stance. He bends his musical talent to the patron's desires, and he makes no bones about it. If we require social orientation—a holding of each other to norms that as norms are prior to any of our particular holdings but are not there outside the institutionally anchored institutions of mutual recognition—then the nephew's reply to any of his critics is that this is exactly what he does and that the institu-tion to which he orients himself is the market. (In a more fastidious mood, he might add that he is also mildly committed to the rule of law taken as a system of constraints necessary for that market to function.)

To orient oneself through a world with no obvious signposts in it, one needs to be flexible. Mastering one genre of music is of no use if the patrons demand another. Thus, for the nephew, what might otherwise be seen as spineless flexi-bility is in fact a virtue, a disposition of character that enables him to succeed in the world in which he lives. In the market in which the nephew lives, what seems to be at work, after all, is not so much an orienting set of norms as a strategic system of social coordination, and flexibility is a virtue of agents in such markets. (Where the whims of patrons change, it is best to be able to move quickly to sat-isfy the whims of other patrons. Thus, it is best to learn lots of easily transferable musical "skills" at the outset.)

To the narrator of the story as the observer (who professes both a fascination and a deep unease with the nephew, at times seeing him as only an aberration, an odd character, and at times seeing him as perhaps in touch with a deeper truth about the world in which they both live), the nephew does not seem to be leading his own life but to be only drifting. The nephew himself, on the other hand, has no such trouble—at least overtly—with his outlook. For the nephew, "leading one's life" (or self-determination) is in fact nothing more than good administration of one's time: One ducks the obstacles coming one's way, and to the extent that one succeeds in ducking them, one successfully manages to achieve one's goal. It is to this end that the nephew prizes his skills of improvisation—what musician doesn't?—and he sheds one musical persona to take on another as the task demands. The nephew shows the limits of any kind of emphasis on personal authenticity as a measure of how true one's life is. If authenticity consists in having an undistorted relation to one's own nature, then the nephew perhaps comes closest to being an authentic individual. He knows exactly who he is, and he makes no bones about it to others. Of course, that does not address the question of whether his own nature is itself distorted, but that is another matter.

## 2: Civil Society and the Balance of Interests

Part of the strength of the modern world, so Hegel thought, was that the possibility of living the life of the nephew had been effectively incorporated into the kind of loosely structured, semipublic, semiprivate realm called "civil society." As so incorporated, it deflected the worries about having it populated by characters such as the nephew.

As Hegel understood the conditions of the ancient world, the family was more or less the unit of economic production, and the competition among families for power and prestige was held in check by some political body (the *polis* or the "state"). However, in the modern world, there is a social context that stands between such political arrangements and the family: "Civil society" is a social arrangement populated neither by the citizens of a *polis* nor by the "subjects" of a sovereign, but by the free "burghers" of modern European life. Likewise, in modern life the "family" becomes an arena of ethical interests of a different sort, where certain facts about human life—such as the difference between the sexes and the need for children to have the proper environment and protections—are sublated into a conception of an egalitarian relation between the sexes and the education to independence on the part of the children. (Unfortunately, Hegel's own version of what counts as an egalitarian conception of the relation between the sexes is so outlandish by contemporary standards that he makes it difficult to see how that counted as egalitarian. Nonetheless, it is crucial to his view that the family is an institution where the "universal" demands on modern agency are supposed to find their initial shaping and therefore cannot be an institution based on domination.)[9]

Civil society involves a competition among interests held together precariously by a commitment to civility in its interactions. Not all those interests can easily be balanced since, as a competitive arrangement, it has winners and losers, which typically see their interests in very different ways. To make "civil society" work, a kind of statelike governmental apparatus—the *Notstaat*, the "state based on need," a version of the classic liberal state—almost naturally arises and lays claim to the authority to preside over matters such as the construction and maintenance of public goods such as roads and bridges, the regulation of commerce, and provision of clean drinking water.

Moreover, in addition to this arrangement for setting regulations and enforcing them, civil society also requires a set of private associations that help to stabilize and make civil society inhabitable; for example, they safeguard the interests of their members, and they sustain the standards and ethics that are taken to be appropriate to the association. In thus learning how to inhabit his status in civil society, the burgher acquires a more determinate sense of what it means to be a good administrator, a good accountant, a good craftsman, or a good mechanic. The burgher also gets a sense of when it is permissible or even expected that one should favor, say, his own clients over others and when such favoritism is out of place. In thus acquiring those kind of skills necessary to move around successfully in civil society, the burgher actualizes in a more nearly complete way the general conception of what it is to be a moral agent and an ethically upright person as he learns to make more particularized judgments. He also acquires both the sense and the skills of what it means to lead a successful life (where success is measured in terms of actualizing a set of concepts that "make sense," in other words, are rational). In being an ethical burgher, he thus also becomes more of a fully realized moral subject.

Because civil society involves both a competition among interests and a continual balance to be struck among those interests, civil society has no measure within itself by which to strike a rational balance. The antinomies of civil society form the basis of much political philosophy—as it gets expressed in various theories of how to best strike the balance that the "state based on need" must do and to strike a balance that is consistent with protecting the abstract rights of individuals, their moral status, and the interests of civil society itself (taken as a whole).

Hegel's rather controversial thesis is that civil society, as a collection of interests that come together only in the most general sense that each has a stake in seeing civil society function well as a whole, is itself incapable of providing a principled way in which those interests do not devolve into mere clashes of power. Those members of civil society with more wealth and consequently more power will tend to skew the decisions taken by the "state based on need" for their own ends, and there is no standard within the practices of civil society other than something very abstract (such as "the common good") that can show that any particular balance should be struck. Moreover, civil society can remain in its precarious equilibrium (and therefore remain "civil") only if there is motivation on the part of the all the parties to see the balance struck as fundamentally fair.

## 3: Making the Sale and Getting at the Truth

As virtually every commentator since Hegel's own day has noted, Hegel thought that the market played a distinct and positive ethical role in modern life. Its importance lay not only in its increased productive capacities but also in its underwriting of the normative status of individuality itself. The stress on the market also provokes the obvious question: Should the balance to be struck among the various interests in civil society simply be the balance that emerges out of the anonymous working of market forces (the "invisible hand")?

Since the market functions efficiently only when each makes a choice for his own advantage without having to take into account any further informal commitments—markets ideally rely on formal commitments, namely, contracts—purely market-based activities of giving and asking for reasons do not seem to rely on any further set of commitments. For that reason, Hegel concluded that market life was, at least on its face, not itself ethical at all. It involves no substantive final ends other than the formal end of individual freedom of choice. It offered no orientation except for the demand, as it were, that people become more and more like the nephew and maintain a certain flexibility while accepting as an unavoidable social necessity the threat of a kind of directionlessness for one's life. While the market plays a crucial role within ethical life since the increase in wealth and innovation it spurs makes people's lives go better, at same time, it is a threat to the civility of civil society since, with its clear-eyed emphasis on strategic behavior, it marks the point at which anything like "ethical life" (in Hegel's sense) seems to be lost altogether.[10]

In particular, the great inequalities of income and wealth that accompany industrialization threaten to undermine the fragile bonds that hold civil society together at all. Hegel spends quite a bit of time lamenting the formation of what he calls, in the idiom of his day, "the rabble." The industrialization of society, with its replacement of men by machines, reduces some people to having no further stake in civil society's functioning well. Alienated from their work, reduced to poverty, lacking any good health care, and eventually "possessing neither capital nor skills," they fall into despair.[11] A member of the so-called rabble feels no obligation to civil society because he receives so little respect from it.

This lack of commitment, however, is not confined to the "rabble." It also extends to the rich, who, although they obviously do have a stake in civil society, nonetheless often believe that they can buy their way out of any particular responsibility: "The rich," Hegel says, "think everything is for sale."[12] Their own amour propre tends to motivate them to think that they have no responsibilities for the overall maintenance of civil society, even though their wealth derives from civil society, and given their power, they tend to see everything as a commodity they can buy or sell. There is, Hegel observes, "also a rich rabble."[13] Thus, the practical need to reduce inequality of income and wealth is obviously present, but the exact balance cannot be determined by an a priori formula. In other words, there can be no "metaphysical" or purely philosophical answer to the question of how much inequality is permissible.[14] What the just distribution of wealth involves includes how the concept is to be actualized, and that involves a consideration of how people's lives fare in that social order.[15]

Furthermore, life in the market, and therefore in civil society as a whole, revolves around a certain theatricality.[16] It presents us with a *Schauspiel*, a "spectacle" or "theater piece," in which what is on view is "extravagance and misery as well as of the physical and ethical corruption" of the civility of the society in which it is embedded.[17] Such a form of theatricality—where each burgher puts his own amour propre into play while at the same time learning to curb it to be successful in civil society—provides rich material for the nineteenth-century novel, but anything like an aesthetic justification for it is out of the question.[18] (Not surprisingly, perhaps, he reserves most of his comments on that kind of theatricality for his lectures on how this makes its appearance in the artworks of his day.)[19]

For the actors in the market to grasp the way in which they offer reasons to each other in their interactions within the market, they have to presume some prior set of norms that do not beg the question about whether and under what conditions these interactions are legitimate. (The answer to the question "Are market norms justified?" cannot be answered by appealing to the norms of the market to settle the question unless one just wants to evade the issue altogether. For that matter, even the most basic of market institutions, that of private property, itself requires a distinction of "mine" and "yours" that is already at work in markets and hence cannot be used to justify them without also begging the question.) Moreover, there has to be a kind of unintelligibility that attaches to purely market-based solutions.[20] One justifies one's actions in terms of what is to one's personal advantage, but for either the rich or the poor who happen to be exercising their right to sleep under bridges, the idea that personal failure is to be justified by its contribution to one's own advantage or that it is an enriching part of the story of the larger good must seem hard to comprehend.[21] Indeed, for Hegel, the very idea that the justifying final end of life would be that of continually increasing capital would seem so obviously false that it would not be worth going to the trouble of presenting an argument against it. What must justify the theatrical spectacle of civil society must be some larger ethical ends of which it is a key component.

The dynamic of civil society left to itself leads to a full state of alienation. It creates a "rabble" who have no stake in the life of the community and an extremely wealthy class (the "rich rabble") who think that everything can be bought. What would be lacking in a full state of alienation would be any sense of the truth of the social facts at issue or their intelligibility. For a whole society of Rameau's nephews, one would have to have agents who had as their first premise (and probably only basic premise) of practical reason only the final end of "Do what it takes to make the sale," together with whatever subsidiary principles were necessary for sustaining that set of interactions.

Now, there is nothing philosophically or transcendentally impossible about such a form of life. (There may be some kind of deep-seated facts about human psychology that would make it more difficult to achieve, but that is another issue.) In such a world, agency would take a much different shape than what Hegel thought it would have to take under modern conditions. "Drift" would be the de facto course of human life. "Management of risk," rather than something like "self-determination," would be the guiding image. The ability to shed one's past and move on without either regret or much difficulty would be a condition of success.[22]

There would be also various virtues associated with it. No doubt, sincerity as the uninhibited expression of one's thoughts would be counted (since therefore one would always know with whom one was dealing) and even constancy of commitment to beliefs, ideals, and the like would not be as highly praised but would still retain value as indicators of how much risk a person would be undertaking with another person.[23] In such a world, everybody becomes, as Hegel says, a "player." The whole is a game, and the point is to master the rules and not only win at the game but, as Hegel says, "to win within the constraints of the moment."[24] This, of course, requires a change in the agent's relation to time. Such an agent must be willing to cut off his relation with the past when a new game calls. He can have long-term strategic plans, but when the game changes, he must be ready to drop the old one and move on. In such a world, lack of consistency would not in particular be a vice in either personal or political life. In such a world, Rameau's nephew would finally be the rather ordinary figure he claimed to be in the dialogue.

Hegel thought that was the trajectory on which the ancien régime was headed, and he originally thought that the collapse of its authority right before and after the French Revolution had more or less cleared the way for a more complex and freer form of life based on certain more or less liberal ideals—including a shared commitment to a constitutionalist state with representative government—all of which were to be held in place as "moments" of a form of ethical life as oriented to certain key goods. As he began to work out his mature views in the context of the political repression of the 1820s, he began to see more and more an updated version of this kind of alienation making its appearance in the early stages of industrialization.

In fact, drift, emphasis on the short term, and cultivation of the skills necessary to "move on" look more and more like the world of globalized capitalism that was being born within Hegel's world, and, as it has taken shape, that world looks less and less like a Hegelian concord among various elements held in tension. It is no wonder that since Hegel's time, many people—from the young left-Hegelians of the 1830s and 1840s to more contemporary figures such as Theodor Adorno—have basically taken large chunks of Hegel's critique of the ancien régime and turned it against his own solution. What Hegel found lacking in the ancien régime, they found lacking in the social system that replaced it.

Some, such as Alasdair MacIntyre (at least at one point in his career), have largely taken on board his analysis of the movement of European history since the Greek world as having brought about a thinning out of ethical life and an establishment of "individualism" but denied that there is any reconciling *Sittlichkeit* that could be available for the moderns (thus, in effect, turning Hegel's criticisms of the ancien régime against the very modern world that Hegel defended). Where does that leave Hegel?

## B:  Power: The Limits of Morality in Politics

The other commitments that have to function as already at work for the market both to take hold and to be effective have to do with constitutionalism and the rule of law. (Hegel also calls this a matter of "patriotism," which he characterizes not as the willingness to indulge in heroic action but in the day-to-day life of a citizen who takes these commitments to heart; it consists in a commitment to the conceptually articulated constitution rather than to the "organism" in the Greek sense.)[25] Political life ("the state," in Hegel's parlance) sublates the other ways of living in society; that is, it circumscribes their authority, but it neither absorbs nor erases them.

The "state" is thus the social space in which the "burghers" of civil society become "citizens" and thus come closer to actualizing their freedom. To mark that distinction, Hegel in several places distinguishes the "burgher" (*Bürger*) of civil society (*bürgerliche Gesellschaft*) from the political citizen, for which he uses the French term, *Citoyen*.[26]

"Citizen," like "burgher," is a status that exists through a network of recognition. What distinguishes citizens from burghers is the subjective identification on the part of each individual with something like a common project of his or her cocitizens and a common commitment to the success of the project (which includes the idea that its citizens are to have successful lives). Thus, for there to be citizens at all, there must be those common commitments themselves, and to live in light of those commitments that are known to be shared is to live a "public life."[27]

To be a citizen is to be committed to living one's life under the rule of law in such a way that, first, the laws themselves are not supposed to represent the interests of only some members of civil society and, second, the citizens are to see those laws as constrained by the more substantive commitments of the citizenry at large (in particular, as constrained by the commitments to rights, morality, and so on and to the conditions under which successful lives can be led).[28]

Members of the Greek *polis* were such citizens. Likewise, modern agents have the right to be citizens and not merely "subjects" of a sovereign if they are to live in a way that is consistent with the overall purposes fulfilled by "abstract right" and "morality."

However, citizenship cannot be a matter merely of having "abstract rights" and being a "moral agent." It is a status belonging to a different context. To the extent that one is a "citizen," one does indeed seek to actualize the idea of living a "universal life," but not in the strictly moral sense. Burghers become citizens by virtue of both seeing themselves as involved in the common life and actually participating in the common life, which consists in subjecting the balance that civil society requires to a measure that is not that of the play of power and interest that accompanies the competition within civil society. For example, the need to prevent great extremes of inequality of income and wealth requires the political state to intervene, since some standard other than that of an "interest" itself must be decisive in determining how such a balance of interests is to be struck that is compatible with lives carried out in terms of rights and morality. Or if the language of interests is to be kept, there must be a political interest, not a moral interest, that is decisive for striking that balance. A moral interest lies in acting according to a principle that is valid for all rational agents. The political principle, on the other hand, has to do with the arrangements and coercive power of a particular group, namely, "this" state as different from other states. When a government is entitled to use coercive force to compel some people to do something that they otherwise would not do or do not want to do is a question with moral overtones, to be sure, but whose answer comes out of a different context.

For Hegel, the question of politics therefore comes down to the issue of how "this" group can form itself so that certain coercive measures can be taken by the state that make actual not only "abstract right" and "morality" but also things like equality between the sexes and the good functioning of "civil society," and, if it is to be consistent with those other statuses, to do so in a way that preserves what those other spheres are about while at the same time circumscribing the authority of those other spheres. The political state is to do this—to carry out the sublation of the other spheres—not, as it were, by subsuming and swallowing the other spheres but by providing a different context in which the oftentimes competing demands of rights, morality, family life, and commercial life play themselves out in terms of a rule of law that, once again, does not ignore these other spheres but whose principles nonetheless make different claims than do those other spheres. The laws of the state require a legitimation strategy about putting people under obligations they otherwise might not have, whereas morality requires an argument about what is ultimately obligatory (or permissible or forbidden).

Thus, political decisions have to be made about what is best for the state—whether these or those roads should be built, whether there needs to be a more or less aggressive intervention to prevent certain types of economic inequality from rising so high it threatens the continued vitality of the political unit, and so on—and those decisions must also be coercively enforced if the interests of the stronger are not simply to ride roughshod over the interests of the more vulnerable (as would happen if "civil society" and the "state based on need" were left to their own devices and were not sublated by a properly functioning political state). That some people's particular interests are set aside and that the state enforces that decision is itself not a moral claim, but neither is it independent of moral claims. It is a different type of claim.

The principles appropriate to the "state" are also not moral principles in that what is required of a citizen—that he or she take a special concern for his or her own political community, even at the expense sometimes of members of other communities—is not itself a universal moral demand. It is, in Hegel's own specialized vocabulary, an "ethical" demand. For example, although no moral agent can make an exception for himself vis-à-vis the demands of morality, the members of a family are more or less expected to take a special interest in their own kind; the burgher is more or less expected to look after his own idiosyncratic interests in his life in the semipublic, semiprivate world of civil society; and it takes nobody by surprise that the citizens of a state show special concern for the other citizens of just their state. Only when the state manages to harmonize those interests in such a way that it seems that only within such an arrangement can the bulk of the citizens live a successful life—achieve goals that are worth achieving—can the state be considered itself a success. (Needless to say, Hegel is skeptical about whether all attempts to reconstruct special obligations—say, to one's family—as merely being applications of some universal rule can be really successful. The special obligations of "ethical life" are the conditions for the actualization of universal moral claims, not the application of independent moral rules.)

Although the modern state cannot (on Hegel's terms) possibly be constructed as a direct democracy, it nonetheless must have elements of direct democracy within it, since the modern state is an institution whose actuality—whose effectiveness—must incorporate the demands of individuals with universal abstract rights and a universalist morality. That, in turn, means that each individual has the right to exercise his "conscience," or, to put it anachronistically, each individual has the right to determine what is his own good consistent with the right of others to do the same. This conception of each individual as possessing infinite worth—the historical, Kantian conclusion drawn from the Socratic "invention" of morality—means that individuals must be entrusted with the ability to lead their own lives, rather than having external authorities decide for them how they are to be led. However, in a large state, that kind of purely liberal demand for the right of individuals to settle on what counts as their own goods is, if pushed to its logical conclusion, simply unworkable, since virtually any governmental decision will interfere with somebody's right to do so. Thus, so Hegel thought, the place for such direct democracy had to be at the level of localities organized along the lines of the prerevolutionary "estates" (*Stände*), where self-governance was to take place. It was there that the "democratic principle" was to find its actualization.[29]

Hegel's own characterization of the state thus fairly well sidesteps the issue of whether he should be described as a "liberal" or a "republican," for although he believes that protecting rights and due process is obviously crucial (which sounds liberal) and although he believes that citizen participation is also central (which sounds republican), he also thinks that the crucial overall issue is how freedom is to be actualized. For the state to protect rights or see to it that citizen participation in public life is efficacious, the political state itself must also be a means of both creating and limiting power. This is, of course, only to be found in a constitutional state since a constitution sets out the laws and principles that, in having as an obvious goal the protection of rights of citizens, also creates a power that sustains or even produces the conditions under which civil society can grow more prosperous.

Since the state must be able to create power if it is to be actual, this also makes political considerations different from moral considerations. Morality is more about setting limits to power, but politics involves an entity—the government—coercing people into doing things they otherwise would not choose to do. The deployment of such state power therefore has to have some kind of legitimation behind it, and for that to be the case, it must be actually viewed by the populace as legitimate and not merely measure up to the standards of a theory.[30] Legitimation works only if it is recognized legitimacy, whereas moral norms may be in force even where there is either little recognition of them or little hope of their being actualized.

Politics is not therefore just about rights and obligations. If it were, then "abstract right" and "morality" would exhaust all there is to say about it. Politics is just as much about the use of power, the creation of power, and the restraints on power. Moreover, the deployment of power and the restraint of power are themselves conditional on the kind of ethos (as the habits, interests, and dispositions) of the citizenry at hand. Legitimation depends not on what people would on reflection and in perfect conditions rationally accept—even if one could work out all the elements of that counterfactual—but on what they can accept within the conditions of life in which they find themselves, and on how deep the commitment to rationality runs in their lives. Like "morality" and all the aspects of "ethical life," legitimation requires not only theoretical but also practical truth.

So Hegel's thesis goes, states based on constitutions that have the realization of freedom as their animating idea—or more specifically, where the ethos of appealing to reason instead of blind tradition or supernatural authority is really at work in the ethos of a people[31]—are the states that have more power and hence are more prosperous. Political freedom and the power it creates are essential both for prosperity and for the protection of rights.[32] A weak state can neither protect rights nor create or sustain the conditions under which wealth can be generated. In fact, the great strength of the modern state, Hegel stresses in several places, lies in its ability to accept great differences within itself, including those who question the power of the state itself and even reject key parts of it.[33] A weak state cannot do that.

## 1: Bureaucratic Democracy?

For a modern, bureaucratic state based on expertise (where officials supposedly rise through the ranks of government organization not on the basis of their noble titles, that is, family past, but on their learning), this gives rise to a new problem in modern states, namely, that of domination of the citizenry by the officials of the state and how the state may be organized so that it adequately deals with this problem. Hegel's own suggestions for how this is to be concretely carried out display, of course, many of the idiosyncrasies of his own time, but the general view of how a free people is to be actualized in the political circumstances of a state that organizes and creates power is at least partly democratic in spirit. There must be public reasoning about the ends of politics, and there must be an effective system of accountability that makes this space of public reasoning effective. Moreover, there is no a priori way of thinking this problem through to its conclusion. Rather, there are the abstract meanings of what it is to be a rights bearer, a moral agent, a member of a modern family, a child or young person facing the hurdles of education, a burgher, and a citizen, and there are all the ways those abstract meanings are concretely actualized within a people who have committed themselves to freedom and the ways the abstract meanings themselves are transformed by the concrete manner in which they are realized.

However, that brings in its wake a new problem of oppression of the citizenry by bureaucratic officials appointed by merit. Oppression of subjects of the sovereign by officials appointed by the sovereign is, of course, an old problem. Where the legitimacy of the state does not depend in any sense on the "democratic principle" of political organization, this poses only practical and not deeply conceptual problems. However, the newer and more deeply conceptual problem for modern states has to do with the rise of an administrative bureaucracy that rules in the name not of aristocratic or familial background but a claim to superior expertise, which itself rests on the scientific education of the officials in question. Decisions such as how best to deal with problems in the water supply or which steps are to be taken to encourage economic development need to be taken rationally in light of facts that are difficult to gather and equally difficult to assess, and that means ultimately that the state will have to decide on policies that will not be to the liking of at least some of its citizens and that these decisions will be made by officials on grounds that are difficult to state publicly (not because they are embarrassing but because they require a certain expertise even to understand). Moreover, the capacity of the bureaucratic officials to make policy and have it coercively enforced makes it seem that they at least have the possibility of imposing their "arbitrary wills" (*Willkür*) and of "oppressing citizens."[34] In an aristocratic state, this is not a particular problem, since the push toward publicly accessible standards is not as intense. In modern states, where each individual is taken to be of "infinite worth," it becomes much more problematic. In addition to the age-old problem of state officials using their office to promote their own interests, in the modern state, even with a relatively uncorrupt bureaucracy, the demands of reason push the bureaucracy toward a conception of the state as a "whole" that is abstract (in Hegel's usage of that term) and therefore oppressive.

This particular problem of legitimacy is a conceptual problem at the heart of the empirical, factual development of the modern state. For the state to have the power of being able to actualize rights and so forth, it must be able to make policy that is rational and effective, and this requires expertise at the levels of policy making and execution of policy. Nonetheless, the policies adopted by the officials must also be legitimate; that is, they must have an actuality, an effectiveness so that they do not in turn alienate the citizenry. In turn, this means that there arises a tendency in the modern state for the officials to rule in the name of reason alone, and whatever the rationality of their policies may be, such policies are thereby divorced from the public's comprehension of them. Partly for this reason, so Hegel says, the civil service is supposed to be the "universal estate" since their decisions are supposed to further the state's interest as a rational project.[35]

However, the reality is that the bureaucrats of the "universal estate" do, of course, have their own interests or represent particular interests, and they often to seek to put those interests into practice by phrasing their decisions in a learned jargon that, as Hegel likes to say, sounds to the public's ear necessarily more like "underworld jargon" or "thieves' slang" than it sounds like reasoned argument.[36] Where that is the case, what follows is, of course, the increasing detachment of the populace from such politics, and when that happens, the legitimacy of the state as resting on its being seen as rational by the citizenry begins to fade. "For some time now," Hegel says, "organization has always been directed from above....Yet it is extremely important that the large mass of the people (*das Massenhafte des Ganzen*) be organic, because only then do they become a power (*Macht*)....Legitimate power is to be found only when the particular spheres exist in an organic condition" (where the reference to the "organic" is to be understood as exhibiting a concretely rational structure—that of "the concept").[37] However, within that concept of an "organic" structure of political life, Hegel lacked any fully worked out conception of the "public" sphere as a distinct sphere on its own. Now, the conception of such a sphere is already there in his thought, but, to use his own terms, it is there only *an sich*, "in itself," in his conception of the "democratic principle" in political life and has yet to find its "actualization." It appears rather clearly in his commitment to public discourse in the assembly of estates as a "learning process" by which the wider public is helped to reason together about such political matters and in his conception of how the shaping of public opinion and the decisions about policies cannot be matters of simply interpreting or bringing to voice an already shaped opinion hitherto existent "out there," but in producing something new and more reasoned in the give-and-take of such debate.[38] The public proceedings of the assembly of estates are supposed to give a new shape to the face-to-face deliberations of the ancient *polis*.

In terms of its sources, Hegel's view of the state is his own sublation of Aristotle, Kant, and Rousseau (more as the author of the *Government of Poland* and not so much the *Social Contract*), all stirred together within Hegel's own social and historical conception of agency.[39] Once seen in that light, Hegel's rather stubborn antidemocratic stances look very much less antidemocratic and, as Jean-François Kervégan has argued, look more like various contemporary accounts of the functioning of modern bureaucratic representative democracies.[40] Especially in his lectures, Hegel stressed the need for democratic politics to bubble up in the various organizations of local life, even though the complexity of modern life—with its emphasis on individual liberty, the necessity for complex legal arrangements, and a vibrant, creative, and destructive (although rationally regulated) market economy—makes necessary a certain level of expertise at the top. On the other hand, there also has to be a protection from the tendency of political officials (at the level of both the political state and the "state based on need") to want to regulate absolutely everything in the interest of "wholeness." "Public life should be free," he noted, but the civil service bureaucrats, necessary as they are, will always be tempted to overregulate public life in the name of some abstraction and as an attempt to bring all the parts into an abstract unity. As an example, Hegel cites Fichte's proposal to require people to have their passports or identity papers with them at all times ready and available for police inspection. This would, he says, only result in the state becoming "truly a vessel of galley slaves, where each is always supposed to be exercising oversight over the other."[41]

This is part and parcel of Hegel's "historical" conception of political life. What is possible in political life is a function of the historical context. Without the kind of conceptual innovations that come at a later stage of development, some kinds of considerations cannot be on the table. However, once a genuine conceptual innovation has been instituted, it casts the discussions of the past in a new light, since, given the terms of the innovation, those discussions may now appear as irrational, whereas before the innovation, they might have appeared as, say, problematic (because of the tensions coming to light in them) but not as therefore at odds with the bounds of rationality itself. Such is the case with the modern political and democratic organization "from below" of its citizens. (It is, of course, always tempting to imagine ourselves going back in time, standing before, say, Henry VIII, and morally criticizing him for his mistakes, but that is because we bring our innovations with us, and we also bring the historical experience of what worked and did not work with us. That is exactly the kind of moralistic approach Hegel wishes to avoid.)[42]

## 2: The Nation-State?

Nonetheless, however close Hegel's conception of the state may be to modern conceptions of bureaucratic democracy, the orthodox Hegelian state as Hegel envisioned it still has its genuine political decisions being taken at the state level, where proper bureaucrats, with the proper degrees from the proper universities, where they were taught by the proper professors, do what is required of them by virtue of the rationality they are supposed to embody. Even though Hegel himself may have grumbled about the "top-down" governance he saw in the German states of his own time, in his own conception of the state, he still displayed a relatively strong mistrust about giving the "people" full political liberty in the sense of having the power to fill public offices. Only the well-trained expert, or at least the man of high standing, should be making the real political decisions. In this respect, Hegel was fully in keeping with his own time, which by and large strongly resisted extending the franchise to males without property and also by and large thought that extending it to women and those of non-European descent was simply out of the question.[43] Thus, whereas Hegel's conception of the state has room for republican conceptions of citizen participation and freedom from domination, together with liberal conceptions of protection of rights, he has little to no place at all for any form of a populist conception of citizen participation. He took his commitment to politics based on rationalism—the giving and asking for reasons, rather than any kind of summing up of de facto interests—to preclude such populism. Indeed, his position on the civil service as the "universal estate" is precisely meant to set sharp limits to any form of populism.[44]

However, this also put a certain nervous tension into elements within the core of Hegel's thought. Hegel distrusted nationalism, and he particularly distrusted the rising German nationalism of his own time. All the nationalist talk of *Deutschtum* (German-dom), he said, was at its heart just *Deutschdumm* (German-dumb).[45] Nonetheless, he also thought that the only possibility for such a constitutional state with representative government had to be in its being rooted in something like a nation-state. Only by being rooted in some concrete national ethos could the dispositions and habits of citizens and burghers make this kind of political and social order workable. However, if this type of appeal to something like ethos and mores was to be consistent with the conceptions of rights-bearing, moral individuals, it also had to be the case that these ethos and mores had to be modern, "the modern" had to be demonstratively superior to what had preceded it, and, so Hegel thought, ultimately non-European nations, such as India or China, also had to be ruled out as offering possible alternatives to European social life as it had recently taken shape. He also thought that by the early nineteenth century, the different nation-states of Europe were all at their basis now committed to the same overall modernist scheme of actualizing freedom, and thus the appeal to more particularistic items such as "national ethos" would not become the highly one-sided and partial assertion it might otherwise seem to be.[46]

The very nature of a "people" has to do with their common commitments, not from any ethnic essence—a "people" is, in Hegel's terms, "a unity in regard to customs, culture, etc., and this unity is existing substance" (i.e., a set of learned dispositions and habits)[47]—but a people is thus also constituted by its being a distinctive national type.[48] Hegel had no truck with those who thought there was a German racial essence that was best captured by something like the *Nibelungen* saga. The *Nibelungenlied* in particular, he thought, had been swept aside by history and Christianity as having any key importance for German identity.[49] The differences of ethos among, say, Britain, France, and the German states were thus at best contingent differences floating at the surface, not differences in the more ground-level commitments to basic rights, morality, civil society, and the like. Indeed, so Hegel falsely thought, after the post-Napoleonic settlement, since war between European states would have been so irrational, it had become simply out of the question.[50]

That Hegel clearly underestimated the destructive power of the nation-state does not need much argument. Hegel's mistake is even more peculiar in that he also recognized the way in which the founding principles of the modern nation-state, with its twin commitment to local democracy and rule by modern expertise at the level of the "state based on need" and the political state, were already in rather sharp tension with each other. On the one hand, the politically formed nation-state presents its members with specific obligations to a particular state. On the other hand, those members are also to think of themselves as moral agents whose end is universal, not specific. Hegel simply did not fully comprehend how the memory of the "warmth" of Greek life—or even when it was not the memory but the inchoate feeling about restoring the mythical reality of such face-to-face warmth—could be, when translated into the form of an ethnic nation-state, fully and totally catastrophic.

Now although Hegel's argument throughout was that an agent can actually (that is, effectively) be such a moral individual only within the context of a modern nation-state, he also recognized the pull of the opposite view, that of seeing oneself not as a "national" but as a "cosmopolitan." Although his infrequent mentions of cosmopolitanism are usually slightly dismissive, what he sees as the defect of cosmopolitanism is that it lacks a clear sense of how to actualize any such cosmopolitan scheme in contemporary circumstances. However, in Hegel's view, the lack of any such clear scheme for actualizing a world government in no way rules out a commitment to universal human rights: "*A human being counts as such because he is a human being*, not because he is a Jew, Catholic, Protestant, German, Italian, etc."[51] If nothing else, the commitment to full human rights was and remains in far greater tension with the nation-state than Hegel himself credited. That particular Hegelian sublation has not quite worked out in that context as it was supposed to do. However, Hegel's argument that both must be balanced pragmatically—as a balance between two requirements that lack a common metaphysical measure—retains its force despite Hegel's overly optimistic assessment of the possibility of the nation-state.

*Notes*

1. See, for example, Hegel, *Vorlesungen über die Philosophie der Geschichte*, 12, p. 458; Hegel, *The Philosophy of History*, p. 381: "Subjective spirit...its finitude begins to come out within this distinction, and, as the same time, contradiction and the appearance of alienation commences...and the deeper goes the truth to which spirit in itself relates itself...the more alienated it is in its own eyes within this present moment. However, it is only from out of this alienation that it attains its genuine reconciliation."

2. See Rahel Jaeggi, *Entfremdung: Zur Aktualität eines sozialphilosophischen Problems (Frankfurter Beiträge zur Soziologie und Sozialphilosophie*; Frankfurt am Main: Campus, 2005), p. 189.
3. Hegel's own view thus differs slightly, or so it seems, from the alternative view proposed by Rahel Jaeggi in her work (ibid.). For her, the issue about alienation has to do not with, as she puts it, the actualization of determinate values but the *way* in which they are actualized. See ibid., pp. 54, 184. For Hegel, although it partly has to do with the way in which they are actualized, it more definitely has to do with the status of the values themselves. For Hegel, the lack of an "appropriation as making-it-your-own" (in Jaeggi's use of the German *Anneignung*, which cannot be adequately translated simply as "appropriation") has to do with the very norm itself being appropriated, not just with the way it is appropriated. The norm is alienating if it requires, within the conditions of mutual recognition, an incompatibility of holding oneself and others to such a norm within the facts of the world.
4. Hegel, *Phänomenologie des Geistes*, p. 389 (¶525): "From the aspect of the return into the self, the *vanity* of all *things* is its *own vanity*, that is, it *is* itself vain. It is the self existing-for-itself, which does not merely know how to evaluate and how to chatter about everything but which also knows how to convey wittily the fixed essence of actuality as well as the fixed determinations posited by judgment, and it knows how to speak of them in their *contradictions*. This contradiction is their truth.—Considered in accordance with its form, it knows everything to be alienated from itself."
5. Bernard Arthur Owen Williams, *Truth & Truthfulness: An Essay in Genealogy* (Princeton, N.J.: Princeton University Press, 2002), xi, 328 pp., whose own reading of the dialogue, while otherwise so insightful, seriously misreads Hegel's own interpretation of the dialogue. He seems to have taken Lionel Trilling's account of Hegel's account as summing up Hegel's own views and critiqued that. See Lionel Trilling, *Sincerity and Authenticity* (Cambridge, Mass: Harvard University Press, 1972), 188 pp.
6. Hegel, *Vorlesungen über die Philosophie der Geschichte*, 12, p. 312; Hegel, *The Philosophy of History*, p. 255.
7. See the helpful discussion in Sally Sedgwick, "The State as Organism: The Metaphysical Basis of Hegel's Philosophy of Right," *Southern Journal of Philosophy*, 39 (suppl.) (2001), 171–88; she brings out the relation between Kant's conception of teleology as something that is both cause and effect of itself and Hegel's idea of the state as having an organic structure. Robert Pippin offers reasons that count against all so-called metaphysically organicist interpretations in *Hegel's Practical Philosophy: Rational Agency as Ethical Life* (Cambridge: Cambridge University Press, 2008).
8. The necessity of both the objective and subjective conditions of legitimacy was already stressed by Frederick Neuhouser, *Foundations of Hegel's Social Theory: Actualizing Freedom* (Cambridge, Mass.: Harvard University Press, 2000), xiii, 337 pp. See also Pippin, *Hegel's Practical Philosophy*.
9. Since Hegel's own views about women are by contemporary lights so preposterously sexist, the idea that he was seeking any kind of egalitarian conception of family life may very well sound like an equally preposterous interpretation. However, his writings and especially his handwritten marginalia to the *Philosophy of Right* make it clear that this is what he saw himself as doing. Thus, in the marginalia to ¶167 of the *Philosophy of Right*, Hegel muses: "The man according to his individuality—the wife to be placed as his equal and to be *equally respected*—not higher.... Equality, the sameness of rights and duties—the man [the husband] should not count for more than the woman [the wife]—not subordinate." Hegel, *Grundlinien der Philosophie des Rechts*.
10. Ibid., §181; Hegel, *Elements of the Philosophy of Right*, p. 219: "This relation of reflection accordingly represents in the first instance the loss of ethical life."
11. See Karl-Heinz Ilting, P. Wannenmann, and C. G. Homeyer, *G. W. F. Hegel, Die Philosophie des Rechts: Die Mitschriften Wannenmann (Heidelberg 1817/18) und Homeyer (Berlin 1818/19)* (Stuttgart: Klett-Cotta, 1983), 399 pp., §118, p. 138. Georg Wilhelm Friedrich Hegel, P. Wannenmann, and Ruhr-Universität Bochum. Hegel-Archiv., *Lectures on Natural Right and Political Science: The First Philosophy of Right: Heidelberg, 1817–1818, with*

168 HEGEL'S NATURALISM

*Additions from the Lectures of 1818–1819* (Berkeley: University of California Press, 1995), x, 356 pp., p. 210. The alienation from the work is discussed by Hegel when he speaks of the "deadening" (*Abstumpfung*) of the workers in a modernized industrial facility: "Factory workers become deadened and tied to their factory and dependent on it, since with this single aptitude they cannot earn a living anywhere else. The factory presents a sad picture of the deadening of human beings." See Hegel, Wannenmann, and Ruhr-Universität Bochum. Hegel-Archiv., *Lectures on Natural Right and Political Science*, pp. 176–77; Ilting, Wannenmann, and Homeyer, *G. W. F. Hegel*, §101, p. 118. The reference to "health care" comes when Hegel remarks: [Those in poverty] "are at a great disadvantage in religion and justice and also in medicine because it is only from the goodness of their hearts that physicians attend them, and the hospital authorities also take a great deal off their patients for their own profit." See Ilting, Wannenmann, and Homeyer, *G. W. F. Hegel*, §118, p. 138; Hegel, Wannenmann, and Ruhr-Universität Bochum. Hegel-Archiv., *Lectures on Natural Right and Political Science*, p. 210.

12. "The rich view everything as on its own buyable, because the rich person knows himself to be the power of the particularity of self-consciousness. Wealth can thus lead to the same mockery and shamelessness as that of the poverty stricken rabble." See Georg Wilhelm Friedrich Hegel and Dieter Henrich, *Philosophie des Rechts: Die Vorlesung von 1819/20 in einer Nachschrift* (Frankfurt a. M.: Suhrkamp, 1983), 388 pp., p. 196.

13. Georg Wilhelm Friedrich Hegel and Hans-Georg Hoppe, *Die Philosophie des Rechts: Vorlesung von 1821/22* (Suhrkamp Taschenbuch Wissenschaft; Frankfurt am Main: Suhrkamp, 2005), 236 pp., p. 222.

14. Hegel speaks against such inequality in many places. For example, "In republics an inordinate increase in wealth is dangerous, so legislators have sought to counteract it." See Ilting, Wannenmann, and Homeyer, *G. W. F. Hegel*, p. 122; Hegel, Wannenmann, and Ruhr-Universität Bochum. Hegel-Archiv., §104, p. 184.

15. It is natural to think that Hegel is somehow ahead of his time here in his critique of the growing alienation and impoverishment of the workers and his assaults on the arrogance of the rich. Maybe he was, but in his own mind he was simply repeating the same points raised by Aristotle in the *Politics*, 1295b. Aristotle and Richard McKeon, *The Basic Works of Aristotle*.

16. This has to do with what Rousseau called amour propre, which Kant redescribed as our *humanity*, that is, "the inclination *to acquire worth in the opinions of others*," an inclination that inevitably develops into a contest for social superiority, which in turn leads inevitably into "the unjustifiable craving to win [worth] for oneself over others." The possibly corrosive effects of such amour propre are countered, Kant thought, in what he called *personality*, the respect for the moral law, which, unlike Rousseau's *amour de soi*, cannot be given an explanation in terms of any natural desire. See Immanuel Kant et al., *Religion within the Limits of Reason Alone* (Harper Torchbooks. The Cloister Library; New York: Harper, 1960), pp. cxlvii–cliv, 22.

17. Hegel, *Grundlinien der Philosophie des Rechts*, §185; Hegel, *Elements of the Philosophy of Right*, pp. 222–23.

18. Hegel also notes how such a craving for luxury also provided the rich material for ancient Roman satire: "Roman satirists made lots of fun about this multiplication of needs, where sometimes a hundred people had to be put to work to satisfy a momentary need, all of which overlooked the fact that these hundred people also had their own needs." See Ilting, Wannenmann, and Homeyer, *G. W. F. Hegel*, §98, p. 115.

19. The importance of the "theatrical" in Hegel's works is one of the main themes in Christoph Menke, *Tragödie Im Sittlichen: Gerechtigkeit Und Freiheit Nach Hegel* (Frankfurt am Main: Suhrkamp, 1996). Menke thinks that the theme of theatricality provides Hegel with an entry into opposing two forms of freedom to each other (autonomy and self-actualization) that are reconciled in the "modern subject" by the concept of a "post-hierarchical sovereign subject." It is, however, unclear if Hegel thought that the modern subject was sovereign at all, or, rather, as he puts it at the end of the preface to the *Phenomenology*, "the share in the

total work of spirit which falls to the activity of any individual can only be very small." See Hegel, *Phänomenologie des Geistes*, p. 67 (¶72). Individuals are, as he puts it in his 1826 lectures, only "fragments."

20. On the unintelligibility of the market to "pure reason," see Hegel's remark in *Grundlinien der Philosophie des Rechts* (7), §184; *Elements of the Philosophy of Right*, p. 221: "Reality here is externality, the dissolution of the concept, the self-sufficiency of its liberated and existent moments."

21. With apologies to Anatole France, who claimed that the majesty of legal equality was that it forbade both rich and poor from sleeping under bridges rather than giving them the right to it.

22. The idea of the efficient manager as one of the "shapes of consciousness" of modern market life was, of course, made famous in philosophy by Alasdair MacIntyre, *After Virtue: A Study in Moral Theory* (Notre Dame, Ind.: University of Notre Dame Press, 1981), ix, 252 pp. MacIntyre calls such a shape a "character." Seen from a high-altitude vantage point, *After Virtue* in effect follows the same line of argument Hegel makes in his *Phenomenology* as he develops the book up to the alienation of the ancien régime. What MacIntyre calls a "character" in his book matches up in a rough-and-ready way to what Hegel calls a "shape of consciousness" in his own book. The idea of drift also features prominently in Richard Sennett, *The Culture of the New Capitalism* (Castle Lectures in Ethics, Politics, and Economics; New Haven, Conn.: Yale University Press, 2006), 214 pp.

23. Williams, *Truth & Truthfulness*, argues both for this as capturing the most interesting sense of sincerity and as being well illustrated by the nephew.

24. Hegel and Hoppe, *Die Philosophie des Rechts*, p. 230: "The individual, who is here bereft of a corporation, nowadays has to fend for himself, and he is a case of being a player [gambler].— he must seek at this moment to win, and he is led to make demands in the most egregious ways." *Spieler* here would be more normally translated as "gambler," but that would fail to bring out the kind of theatricality Hegel is trying to illuminate here. The *Korporation* of which he speaks is, of course, not the modern limited-liability corporation of capitalism but the older medieval and early modern guildlike group to which various artisans typically belonged.

25. The parallels with Jürgen Habermas's well-known appeal to "constitutional patriotism" are obvious and only barely need pointing out. Hegel himself notes, "Patriotism is frequently understood to mean only a willingness to perform extraordinary sacrifices and actions. But in essence it is that disposition which, in the normal conditions and circumstances of life, habitually knows that the community is the substantial basis and end. It is this same consciousness, tried and tested in all circumstances of ordinary life, which underlies the willingness to make extraordinary efforts. But just as human beings often prefer to be guided by magnanimity instead of by right, so also do they readily convince themselves that they possess this extraordinary patriotism in order to exempt themselves from the genuine disposition, or to excuse their lack of it." See Hegel, *Grundlinien der Philosophie des Rechts*, §268, p. 413; Hegel, *Elements of the Philosophy of Right*, p. 288. Jean-François Kervégan points out that, contra Hegel's reputation for warlike bellicosity, Hegel explicitly claims that bravery in battle is only a formal virtue and hence cannot be a motive for normal action. See his discussion of political virtue in Kervégan, *L'Effectif et le Rationnel*, pp. 343–59.

26. In civil society, Hegel says that "the basis here is an external civil (*bürgerliches*) relationship...here the burgher is a *bourgeois*.... The third stage is public life (*das öffentliche Leben*), where life in and for the universal is the aim...where the individual exists for universal life as a public person (*Person*), in other words is a *citoyen*." See Ilting, Wannenmann, and Homeyer, *G. W. F. Hegel*, pp. 93–94; Hegel, Wannenmann, and Ruhr-Universität Bochum. Hegel-Archiv., *Lectures on Natural Right and Political Science*, §72, pp. 137–38.

27. See also Neuhouser, *Foundations of Hegel's Social Theory*, and Pippin, *Hegel's Practical Philosophy*, for other statements within the same family as this view.

28. "And no interests of the one class (*Stand*) may be exalted at the expense of those of another class (*Stand*)." See Ilting, Wannenmann, and Homeyer, *G. W. F. Hegel*, p. 141; Hegel,

Wannenmann, and Ruhr-Universität Bochum. Hegel-Archiv., *Lectures on Natural Right and Political Science*, §120, p. 216.

29. "This is the point of view of right, that individuals have the right to administer their resources, while the ethical aspect is that, in their corporation, citizens find a state in the government of which they are the co-rulers, and in which they carry their particularity over into the universal. Nowadays governments have relieved the citizens of all these cares for a universal. But this is the democratic principle, that the individual should share in the government of local communities, corporations, and guilds, which have within themselves the form of the universal." See Ilting, Wannenmann, and Homeyer, *G. W. F. Hegel*, p. 168; Hegel, Wannenmann, and Ruhr-Universität Bochum. Hegel-Archiv., *Lectures on Natural Right and Political Science*, §141, p. 261. Hegel also notes: "And the fact that the particular spheres are necessarily self-governed constitutes the democratic principle in a monarchy." In Ilting, Wannenmann, and Homeyer, *G. W. F. Hegel*, p. 168; Hegel, Wannenmann, and Ruhr-Universität Bochum. Hegel-Archiv., *Lectures on Natural Right and Political Science*, p. 260.

30. "The principle of the modern world requires that whatever is to be recognized by everyone must be seen by everyone as entitled to such recognition. But in addition, each individual wishes to be consulted and to be given a hearing." See Hegel, *Grundlinien der Philosophie des Rechts*, §317 *Zusatz*; Hegel, *Elements of the Philosophy of Right*, p. 355.

31. Thus, Hegel notes: "Freedom must *be*, not in the sense of contingency but in that of necessity. Its actual being consists in its inner organization. A people is rational only to the extent that its constitution is rational." See Ilting, Wannenmann, and Homeyer, *G. W. F. Hegel*, p. 140; Hegel, Wannenmann, and Ruhr-Universität Bochum. Hegel-Archiv., *Lectures on Natural Right and Political Science*, p. 227.

32. Hegel thus distinguishes between "civil" and "political freedom": "Civil freedom in regard to the administration of justice and political freedom are necessary moments.... Political freedom is likewise very important, and where it is lacking, where it is suppressed, the state declines." See Ilting, Wannenmann, and Homeyer, *G. W. F. Hegel*, p. 140; Hegel, Wannenmann, and Ruhr-Universität Bochum. Hegel-Archiv., *Lectures on Natural Right and Political Science*, §120, p. 214.

33. In §270; Hegel, *Grundlinien der Philosophie des Rechts*; Hegel, *Elements of the Philosophy of Right*, p. 295, he says: "Of Quakers, Anabaptists, etc., it may be said that they are active members only of civil society and that, as private persons, they have purely private relations with other people.... Only if the state is strong in other respects can it overlook and tolerate such anomalies, relying above all on the power of custom and the inner rationality of its institutions to reduce and overcome the discrepancy if the state does not strictly enforce its rights in this respect"; and §260: "The principle of modern states has enormous strength and depth because it allows the principle of subjectivity to attain fulfillment in the *self-sufficient extremes* of personal particularity, while at the same time *bringing it back to substantial unity* and so preserving this unity in the principle of subjectivity itself." Hegel, *Grundlinien der Philosophie des Rechts*, p. 407; Hegel, *Elements of the Philosophy of Right*, p. 282.

34. Hegel notes that "one of the greatest ills that can befall states, namely that the class of officials...may become remote and alien, and, by its skill and education and use of official authority, may provide a channel for arbitrary will (*Willkür*) and the oppression of citizens." See Ilting, Wannenmann, and Homeyer, *G. W. F. Hegel*, p. 172; Hegel, Wannenmann, and Ruhr-Universität Bochum. Hegel-Archiv., *Lectures on Natural Right and Political Science*, §145, p. 267.

35. Hegel, *Grundlinien der Philosophie des Rechts*, §205; Hegel, *Elements of the Philosophy of Right*, p. 237. "The universal estate has the universal interests of society as its business. It must therefore be exempted from work for the direct satisfaction of its needs, either by having private resources, or be receiving an indemnity from the state which calls upon its services, so that the private interest is satisfied through working for the universal."

36. "Die Bürger sieht schon ihre Sprache für ein Rotwelsch an, wie eine Gaunersprache." See Ilting, Wannenmann, and Homeyer, *G. W. F. Hegel*, p. 173; Hegel, Wannenmann, and

Ruhr-Universität Bochum. Hegel-Archiv., *Lectures on Natural Right and Political Science*, §145, p. 269.

37. "For some time now, organization has always been directed from above...yet it is extremely important that it [this act of organizing] become organic, for only then do they constitute a power or force....Legitimate power is to be found only in the organic conditions of particular spheres." See Hegel, *Grundlinien der Philosophie des Rechts*, §290; Hegel, *Elements of the Philosophy of Right*, p. 331.

38. Hegel, *Grundlinien der Philosophie des Rechts*, §315 *Zusatz*; Hegel, *Elements of the Philosophy of Right*, p. 352: "The public nature of the Estates-assembly is a great spectacle of outstanding educational value to the citizens, and it is from this above all that the people can learn the true nature of their interests. As a rule, it is accepted that everyone already knows what is good for the state, and that the assembly of the Estates merely discusses this knowledge. But in fact, precisely the opposite is the case, for it is only in such assemblies that those virtues, abilities, and skills are developed which must serve as models....Nevertheless, such publicity is the most important means of education as far as the interests of the state in general are concerned. In a people where this publicity exists, there is a much more lively attitude towards the state than in one where the Estates have no assembly or where such assemblies are not held in public."

39. Hegel's discussions of the issue of the democratic elements in a large state seem quite obviously indebted to Rousseau's own discussion of it and his idea of a second-best alternative in the notion of representative government bound together with a lively local democratic practice in his work on *The Government of Poland*. Hegel does not, as far as I can tell, mention this work by Rousseau, but given his strong admiration of Rousseau and the similarities, it is difficult to avoid the conclusion that this is one of his major resources for his argument.

40. In *L'Effectif et le Rationnel*, his rightfully lauded study of the *Philosophy of Right*, Jean-François Kervégan argues that Hegel's version of the bureaucratic state actually has more in common with the kinds of large-scale bureaucratic democracies than Hegel has been given credit for.

41. Ilting, Wannenmann, and Homeyer, *G. W. F. Hegel*, p. 139; Hegel, Wannenmann, and Ruhr-Universität Bochum. Hegel-Archiv., *Lectures on Natural Right and Political Science*, §119, p. 212.

42. As one of many examples of Hegel's distaste for such moralism, there is his oft-cited remark, "What schoolmaster has not demonstrated of Alexander the Great or Julius Caesar that they were impelled by such passions and were therefore immoral characters?—from which it at once follows that the schoolmaster himself is a more admirable man than they were, because he does not have such passions (the proof being that he does not conquer Asia or vanquish Darius and Porus, but simply lives and lets live)." See Hegel, *Vorlesungen über die Philosophie der Weltgeschichte: Berlin 1822/1823*, pp. 102–3; Hegel, *Lectures on the Philosophy of World History: Introduction, Reason in History*, p. 87; Hegel, *Vorlesungen über die Philosophie der Geschichte*, p. 48; Hegel, *The Philosophy of History*, p. 32.

43. Kervégan notes that Hegel's own arguments about democracy do not deal with the idea of universal suffrage (which, as Kervégan notes, was rejected by almost all the liberal bourgeoisie of the first part of the nineteenth century) but only the idea of each individual's political participation being exhausted by his casting his one, single vote. This level of participation is too small to be effective, so Hegel thought. The political order cannot be separated from the social order even though both can be distinguished, and the "political identity, guaranteed by the institutions of the state, prevents the always possible degradation of social competition into civil war." See Kervégan, *L'Effectif et le Rationnel*, p. 301.

44. This is a distinction drawn by Henry S. Richardson, *Democratic Autonomy: Public Reasoning about the Ends of Policy* (Oxford Political Theory; New York: Oxford University Press, 2002), xii, 316 pp., although not with respect to Hegel.

45. Georg Wilhelm Friedrich Hegel, Johannes Hoffmeister, and Friedhelm Nicolin, *Briefe von und an Hegel* (Philosophische Bibliothek; Hamburg: F. Meiner, 1969), 4 v. in 5., vol. 2, #241;

Georg Wilhelm Friedrich Hegel, Clark Butler, and Christiane Seiler, *Hegel, the Letters* (Bloomington: Indiana University Press, 1984), xiv, 740 pp., p. 312.

46. "The European nations form a family with respect to the universal principle of their legislation, customs, and culture, so that their conduct in accordance with its form of international law is modified accordingly in a situation which is otherwise dominated by the mutual infliction of evils." See Hegel, *Grundlinien der Philosophie des Rechts*, §339; Hegel, *Elements of the Philosophy of Right*, p. 371.

47. Ilting, Wannenmann, and Homeyer, *G. W. F. Hegel*, p. 148; Hegel, Wannenmann, and Ruhr-Universität Bochum. Hegel-Archiv., *Lectures on Natural Right and Political Science*, p. 227.

48. Hegel distinguishes between a "people" (a *Volk*) as held together by common commitments, and a "nation" (in his German, a "*Nation*") as having a very specific ethos (a kind of "this is just the way we do things"): "A people is a single entity, and it is only through determination and particularity that individuality has existence and actuality. Each people accordingly has its determinate anthropological principle which is developed in its history and in accordance with its form which it is a *nation*." See Ilting, Wannenmann, and Homeyer, *G. W. F. Hegel*, p. 190; Hegel, Wannenmann, and Ruhr-Universität Bochum. Hegel-Archiv., *Lectures on Natural Right and Political Science*, §159, p. 297.

49. "The story of Christ, Jerusalem, Bethlehem, Roman law, even the Trojan war have far more present reality for us than the affairs of the Nibelungs which for our national consciousness are simply a past history, swept clean away with a broom. To propose to make things of that sort into something national for us or even into the Book of the German people has been the most trivial and shallow notion." See Georg Wilhelm Friedrich Hegel, *Vorlesungen über die Ästhetik III*, ed. Eva Moldenhauer and Karl Markus Michel, 20 vols. (Theorie-Werkausgabe 15; Frankfurt a. M.: Suhrkamp, 1969), p. 347; Hegel, *Aesthetics: Lectures on Fine Art*, p. 1057.

50. Although Hegel realized that war was not legally ruled out among European nations (because there was no higher power to enforce such a view), it was, he obviously mistakenly thought, de facto ruled out: "For in Europe nowadays each nation is bounded by another and may not of itself begin a war against another European nation; if we now want to look beyond Europe, we can only turn our eyes to America." See Hegel, *Vorlesungen über die Ästhetik III*, p. 353; Hegel, *Aesthetics: Lectures on Fine Art*, p. 1062.

51. The full quote: "*A human being counts as such because he is a human being*, not because he is a Jew, Catholic, Protestant, German, Italian, etc. This consciousness, which is the aim of *thought*, is of infinite importance, and it is inadequate only if it adopts a fixed position—for example, as *cosmopolitanism*—in opposition to the concrete life of the state." See Hegel, *Grundlinien der Philosophie des Rechts*, §209; Hegel, *Elements of the Philosophy of Right*, p. 240.

# 7

# Conclusion

*Hegel as a Post-Hegelian*

## A: Self-Comprehension

Central to Hegel's overall set of claims is something like this: If for a modern agent to understand himself, he must take on the commitment that his final end (his basic, ground-level understanding of what it means to be human) is that of being at one with himself in terms of freedom (and not, for example, as mere submission to an authoritative tradition), then the fragmentation and pluralization of goods in modern life can be rethought, and there emerges a kind of reconciliation to our own fragmentation that would otherwise not be possible. Unlike happiness, this final end of freedom can be sufficiently harmonized with others also holding this final end. Whereas it might actually be the case that an Aristotelian agent in a classical *polis* would actually need there to be slaves to do the dirty work that frees up the philosopher for contemplative tasks, there is no good reason, a priori or otherwise, to think of self-comprehension in the same way. It is false that one understands humanity better only when other humans understand themselves worse.[1] Self-comprehension as equally free does not require the oppression of others.

Despite the impossibility of establishing anything like Greek democracy, the concrete possibility nonetheless remains in modern social life for a kind of complex cooperative activity in which each can be a law unto himself in that each can shape his life in terms of goods that are to a great extent idiosyncratic to him.[2] When one does so, one is at one with oneself in a free manner, which, to use Hegel's paraphrase of Aristotle's conception of the final end of life, is "the energy of the (complete) life willed for its own sake."[3] This role of "ethical life" is to provide those kinds of orientations that actualize such a sense of being at one with oneself by standing in the right relation to others.[4]

Nonetheless, the final end of being at one with oneself cannot be achieved, or be achieved fully or in the right degree, in post-Greek political life. The political and social world of modern European life is, like its predecessors, all too finite—

too much bounded on all sides by contingency—for there to be within it a full way
of being at one with oneself. Indeed, in the practical world in general, there simply
is no way for self-conscious life, except in rare moments, to be fully at one with
itself in a true way. Where there is no possibility of seeing the world as a whole as
an organic unity, there is no possibility of overcoming that fragmentation.

What is the shape of the life that is willed for the sake of being at one with oneself with the self-consciousness that also comes with the conviction that this is
not fully realizable in the life of the practical "every day"? Hegel's answer comes in
a description of such a life within a modern context (in his comments on Dutch
painting):

> Man always lives in the immediate present; what he does at every
> moment is something particular, and the right thing is simply to fulfill
> every task, no matter how trivial, with heart and soul. In that event the
> man is at one with such an individual matter for which alone he seems to
> exist, because he has put his whole self and all his energy into it. This
> growing-together [between the man and his work] produces that har-
> mony between the subject and the particular character of his activity in
> his nearest circumstances which is also an intimacy (*Innigkeit*) and which
> is the attractiveness of the self-sufficiency of a total, rounded, and per-
> fected existence on its own.[5]

The truly free person will be at one with himself or herself, not in the sense that
truly free persons get everything they desire (or even get everything they consider desirable) but in the sense that they can be confident that whatever life's ups
and downs may be, their own choices are made in light of a final end that is
self-sufficient, rationally intelligible, and therefore "infinite." Moreover, truly free
persons are said to be fully "in" their actions, in this case "with heart and soul," in
which they and their activities begin to knit themselves into a whole. However,
since each individual is in Hegel's own description now a fragment, his or her life
is thus also composed of fragments.[6] Is a free person also a fragmented one?

## 1: Hegelian Amphibians

On Hegel's view, which only really comes to full display in his Berlin lectures in the
1820s, one of the deeper pathologies of modern European life is its widespread
failure to come to grips with these tensions inherent in that form of life and that,
rather than seeking a sublation of those tensions within a more comprehensive
vision of self-interpreting agency and in the limited although necessary aspirations of political and social life, a large element within it instead longs for some
state of resolved tension, a new golden age or a utopia yet to come, which, instead
of sublating these tensions, seeks to overcome them or transcend them. The way
this demand for reconciliation and this feature of life feed on each other is itself

the basis of the perpetual temptation to push toward the disaster that lies in any attempt to fashion a politics that would make us completely whole again.[7]

As Hegel makes clear, in his view, in any political situation, including the modern arrangement of rights, civic associations, and constitutional government, the demand for such wholeness is ruled out more or less conceptually:

> The content of this freedom and satisfaction remains *restricted*, and thus this freedom and self-fulfillment retain too an aspect of *finitude*. But where there is finitude, opposition and contradiction always break out again afresh, and satisfaction does not get beyond being relative. . . . It is only the rational freedom of the *will* which is explicit here; it is only in the *state*—and once again only this *individual* state—and therefore again in a *particular* sphere of existence and the isolated reality of this sphere, that freedom is actual. Thus man feels too that the rights and obligations in these regions and their mundane and, once more, *finite* mode of existence are insufficient.[8]

Since all states are, in Hegel's terms, finite, there can be no regime that can make people whole—a conceptual impossibility that does not, of course, rule out the continual reanimation of a desire to have such a regime. This also implies that the kinds of conceptual dilemmas that are at the heart of the modern state—those having to with, for example, rights themselves, morality, the relation between rights and morality, and also conflicting demands of political affiliation and moral universality—cannot themselves be given a final metaphysical or, in the broadest sense, philosophical solution. The solution to the tensions brought on by the dilemmas must itself be pragmatic, a way of balancing, as it were, incommensurables against each other with an eye on the rationality of the whole in which they make their appearance. In Hegel's slightly misleading terminology, those balances must be struck by "the understanding," whereas the grasp of those spheres as a whole is to be worked out by "reason." In this regard, Hegel, the alleged philosopher of totality, is in this context actually more of a philosophical therapist trying to inoculate us against the temptations toward wholeness in a sphere (the finite) where it cannot be found.

However, as Hegel began to rethink his position in the 1820s, he began to worry whether the kind of individuality that was the consequence of the modern world could actually itself be at home in the world that shaped it and whether it could thus find itself at one with itself in that world. Already in 1820, he noted in the preface to the *Philosophy of Right* that the modern world was characterized by the kind of stubbornness (*Eigensinn*), an "inflexibility" that he had earlier used to characterize the consciousness of the servant (the *Knecht*) in his 1807 *Phenomenology*. However, in that same 1820 comment, he was what might seem surprisingly positive in his characterization of such a state of being "self-willed":

It is a great inflexibility (*Eigensinn*), the kind of inflexibility which does honor to human beings, that they are unwilling to acknowledge in their attitudes anything which has not been justified by thought—and this inflexibility is the characteristic property of the modern age, as well as being the distinctive principle of Protestantism.[9]

Normally, for Hegel, the idea of being so inflexible about one's ends—*eigensinnig*—would be viewed as a kind of defect, a self-willed refusal to be genuinely free.[10] However, the "right of particularity" meant that modern subjects, in refusing to budge from their conviction that their own *Innerlichkeit*, their subjective lives (or, in short, the whole realm of "the private" and of personal feeling), had come to possess a genuine authority in moral matters. Their self-willed resistance to all assaults on that authority was therefore to be applauded. The newly expanded authority for the private lives of such individuals was part of the idea that "the actual is the rational." Modern individuals were educated, as it were, to hold fast to the set of dispositions and habits that came in tandem with the new world of nuclear families rather than clans, of economic production now fully severed in principle from the economy of the household, and of the practical unavoidability of constitutionally ordered political arrangements to cope with this.

The social world in which modern agents orient themselves is thus inherently fraught with the tensions that these conceptual dilemmas bring in their wake. Although one can strike better or worse balances among those tensions, one cannot get beyond them. To provide a metaphor for the kind of oppositions that are present in such a form of life, Hegel noted that such a form of life requires agents to be "amphibians" who must live in two worlds—described by Hegel variously as those of the cold command of duty versus the warmth of the heart, of the "dead inherently empty concept, and fully concrete liveliness," of inner freedom versus outer necessity, and so forth.[11] This opposition is, moreover, not something "invented by witty reflection or the point of view of some philosophical school," but emerges as integral to the experience that agents have with their world. Nonetheless, for modern agents, this kind of tension between being both a "subject" and an "object" has been sharpened.

The life of such modern "amphibians" thus is that of living with the contradictions in the commitments to the unconditioned that are constitutive of agency without succumbing to the obvious temptation to seek a wholeness in practical life—to find a practical truth that somehow resolved the key antinomies of modern life—through some kind of politics or social pressure. What wholeness is to be found simply cannot be found in the state but only in something else—art, religion, and philosophy. To put it into full Hegelian jargon: The whole is to be found in the "Idea," and the political is always only a partial, one-sided, never fully complete actualization of the "Idea." There are normative lines to be drawn about, say, universalist morality and political affiliation, and amphibians can live on both sides of the line.

Such amphibians thus are pushed to rely fully on reason while still carving out an area of freedom that encompassed all the points along the way where reason runs out. The idiosyncrasies of character and taste, the cultivation of particular talents, and the odd obsessions and tics of personality now had a right to their own expression. To act in terms of a law of one's own meant in almost every case not only to act in terms of universal principles but also to be socially licensed to protect and attend to one's own quirks as a mark of one's freedom.

Agents are not in all the aspects of their lives fully rational agents. The "strength and power" of the modern state is that it recognizes the rule of reason, makes it its basic principle, but carves out a licensed area for individuals to be the quirky individuals they are. So Hegel thought only a state with modern families, the spectacle of civil society, and the democratic principle at work in the lives of the citizens could sustain the kind of "second nature" needed to make such a form of life work, make it *wirklich*, actual. In such a setting, individual agents are socially licensed to set their own terms, and within limited ways, each can be a "law unto themselves," that is, possess a license to act in terms of their own individual natures.

To be sure, in the modern setting, this brought new tensions with it. The Greeks had the heroic example before them, and their organic view of the world licensed them to understand it as beautiful, as the spontaneous harmony among different elements. The modern world has no such beauty. The "inner" life defies full aesthetic treatment, and the necessity for bureaucracy and the rule of law defies a full aesthetic presentation of its rational virtues. Even the rather theatrical spectacle of civil society seemed, as pieces of theater often do, to follow a script. Hegel ironically notes that Goethe's novel *Wilhelm Meister* had already more or less laid this out in full view and showed how little this kind of script lent itself to genuinely deep aesthetic treatment, since such modern stories of adventure typically recapitulate in a prosaic, banal fashion earlier tales of knights set out on an adventure. They involve a young person who sows wild oats, gets involved in all kinds of escapades, but then gets a partner, settles down, possibly has a family, and falls into the typical worries of the bourgeois household, and the protagonist "becomes as good a Philistine as the others."[12] This is the prosaic world of the rule of law, bureaucracy, and regulated markets, and the worry about civil society is that tales such as *Wilhelm Meister* only recapitulate such banalities because there is nothing else in it to recapitulate. What such works succeed in doing is, rather than representing our "highest interests" in a more heroic fashion (as the Greeks had done), representing our "highest interests" as lying in an identification with each other, something along the lines of "Oh, Wilhelm Meister is just like me."

Nonetheless, this prosaic world also in principle institutes a way in which individuals can be fully "in" their actions within a social space that licenses agents to give their own idiosyncratic lives such authority. Such a social space provides the normative scope for the way in which a kind of intimacy (*Innigkeit*) with one's otherwise unintelligible actions can be an expression of freedom, not merely of inflexibility or revolt. It provides the democratic background of political life that had its analogue in the way fully individual idiosyncrasy had its run in ancient Greece. If successful, it would mark yet another way in which the Greek experience was being retrieved from its Christian overlay and sublated into a new form of life. Its "prosaic" banality was a problem, but the freedom it created was both fragile and noble in its own way.

In 1820, the set of tensions that accompanied such a way of life, along with the inflexibility that accompanied it, all seemed perfectly manageable, no more than a side effect of the brave new world of reflective individuals. By the late 1820s, the intensity and significance of this inwardness (*Innerlichkeit*) and the equal importance of the rational and administered public world were starting to push in directions that not merely stood in tension with each other but, for the people living in that milieu, felt completely at odds with each other. Could "amphibians" continue to live and succeed in such a world?

Even though the "right of particularity" had been acknowledged in the emerging individualist way of life, the sheer depth of the demand for its satisfaction led in several directions that threatened to undermine the legitimacy of modern life itself. For example, some of the early Romantics (such as Friedrich Schlegel) developed a conception of ironic detachment, that is, a form of "inner" individual wholeness as cut off from the world in which it lived. However, in all its forms, such ironic detachment thins out the self until there is virtually nothing left for it to inhabit.

First, there might be a kind of ironic detachment in conceiving of the self as simply a status, an officeholder of sorts who is responsible only for the commitments pertaining to the office he happens to hold at the moment (and who can in principle hold many, even conflicting offices). Besides reducing the self to a logical point in social space with no filling to it, such a conception also threatened to fashion itself into a form of abbreviated agency that would be the bearer of a kind of empty conformity that itself would threaten to overwhelm bourgeois life, since there can be nothing to it except the offices it fills that are recognized by others as its filling them. It would repeat the failures of the ancien régime without the latter's aristocratic underpinnings.

Second, such a self-conception would thin itself out into the self-conception of an agent who now thinks of himself as having a depth simply too profound to be expressed—who thus becomes a beautiful soul who does nothing simply because there is nothing he can do. Such a beautiful soul can endeavor to make himself the man behind the mask, the "free spirit," that is, the ironist who cannot be pinned down simply because he made it so that there is nothing there to pin down. (To this list, we could add yet another possibility, itself also Romantic, namely, to dream of a life of being fully inhabited with an ideal without much accompanying self-consciousness at all, as Dostoyevsky was to do in *The Idiot*, that is, the idea of an adult with adult possibilities who is in other important respects like a child.)[13]

Third, one might simply acknowledge the full absurdity of modern life (or so Hegel thought the writer Jean-Paul in effect did).[14] If it is only "the individual" who has any significance in a prosaic world of bourgeois families and commerce, if that world is indeed rational, and if in that rational, public world, there is no place for such "an individual," then the whole—the modern world and the individualism that is its condition—is therefore necessarily absurd. This self cannot orient itself at all, but it can at least laugh at itself, although what makes its wit funny is the seriousness with which it has to take itself. It holds itself out as worthy of infinite respect but admits that the world is such as to make such seriousness laughable. It aims for a kind of aristocracy of the spirit that it knows is most likely psychologically unsustainable (except for itself). Such a self-anointed aristocracy presumes that there is a larger purpose in the universe for which nature or God fashioned it to serve but which at the same time it knows (or at least fears) does not exist. Its laughter presupposes that only this aristocracy can really be in on the joke.

In 1828, Hegel outlined what he thought was another alternative, at least for art:

> But if this satisfaction in externality or in the subjective portrayal is intensified, according to the principle of romantic art, into the heart's deeper immersion in the object, and if, on the other hand, what matters to humor is the object and its embodiment within its subjective reflex, then we acquire thereby a growing intimacy with the object, a sort of *objective* humor. Yet such an intimacy can only be partial and can perhaps be expressed only within the compass of a song or only as part of a greater whole.[15]

Hegel's term "objective humor" is almost certainly the wrong term to use. (It makes for "poor copy," as Benjamin Rutter puts it.)[16] Hegel should have called it "irony," but since that term had already been taken by Friedrich Schlegel for his own project, and both because Hegel had brutally criticized it in its various forms and because "irony" suggested a stance to the problems of modern life that was distinctly unserious, "irony" was simply not a choice for him.

Hegel instead describes such objective humor with his own term, "*Verinnigung*," a kind of intimacy.[17] We have such an intimacy with the objects of daily life when "what matters...is the object and its embodiment within its subjective reflex"; that is, in adopting what looks like an ironic stance toward all the otherwise rational activities we pursue in the social world (as described in the 1820 *Philosophy of Right*), we interrupt the familiarity of that world, and the subject who learns to practice such ironic intimacy within his absorption in his daily activities experiences a growing *Verinnigung*, or intimacy, with himself and that world. It is a form of humor in that it unsettles not the way in which our thought of what counts may find no echo in nature but in the way what we take every day to be of infinite importance is itself finite. The aristocrats of the spirit come up against the limited nature of their own lives.

The Hegelian amphibian who lives by the categories of, for example, marriage, the family, his bourgeois occupation, and his status as a citizen must also learn to step back and ask himself several questions—for example, whether he is really living up that status and whether he or the status needs to change—accompanied by the realization that this cannot be an individual commitment alone. That is, no matter how committed one is, one can disrupt that commitment with the reflective turn that asks whether that commitment (say, to marriage) is really "a marriage"—or, to put it in terms of Hegel's own somewhat artificial terminology, whether one's de facto commitments really live up to "their concept." To do that is to acknowledge the always potential gap between, to put it most generally, fact and norm in one's own case and the contingency of the specific shape of the shape one's life has taken.[18] This is one of the many tensions that a Hegelian amphibian learns to live with. In such ironic intimacy, there is no "longing, demanding" for wholeness in social life. The inflexibility that is the strength of the modern world finds its counterpart in a kind of humble humility of the everyday world. The breakage between the individual in his inwardness and the rationality of the world around him is now best lived out in a kind of ironic intimacy with one's world.

Reconciliation of a sort is achieved when the individual faces his world with a new humor, as it were, and a new questioning of his own status.[19] The recognition of the limitations of the familiar leads us to the point where we can learn to live with this kind of disruption—to be at one with ourselves while acknowledging the finitude and limitations of that particular fit. This, of course, requires a shift in focus on the part of the individual, but, just as important, it also demands a rational world itself.

The individual who sees the world through this kind of ironic intimacy (or objective humor) looks at it and asks himself, "How do I face this world, for example, with courage?" For Hegel, that seemed to mean that in our personal lives, we once again have to return to Aristotle and what he had to say about the virtues *and* note that this is the best we can have. But isn't this sacrificing the rigor of the concept? Yes, says Hegel, and, strangely enough, all the better! Hegel notes:

> This principle, that Aristotle determines as the mean (more of a difference of degree) between two extremes, has been, of course, rebuked as inadequate and indeterminate; yet this is the nature of the case. Virtue, and especially determinate virtue, enters into a sphere where the quantitative has its place; thought as such is not here at one with itself since the quantitative boundary is indeterminate.[20]

Freedom is a way of being at one with oneself, but for self-conscious agents in the modern world, one is at one with oneself only in also being an "amphibious" animal, holding fast to the intelligibility of the whole while acknowledging the contingency of what falls within it, holding fast to the demands of reason whose actuality often displays itself in complete banality. This requires one to face life with the virtues: courage, wit, magnanimity, and so forth. In our world, that also requires a will to live with the disruption that the self-conscious interrogation of the virtues—is *this* really civic courage?—brings in its wake. If the successful life is oriented to the concrete statuses of ethical life while preserving the sense of the whole that powers reflection on what it means not only to be a good family member, burgher, or citizen but also to be a good human being, then the modern Aristotelian man or woman of virtue is the "amphibian" of which Hegel speaks. To be virtuous is to know how to strike the balance, the mean, among the unavoidable tensions of modern life. Those tensions are ineradicable but necessary components of modern life. Something like practical wisdom, and not a final metaphysical solution, is the proper response.

This is one of the main senses behind Hegel's infamous "double proposition" with which he began his 1820 *Philosophy of Right*: The actual is the rational, and the rational is the actual. From his own time to our own time, it has brought down a firestorm of criticism on him, since on the surface, his sentence seemed to be saying that what existed (the Prussian state in the 1820s) was perfectly in order or, even worse, that the "right" is simply what the "winners" in history happen to say is right. Hegel himself was stung by the criticism (although he should have realized that this way of putting it was almost certainly going to provoke that kind of reaction).[21] His point, however, was never that the existing political order was all in order, as he himself makes clear.[22] He was arguing for a reconciliation with modern life itself, not with the existing political order or set of social institutions. Modern life was the overall "Idea" that acknowledged that one could be at one with oneself only in a free social order that was rational, but it did not follow from such a view that the Prussian state (or the English, the French, or any state) was therefore entitled to call itself fully rational. The appropriate response to this state of affairs—the rationality of the modern world, coupled with the clumsiness or even outright irrationality of the existing order—was that of ironic intimacy.[23] How was one to take that?

It was unclear how the modern world, in producing individuals who claim such a normative authority for their inner lives, could have the psychological security necessary to deal with the increasing fragmentation of groups within the larger social order. The kind of solidarity required for the equality promised by the original French Revolution also required a kind of loyalty and trust that is only barely possible if any group is seen as merely a faction and therefore lacking in any authority, and no mere analysis of the meaning of, say, "rights" was going to resolve that problem.

The great differences among individuals and their interests continually produces factions, oppositions of interest for which mediation in terms of more general norms is always potentially at issue. By 1831, Hegel seemed to be thinking that many of the problems he thought now belonged clearly to the past, having been set aside by the tumult of the revolution, were themselves reemerging in a different, although still modern form. The amoral assertion of power on the part of modern monarchs and modern states was supposed to have been supplanted by a widespread recognition of the rights of individuals and the necessity for an empowered modern pluralist political community, but instead the modern state seemed to hover continuously between legitimation of itself through reason and legitimation that was no more than the assertion of mere power. For that reason, the various groups in society—classes, the older "estates," and so forth—were plagued by a lack of confidence that their lives really could be successful together, with an accompanying fear that policies were in fact being chosen (or would be chosen) that favored the interests of others under the guise of the interests of the community as a whole (or, worse, they came to believe that the interests of the community simply were identical to their own interests or that it was they and nobody else who were the community).

Just how reconciled should we be to the existing state of affairs? Hegel's point was certainly that we should be reconciled to the modern world, that we could still find a place in a disenchanted nature for ourselves even while acknowledging that nature was deaf to us and did not respond to our aspirations. As his thought developed in the 1820s, it also became apparent that he did not think that we were in any position to be reconciled to modern political life—especially political life in Prussia, France, and Britain in that period—and he more or less made that point explicit at the end of the last of his lecture series.

In 1831, he described life in the current climate in France after the 1830 revolution against the monarchy of the restoration period and the establishment of a new, rather bourgeois constitutional monarchy. France seemed to be tottering back and forth between competing ideals of government: "Each particularization appears as a privilege, but there is supposed to be equality. In terms of this principle, no government is possible. This collision, this knot of this problem stands before history, and it is history which has to loosen the knot."[24]

Since the historical narration about the actualization of the concepts in question—the concepts of freedom, the worth of the individual, the authority of inwardness, and so forth—was not over, it was therefore still unclear if the tensions in those collisions were in fact harmonizable and what such a harmony would concretely look like. It is striking that Hegel did not say that if the French had only read the *Philosophy of Right* more carefully, they might have avoided those problems. Instead, he said that there were problems at work that had not been solved and by implication not resolved in his own work.

Hegel saw the other side of this problem in terms of the growing stress on German ethnicity, a problem he initially thought had to be merely a passing piece of nostalgia that, because of its retrograde nature, would not itself undermine the "universality" a modern political community was aspiring to embody. However, by the late 1820s, it was becoming partially clear that the threat was not going away. As Hegel says in one of his later (and close to last) lectures in 1831, in a pointed reference to the increasingly heated debates about German nationalism in his own day, "On a small scale, interests can be the same. On the large scale, as in Germany, the interests of the Bavarians, the Austrians, the Pomeranians and the Mecklenburgers are highly distinct."[25]

In the conditions where that kind of particularity gains the upper hand, and one group begins to believe that its own interests are the true interests of the whole, then "a justice freed from subjective interest and subjective shape and from the contingency of power" becomes less and less actualizable.[26] Where matters are pushed to the edges of full factionalization, no legitimate government at all is possible, and where no legitimate government is possible, only power prevails, even when that power can lay claim to some kind of lesser legitimacy based only on the stability it offers. In that situation, political life would become no longer the sublation of family and personal life but its competitor.[27] The interest of a mythical national group pressing for its own power is potentially just as disastrous as that of factionalization bringing everything to a halt.

## 2:  Second Nature and Wholeness

Such amphibians live with the idea that the whole is intelligible—that there is nothing in the universe that is so inherently mysterious that it must remain impervious to our rational powers—and equally with the idea that we, of course, have not yet made the whole completely intelligible to ourselves. (Science, art, philosophy, and the like are, of course, not yet over, but the idea that the world is in some metaphysical sense inherently unknowable and must remain a mystery is itself inherently over.) Moreover, the idea that all aspects of our lives can be brought under the sway of reason is also an illusion that is over (if, indeed, it had ever really gripped us at all). From the standpoint of pure intelligibility—the kind that can be systematized into something like the *Encyclopedia of the Philosophical Sciences* or what takes itself to be its contemporary successor, the nonsystematic curriculum of the modern philosophy faculty—the contingency of our day-to-day lives and the various idiosyncrasies and actions undertaken not so much as a response to reasons as reasons but as a response to other only dimly articulated attachments themselves fall out of view. (They appear back in view within the forms of "ethical life," art, and religion, each of which, so Hegel argued, is the necessary background for philosophy.)[28] Such amphibians think philosophically (and aesthetically and sometimes religiously) about what it is to be a minded, human agent; they also think outside of the confines of what it is that they can also think philosophically; and finally, as good amphibians, they understand that without drawing on the contingencies of life, their own philosophical reflections can only be, as Hegel remarks at the very end of the *Phenomenology*, "lifeless" and "alone"—"alone" as cut off from the larger social life of which they are a part and "lifeless" as eventually devolving, outside of those larger connections, into a merely formal enterprise.

Acting in terms of one's own law had been often interpreted as acting in terms of nature or of one's own natural constitution. Especially in the eighteenth century and certainly well into the nineteenth century, there was a growing concern on the part of many to lead lives of less artifice, and this was increasingly identified as living a more natural and therefore freer life. At first in the exaggerated artifice of the ancien régime and then afterward in the barely disguised artifice of bourgeois life, acting naturally came to seem like the only way to escape the kind of alienating stance modern life seemed to require. However, "acting naturally," however evocative and attractive it seems, is also incoherent. It would require stripping off all our second nature back to some more primordial nature and expressing that in our actions (instead of expressing the supposedly phony layers of social artifice we have built up). On the other hand, whereas acting morally in terms of a law one gave oneself as a matter of impartial reason seemed to be a clear alternative to "acting naturally," it also seemed to impose a kind of alienation on the part of individuals toward their more individual, sensuous constitutions.[29]

On Hegel's view, one acts in terms of the nature of that to which one concretely first-personally refers, that is, to oneself and to one's own nature as having practical reason embedded within it.[30] He understood the social and historical achievement of an inflexibility (*Eigensinnigkeit*) about "the right of particularity"—a second nature that actualized the idea of acting by a law of one's own nature—to have thus actualized the Rousseauian ideal of naturalness but not as the actualization of some natural propensity within subjects.

Although the room for the individual to act in terms of his own law and therefore naturally—that is, in terms of a law that is both rational and includes within itself the various quirks and oddities of individual personality—was an achievement to be celebrated as being more rational than its predecessors, it also brought with it what Hegel thinks is a specifically modern problem. The felt demand for wholeness is clearly present in modern life, and it outstrips any possibility of attaining it. This is a rational result, not something to be infinitely lamented.

On the one hand, if we accept that the world is intelligible (which, to stress the point, is not to claim that we now know everything there is to know about it), and if it is ultimately an appeal to reason (and not an appeal to revealed mystery or, say, blind custom) that is required to settle matters, then the "rationality of the actual," as Hegel infamously called his view, will be quite obviously at odds with the manifest irrationality of the world around us. Every day one runs across plenty of examples of behavior that do not seem particularly to be evidence of any rationality but instead seem rather peevish, or driven by blind or almost blind passion, or to be simply heedless in their direction. Shortsightedness and arrogance remain stalwarts of political life. The examples rather quickly multiply.

The demand for wholeness in an individual life metamorphoses quite easily into the demand that the inner lives of agents fit as a piece into their cooperative lives together in the modern world. This is a not uncommon wish but an unrealizable ideal, since the demand for wholeness in the world as a whole in effect can in its actualization only be the imposition of a particular kind of wholeness on very dissimilar people.[31] That kind of demand for wholeness would be, if actualized, the very opposite of "a justice freed from subjective interest and subjective shape and from the contingency of power."[32] Instead, as a demand, it amounts to a call for civil strife, and at its extremes, it invites either civil war or the oppression of some in the name of others.

The inflexibility about the irreducibility of individuality and the demand for wholeness were both equally profound aspects of the modern social space, and the depth of the demands from both directions meant that certain types of human possibilities were to become more or less permanent figures in the modern scene. (They were to be figures in what Hegel in 1807 called "shapes of consciousness.")[33] Such figures feel the demand for wholeness strongly enough but experience the world as sufficiently irrational that they always remain permanently alienated and unable to find a home in that world. For them, it is the whole itself that has gone wrong, and, quite typically, several false solutions suggest themselves. Such figures may come to think that it is up to them and them alone to hold fast to an integrated subjectivity that refuses to bend to that world. (This, more or less, was Hegel's view of his contemporary Romantics and their beautiful souls.) On the other hand, there are those who are more than willing to bring wholeness to the world, usually at the end of the barrel of a gun.[34] And of course, there are all the in-between positions where the demand for wholeness is seen as some kind of infinite longing expressed as a hope for some kind of dramatic experience (a "messianic" event) that will suddenly change everything. Hegel, whose most famous claim is probably the *Phenomenology*'s "the truth is the whole," thought that in modern social life such a demand for wholeness on the part of individuals is ill conceived and, even worse, socially and politically dangerous. It misunderstands the kind of unity that modern social life proposes.

The reconciliatory ideal, on the other hand, is to understand that the actual is the rational (that is, that the world is ultimately intelligible to rational inquiry) and, as Hegel notoriously stressed in his lectures and private conversations, that the rational must also become actual; that is, the social institutions in the modern world must come to terms with the complex demands presented by the form of life in which there are some justifications that appeal to reasons—paradigmatically those of conscience—which, oddly enough, are both required to pass public muster and at the same time are licensed not to be required to do so. One is thus reconciled to a world in which alienation and unintelligibility on a personal level are maintained, yet in which there is good reason to believe that this arrangement is, in principle, rational. A free life is a rational life, even if freedom brings in its wake all sorts of other things that one otherwise might find deplorable.[35]

Hegel's distrust of the ordinary citizen to grasp the complexities of the workings of the political state has, of course, been mirrored in various theories of democracy and antidemocracy since his own time.[36] Hegel's argument (obviously indebted to Rousseau) is that the abstractions of modern life, which require its citizens to show allegiance to large-scale, complex institutions (in short, to large-scale bureaucracies), are incompatible with direct democratic rule, which he also takes, as does Rousseau, to be possible only as a matter of face-to-face joint deliberation. That, however, is ruled out by the abstractness of the modern rule of law and the institutions necessary to make a modern government work within the context of a fractured public. To be a good amphibious citizen, one must learn to live within these abstractions, and Hegel was simply not very clear to himself about how much of that kind of skill could be realized in many people's lives. Likewise, these abstractions of state power cannot be well represented in works of art (or can be represented only badly or even falsely), so they cannot get the intuitive hold on us that other features of modern life—for example, the concern of the lyric poet with love and its tribulations—can have.[37] For Hegel, democracy requires free communication, communicative freedom requires orientation to norms of truth, and the difficulties of communicating the truth embedded in the abstractions that govern modern life require that basic decisions be made by experts. In turn, appeal to expertise alone itself rules out the kind of communicative freedom that would be necessary for a modern democracy and appeal to expertise in the first place.

Likewise, although individual possession of the virtues is crucial for living well in a modern state, if the modern state tries to rule by virtue alone, it becomes a tyranny or worse. Living according to virtue is one thing, but virtue is not a matter of living by abstractions. It requires, as a modified Aristotelian naturalism would have it, a kind of practical skill that resists formal codification and thus is something very different from the abstractions required by the rule of law. The rule of law requires political virtue on the part of citizens, but it also both integrates that virtue into a set of shared political commitments and circumscribes the authority of that virtue. Substituting political virtue for the rule of law (or identifying the two) leads only to tyranny, terror, or breakdown. Hegel took Robespierre's rule in France to illustrate that simple point.[38]

However, modern life does require the acceptance of ourselves as fragments within the abstractions of modern bureaucratic rule, and that also requires a kind of practice of forgiveness and reconciliation for which Hegel argued in the 1807 *Phenomenology*. Each acknowledges his own finitude and partiality, and in doing so, in the give-and-take of their encounter, each forgives the other for having claimed such an absolute status for himself. In religious terms, each acknowledges that he is not without sin, but in the more secular terms favored by Hegel, each acknowledges his own radical fallibility and the temptation to claim a knowledge of the unconditional that outstrips the resources of the individual agent. The "true infinity" the agents seek is to be found within the ongoing interchange itself, insofar as that interchange is oriented to truth.

To phrase Hegel's conclusion in a rather breathlessly abstract manner: Amphibians breathe the thin air lying within the twin commitments to truth ("infinity") and to their own fallibility ("finitude"), to the ideals of reason and the often prosaic and banal world in which it finds its actualization. Their public lives display the same tension. It would be futile to expect politics to abolish that tension, but it would be irrational to think that it could not be made to live with it. The world as we find it is never fully rational, and "who is not clever enough to see a great deal in his own surroundings which is in fact not what it ought to be?"[39] As Hegel phrased the point in his 1819 lectures, we should say that "the actual comes to be the rational," not that we need think that it has ever finally completed its job, or that what is effectively at work in the world is rational at this moment.[40] To understand that requires attention to philosophical argument, but it also requires a form of life of rights-bearing, moral individuals, who acquire a sense of egalitarian right from childhood onward, whose participation in civil society is coupled with a feel for what is practical and workable, and whose political temperament is shaped by a shared commitment to political and social justice. It requires a "second nature" that can live without enchanted illusions but not without ideals and that, like all other human strivings, succeeds only when it also aims at truth.

# B: Final Ends?

To Kant's four questions about philosophy, Hegel supplied rather different answers. Overall, Kant held that the world and ourselves must ultimately be a mystery, even if by virtue of the Kantian critical philosophy, we can understand why it must be a mystery and why in principle the mysteries are not resolvable. At the heart of the mystery is the metaphysical commitment that we are free, rational beings in a world that seems to defy the very possibility of there being anything like free rational beings. Hegel, on the other hand, argued that there is no reason in principle that we should believe that the world must remain a metaphysical mystery to us. (It may remain mysterious in countless other ways, but its alleged metaphysical mystery should be put aside.) The contradictions we encounter when we think metaphysically—that is, unconditionally—about the world at first seem to reveal something about us, not the world, but in thinking about "us," we come to understand that these contradictions also tell us something about our world and in particular about nature, agency, and history.

For Hegel, what counts for us at any point as an unconditional duty is in one sense always relative to the historical space we inhabit. A look at the history of our attempts to make sense of the whole shows that what we took to be the unconditioned was itself in reality only conditional, not in the sense that it referred back to other, deeper presuppositions but in that it was part of a human form of life that had taken the shape it did because of its own peculiar path-dependent development in history and its commitment to a certain view of what was absolute for it. At any given point in the development of a form of life, the whole itself cannot be articulated, not because in all unconcealing there is an element of essential metaphysical concealment from us. We often know what we have meant only after the fact. The logic of a form of life, that is, comes only when the owl of

Minerva starts its flight, not because of any deeper metaphysical concealment of the nature of things but because it is only when its story is over that all of the real-izations of its meanings have been accomplished and we can speak of what it was.

Acknowledging the historical situatedness of any form of life would be, of course, if left at that stage, completely unsatisfactory. If left in that abstract form, it would simply be yet another blandly self-contradictory muddle in the way that all forms of radical relativism are blandly self-contradictory muddles. It might also look as if it were a counsel to abandon philosophy (or metaphysics), since it seems to be saying, after all, that it is an impossible enterprise. Indeed, the kind of skepticism it provokes, as Hegel says in the introduction to the 1807 *Phenomenology*, looks like it is recommending more a path of despair than a path of mere doubt.[41]

To avoid this kind of bland relativism, Hegel's proposal, stated most generally, is to make philosophy the study of the development of the "Idea"—the joint con-ception of our norms, the world, and how the world (as it were) does or does not cooperate with the fulfillment of those norms—as a way of characterizing the point of view in which we acknowledge our own fallibility while at the same time continuing to commit ourselves to a robust conception of truth. Understanding the history of metaphysics as Kant and Hegel did, it involves a reflective view about our own embeddedness in our historical situation as expressing a determi-nate conception of the unconditioned or, in Hegel's terms, the absolute. For our time, that involves our own reflective grasp of our own situation and of how it itself is but a component (a "moment") of our attempt at self-interpretation.

Many of those who followed in Kant's wake took it that the task of grasping the unconditioned had to be itself an infinite task, something we postulated but that in principle could never be completed in human time—the mythical point at which the last metaphysician supposedly finally delivers the knockout argument, and the project is over.[42] Hegel, on the other hand, thought that this task was always in the process of being accomplished and that it is our reflective consciousness of this ongoing process of understanding the world and ourselves as the kinds of creatures who must ask those questions that is the permanent element in the story. As "Idea," we have a view of ourselves and the world as standing in one unity. The finite world is the world in which we live, where our metaphysical speculations inevitably contradict each other and the infinite exists, as it were, as our own reflec-tive consciousness of this finitude. To compress this view into Hegel's own preferred jargon: "Reason is at the same time only the infinite insofar as it is absolute free-dom which consequently presupposes to itself its own knowledge and by that means makes itself finite, and it is the eternal movement to sublate this imme-diacy, to comprehend itself, and to be knowledge of the rational."[43]

Hegel himself had no trouble calling this a religious view of things. Although Hegel's philosophy of religion is an immense topic on its own, Hegel's own views on this, once again, have at least a surface similarity to Wittgenstein's views. Wittgenstein is reported to have said: "I am not a religious man but I cannot help seeing every problem from a religious point of view."[44] Hegel, too, although not being a particularly religious man—at least in terms of displaying any obviously publicly pious outlook—also saw things from a religious point of view, and no reader of Hegel can fail to notice the many religious references scattered through his works.[45]

Although Hegel claimed to be a Christian (and there is no reason at all to doubt his sincerity), his version of God was more a sublated version of Aristotle's god, at least in the last book of the *Nicomachean Ethics*, than it was the God of his earlier theological education at Tübingen. Like Aristotle, Hegel thought that the only intelligible conception of divinity had to be along the lines of a spiritual being thinking eternal thoughts, and, as if to make sure we did not miss his point, Hegel even ended his *Encyclopedia* with a citation from Aristotle's *Metaphysics* about the nature of divinity as lying in thought thinking about itself.

What Hegel's student, Heinrich Heine, said about Germany in general—that it is an "open secret" that "pantheism is the clandestine religion of Germany"[46]—was also true of Hegel. Hegel, of course, always denied that he was a pantheist. After all, if pantheism is the doctrine that everything is god—this pencil, this blade of grass, this rock, this bottle—then, so he would argue, pantheism is simply false, since the divine is supposed to be the essence of things, not just everything in general. In turn, Hegel also held that it is in the essence of things that the world as a whole be intelligible to reason but not that every contingent event is equally intelligible, and thus it is the world as a whole that is divine insofar as it is intelligible that the world includes all sorts of contingency within itself. In addition, Hegel also tended to attribute to pantheism the tendency to sacrifice the intelligibility of the world to an inflated sense of the sublime, a kind of mute awe in the face of the grandeur of the natural world (which is one reason he also thought, wrongly, that pantheism was appropriately the religion of the "mysterious East").

In taking his work to express not only a philosophical but also a religious point of view, Hegel was trying to hold philosophy fast to its traditional Greek concern with rigor and argumentation about the conceptual dilemmas that were its proper domain but equally together with its equally Greek concern with raising issues about the final ends of life. (Whether such a view could really lay claim to calling itself Christian has always been a matter of some well-founded suspicion about Hegel's philosophy of religion from his own day up to our very own.)[47] However, whereas religion seeks to tell a certain type of story about the final ends and where we stand with regard to them, it does not, as Hegel explicitly puts it, speak the truth "in the shape of truth" about this matter. It is philosophy as self-conscious rational inquiry that does exactly that.[48]

For Hegel, the "open secret" of the modern world was that the religion to which it seems to have committed itself takes on this form of a quasi-pantheist commitment to rationality in general. The religious person sees the world as a whole, and the modern religious outlook is to see the world as manifesting a kind of intelligibility about itself. However, this more or less intuitive and emotional grasp of the world as a whole is deficient because it can get no further than the feeling of it and thus does not speak the truth "in the shape of truth." Now, in being a kind of pantheist in that sense, Hegel was certainly not committing himself to anything like the divinity of nature. Nature as a whole aims at nothing, has no overall goal for itself, and is not just incapable of organizing itself into a better version of itself— it is not even comprehensible what the better version of nature could be. Nature is thus a poor choice for divinity. Nonetheless, within nature, there is life, and within life there are self-conscious creatures on at least one planet whose own nature is to seek to comprehend what it is that they are. If there is anything of absolute worth in the world, it is that. It may not fit into any larger purpose for the universe at large, and it may include elements that are not easy to digest (such as the death of friends, family, and lovers), but, from the standpoint of a rational animal, it is nonetheless a good thing that rational beings seek to understand themselves. Understanding nature in this way, without illusions, puts us in the position of being able to inhabit our natural status in a way made difficult by Christian civilization but more at ease in Hegel's developed Greek sense.

From the standpoint of its species, the animal is an end in itself, a *Selbstzweck*, even though it may have no knowledge of itself as such. The animal seeks only to reproduce itself and its species, and its status as an end in itself is almost certainly at odds with the similar status of other animals. Nature has no way of harmonizing prey and predator. It is only when self-conscious animals whose own existence is a problem to them appear on the planet that the intelligibility of the world as a whole, and of their species in particular, becomes anything of an issue. The final end of the world, for Hegel, is that of life assuming the position of *Geistigkeit* (our own mindful agency) and coming to a full self-consciousness, that is, our full awareness of our status as self-interpreting animals, as having always been and always being a problem to ourselves. The world was not designed for us (or for anything else), but we are for ourselves a final end, which makes us natural creatures that are a problem to themselves.

The nature of nature as a whole can be an issue only for such rational, reflective creatures, since the whole cannot be sensibly presented but is available to them only as they think of it. (Hegel fully agrees with Kant that the necessity of intuition for our ordinary understanding of the world means that we cannot in principle achieve any intuitive grasp of the whole.) The whole itself therefore is only "ideally" there for such creatures, who themselves are parts of that whole, and, on Hegel's view, this is as much divinity as one can rationally discern. That the world becomes intelligible to such creatures is to say that such natural creatures can find the world everywhere a rational place, at least in the sense that they can make that world intelligible to themselves—for nature, that is paradigmatically through the natural sciences and through the philosophical reflection on the conceptual problems that arise out of that kind of encounter with nature. That such reflective creatures living in a disenchanted nature can no longer be fully at home in that world is one reason, as we have seen, that something like the Greeks (in their idealized and romanticized shape) continues to remain an object of nostalgia. "If it were permitted at all to have a longing for something, then it would be for such a place, for such circumstances," as Hegel said of the idealized Greeks.[49] They seemed to be at home in their world, but their world was not the world as we have come to know it, and we cannot self-consciously rewind that clock and return to a "Greek" state of cheerfulness about things. Understanding the world as an organic whole is at odds with nature as we now know it.

Since nature as a whole aims at nothing, nature cannot be expected to answer to human aspirations or to cooperate with human wants. It is thus not unexpected that a disappointment with that would be projected onto something else and that we might imagine that there must be something else to the world that does indeed answer to human aspirations—to our "highest needs," as Hegel describes them—and it may even indeed be foolish to think that people will ever want to cease to hope for such a response from the world as a whole. Now, on Hegel's understanding, the religious point of view seeks not merely an understanding of the world as a whole and the place of such self-reflective beings in it. It also wishes to find a reconciliation with it. Hegel thought that philosophy, pursued as a *Wissenschaft* and culminating in an account of ourselves as being at one with ourselves in a certain type of self-interpretation, would, as much as possible, help to satisfy that religious impulse. If the religious point of view aims at seeing how human lives fit into the larger whole, and the larger whole is itself something that is the aim of a certain type of reflective thought, then inevitably philosophy is pushed to consider that in terms of its own internal aim of elucidation and understanding. As we reflect on ourselves and our place in the world as a whole, which in the religious imagination might consist in trying to understand ourselves in terms of God's plan for the world, we find that we are led to think of our lives in terms of a larger set of principles that make sense to us—that is, that are rational—and this is all it could mean to live a life in keeping with these spiritual terms. In the context of modern science, modern economies, and modern bureaucracies, that means learning to live by breathing rather thin air or, as Hegel himself concluded his preface to his 1807 *Phenomenology*, it means acknowledging that "the share in the total work of spirit which falls to the activity of any individual can only be very small."[50]

This self-reflection on the part of natural creatures is the final end of the world, at least in the sense that there is no further purpose outside of that purpose itself and that such a purpose is, or can become, intelligible to itself. Hegel's claim is not that the world was designed in any way to achieve that goal, nor is it a claim that we create the sense of the world (as if we could do that in any such way we pleased). The meaning that we are to find in the world has to do with the facts of our being the primates we are, and although we can sublate some of those facts—we can circumscribe their authority—we cannot ignore them.[51] We are the creatures for whom our existence is a problem, and in becoming self-conscious, we institute a space of reasons that we ourselves do not then control. This space of reasons itself grows out of the kind of normativity that is already at work in animal life, and our ways of instituting forms of mutual recognition give that normativity a shape it cannot otherwise have in animal life, but that does not mean, on Hegel's view, that we can ever leave nature behind. (That would be to conflate sublation, *Aufhebung*, with overcoming, *Überwindung*.) Independent of whether the emergence of life on earth was a likely event or a massively improbable contingency, it is still the case that with the emergence of life, there are goods in the world, and with the emergence of self-conscious life, there are different types of goods to be found in the historical and social world.

In that world, one need not think that we must postulate that in some indeterminate future time, virtue will be rewarded with happiness. To the extent that our social world is at least a partial embodiment of freedom, we can live successful lives in the here and now, and to the extent that our world is not such an embodiment or is a lesser and deficient embodiment of it, we can only lead less successful lives. To make sense of our lives is thus not to go beyond the boundaries of a human life. It is rather to ask how a rational life that is also a human life is to be pursued. (It is to ask how a rational life in the abstract is to be actualized in the context of a human life, with all its contingent accompaniments.) To want any deeper oneness with the world as a whole would be, on Hegel's conception, to mistake the issue. It is to yearn for a oneness that is not possible for a self-conscious creature to have.

Hegel's conception of the religiously spiritual life is one that many (including those in his own family) have found unsatisfying.[52] Those who want more from religion will simply find his views far too weak to be satisfactory; likewise, those who are suspicious about religion in general will most likely find Hegel's conviction about the continuity of his views with a religious outlook far too tepid to be even close to a convincing argument. Hegel's religious views are, in fact, curiously abstract for a philosopher who argued for the primacy of the concrete, even though he devoted much of his energy to showing how all of Christian doctrine could be adapted to this neo-Aristotelian conception of divinity (such as his attempt to show how the conceptual difficulties of the Christian Trinity are best viewed as being only symbolic representations, *Vorstellungen*, of the deeper conceptual difficulties in formulating what it is to be both sovereign and subject of the moral law).[53] Moreover, although he thought that the conceptual space carved out for the authority of "inwardness" would not have taken place except for the entrance of Christianity into Roman life, he did not think that the modern state had to rest its convictions about protecting the right of conscience by appealing to religion to justify those claims. He also thought that religion was important enough that the state should require citizens to belong to "a" religious community but not to any particular one, and he thought this was also consistent with a sharp separation between church and state.[54] Nonetheless, for Hegel, there is nothing outside of this world, no world beyond this world to which we may appeal.[55] Hegel is uncompromising in his insistence that it is philosophical reflection—reason—that has the authority to speak about the truth of religious claims, and he thought that philosophical reflection showed us that something like Aristotle's god is the only true sense we can give to a conception of the divine.

Hegel thus accepts in a sense the Aristotelian conception of contemplation as the highest good but for very modified reasons that lead both to a modified conception of contemplation and to a modified conception of the highest good—or, if we keep to Hegel's terminology, it leads to a sublated conception of contemplation of the highest good. Part of the rhetoric against Hegel's view has traditionally seen this as Hegel's obviously inflated claim to be the overreaching professor claiming to embody the absolute while declaiming from the lectern of the university as he preached to the less informed about the "end of history" or some such thing. In fact, Hegel's point is much different. The highest good consists in thinking about what it means to be a human being in general, and, as we have seen, that in turn requires us to think about what it means in particular to be a good parent, citizen, brother, sister, workman, artisan, legislator, and so forth. Moreover, given Hegel's views on meaning and its actualization, thinking about it also requires actualizing it if one is to ever know what one really thinks about it, since one cannot know the full truth about one's thoughts until they have been made actual.

For those of a postmodern persuasion, Hegel is nowadays often cited as the philosopher of totality, and from that, it is almost always then inferred that any philosophy of totality directly implies, or is rumbling down the road to, or is a short step away from some form of totalitarianism. Now it is certainly true that Hegel claims that the truth is the whole. It is also true that he thinks that the whole is such that it is only within it—namely, in our embeddedness in various structured dependencies—that the modern conception of being an individual is not merely possible but actual.[56] However, Hegel is as much a philosopher of individuality as he is of quasi-organic unity, since he thinks that the success of the modern world lies in its capacity to sustain the very fragile status of being an "individual," which is possible only under the conditions that sublate the older ideal of "organic unity" into the "unity of the concept." The independence for which the "individual" strives within such a context is sustainable—can be real, actual—only from within the complex patterns of mutual dependence that sustain such statuses. Hegel's point is not the claim (true enough on its own) that our finitude makes us ineradicably dependent on each other for emotional and material ends. It is the more radical point that our very metaphysical status as the agents we are is realizable only from within these complex social dependencies within the fabric of recognition. This transpires within a disenchanted nature, devoid of either a full-blown Aristotelian or Christian teleology, but not in a nature devoid of goods and evils, where the concrete shape of those goods and evils is always determined by the form of life in question.

Hegel is also almost always cited not only as a philosopher of totality but also as a thoroughly teleological thinker. However, in one important way Hegel is not a teleological thinker at all. If one takes teleology in its most obvious sense—namely, that of explaining an action in light of the purpose at which the action was aiming—then there is very little overt teleology in Hegel's thought except for the explanation of human action. Nature aims at nothing, and there is no goal for which nature was designed. Likewise, there is no superagent in history aiming at a goal and manipulating events to arrive there. History aims at nothing. Instead, in history, there is a kind of logic such that spirit, after having gone through several steps, finds itself in a position that was rationally compelled for it, given its path-dependent development, but at which nobody (not even the fictitious super-subject) ever aimed.

Nor does the modern period in history fulfill a metaphysical need within human life that has only recently blossomed into completion. For Hegel, the metaphysics of potentialities and their actualization was to be replaced by the complex histories of the actualizations of meanings. Likewise, in nature there are functions that have a teleological structure to them—the eye functions as a way of seeing, which most likely is selected because it increases the survival chances of that collection of genetic material—but there is no designer who made them with any goal in mind. Teleology in that sense depends on there being organic life, but organic life does not appear on the planet to fulfill a goal, even if there is a logic to the explanation of organic life that requires us to look to these functions in nature to get our accounts in order. If history turns out to be about how humans come to an understanding of themselves, then there is a subject of history but only as a late achievement of sorts, not as anything that was already there directing the show from the outset. To say that history has been about *Geist* coming to a full self-consciousness is not to describe a metaphysical process completing itself but instead to state a new commitment that has only now emerged, namely, that we now must think of humanity as a whole and that our ideals likewise have from now on to do with the actualization of the idea of the "universal" instead of that of a tribe, a nation, or even that of a whole culture. Prior to this new commitment, there was no subject of history.[57]

Hegel also thought that the period had arrived when the idea of a national philosophy—German, French, British, and so on—was over. As he says rather obliquely near the end of the *Phenomenology*, "hence, as long as spirit has not *in itself* brought itself to consummation as the world-spirit, it cannot attain its consummation as *self-conscious* spirit."[58] As just said, this reference to the world-spirit expresses a new commitment, not the recognition of a metaphysical fact that was always there.[59] To say that "spirit" had to become "world-spirit" was to say that philosophy, as *Wissenschaft*, can no longer concern itself exclusively with specifically European matters. Now, although Hegel himself attempted that in his lectures in Berlin, where he drew out the historical nature of politics, art, religion, and philosophy, nonetheless, when judged by any fair standard, his own efforts are clearly marred both by his own lack of understanding about the ways of life of China, Africa, India, and Japan and equally by his own ill-formed prejudices about all of them. But since, after all, "the universal *Geist* does not stand still," one has Hegel's permission for not staying put with all the ways in which Hegel fell short of his own standards.[60]

At this time in history, so Hegel thought, we have finally reached the point where an authentic understanding of the Greeks was now effectively realized. Having thrown mythology aside, the ancient philosophers, Hegel says, "presupposed nothing but the heavens above and the earth below" and in that "substantive environment" thereby achieved a kind of free thought, something that the later scholastic philosophers could never achieve, since they "absorbed their content as given content, and, to be precise, as content given by the church."[61] Having finally come to grasp ourselves as self-interpreting primates who live within the conceptual determinations of a disenchanted naturalism, we find ourselves in a similar position to those Greeks. Like the ancients, we, too, need not presuppose anything but the heavens above and the earth below, but as we begin doing philosophy and searching for the unconditioned, the absolute, we are more like a people "freely disembarking into the wide-open, with nothing below us and nothing above us."[62] However, in rediscovering the Greeks within a disenchanted nature, we have also entered into a project where, as Hegel puts it, we are now "alone with ourselves," and where this aloneness constitutes a "pure being-at-one-with-oneself."[63] Nature may be silent about our aspirations, but there is a limited way in which we remain an *Endzweck*, an end in itself, for ourselves in nature. The world was not designed for us, nor is there necessarily any larger purpose in nature that we fulfill. We are our own purpose, but that rational purpose is both our nature and intelligible to itself. For the "amphibians" we have come to be, that should suffice. (No doubt, Hegel would be very taken with W. H. Auden's line, "Find the mortal world enough.")

Almost at the very end of the *Critique of Pure Reason*, Kant, who had just spent several hundred pages demonstrating the impossibility of achieving the aims of traditional metaphysics, noted that despite its impossibility, "we shall always return to metaphysics as to a beloved one with whom we have had a quarrel. For here we are concerned with essential ends—ends with which metaphysics must ceaselessly occupy itself, either in striving for genuine insight into them, or in refuting those who profess already to have attained it."[64] For Hegel, Kant's critique of all philosophy that seeks to free itself from its link to experience, together with the realization that we cannot do without such philosophy, meant that philosophy now became aware of itself in a way it had not since the Greeks. It had to realize that it drew its strength, as it were, not merely from itself but from the other modes in which such human mindful agency displayed itself. For the philosophy of nature, that meant both the sciences together with the more poetic explorations of nature. For the philosophy of mind, it of course meant the human sciences but, even more particularly, the practices of art and religion. It also meant that as exploring the social space of human mindful agency, philosophy had to become historical. To put it anachronistically, philosophy had always been and had to strive to remain interdisciplinary if it was to be part of life.

Near the end of his life, one of Hegel's acquaintances asked him if his dialectic meant that there would be no progress after him, and Hegel told him that of course it did not and that the future would come up with forms of life that he could not possibly anticipate.[65] After all, how could the process of self-interpretation for a primate that remains a problem to itself ever come to an end on its own accord? How could we know what we meant until we had seen its actualization? In effect, all Hegel thought he could say about that point was exactly how he concluded his lectures on the history of philosophy at Berlin: "It is up to this very point that philosophy has now arrived,"[66] and, obviously, the rest is still to be written. No doubt, we shall always return to metaphysics even if we believe in advance that we will be disappointed. However, at least we now know who we are: "Alone with ourselves," we are the kind of creatures for whom this is a problem and will remain so, and at least that much counts as "absolute."

## Notes

1. There are no major commentators I know of who defend Aristotle on this point. Hegel, on the other hand, thought that although Aristotle was wrong in holding these views, such views were nonetheless consistent with Greek life. Lear, in *Happy Lives and the Highest Good: An Essay on Aristotle's Nicomachean Ethics* (Princeton, N.J.: Princeton University Press, 2004), argues that the goal of contemplation does not entail slavery, as does Kraut, *Aristotle: Political Philosophy* (Oxford: Oxford University Press, 2002), who argues that on his own terms, Aristotle should not have endorsed slavery, especially not the idea of natural slaves.

2. See Aristotle, *The Nicomachean Ethics*. "The refined and well-bred man, therefore, will be as we have described, being as it were a law to himself" (Book IV, 8, p. 104).

3. Hegel, *Vorlesungen über die Geschichte der Philosophie I*, p. 222.

4. See Hegel, *Grundlinien der Philosophie des Rechts*, §7, Zusatz; Hegel, *Elements of the Philosophy of Right*, p. 42: "Then the third moment is that 'I' is at one with itself in its limitation, in this other; as it determines itself. It nevertheless still remains at one with itself and does not cease to hold fast to the universal. This is the concrete concept of freedom, whereas the two previous moments have been found to be thoroughly abstract and one-sided." On the necessity of mutual dependency, see also Frederick Neuhouser, *Foundations of Hegel's Social Theory: Actualizing Freedom* (Cambridge, Mass.: Harvard University Press, 2000), and Robert Pippin, *Hegel's Practical Philosophy: Rational Agency as Ethical Life* (Cambridge: Cambridge University Press, 2008).

5. Hegel, *Vorlesungen über die Ästhetik III*, p. 62; Hegel, *Aesthetics: Lectures on Fine Art*, p. 833.

6. Hegel, *Vorlesungen über Die Philosophie der Kunst (1826)*, p. 77.

7. Benjamin Rutter brings this out in his discussion of the tension at work in Hegel's conception of a state as embodying a "nation." See Rutter, *Hegel on the Modern Arts* (Cambridge: Cambridge University Press, 2011).

8. Hegel, *Vorlesungen über die Ästhetik I*, pp. 136–37; Hegel, *Aesthetics: Lectures on Fine Art*, pp. 98–99.

9. Hegel, *Grundlinien der Philosophie des Rechts*, p. 27; Hegel, *Elements of the Philosophy of Right*, p. 22.

10. See Hegel, *Nürnberger und Heidelberger Schriften 1808–1817*, ed. Eva Moldenhauer and Karl Markus Michel, 20 vols. (Theorie-Werkausgabe 4; Frankfurt a. M.: Suhrkamp, 1969), p. 226. "The absolutely free will is also different from... being **self-willed**. This latter has in common with the absolute will that it is concerned not so much with the matter at hand as with the

will as will, precisely that its will be respected. The self-willed person sticks merely with his will because it is his will without having a rational ground for it, i.e., without being concerned that his will is something universal."

11. Hegel, *Vorlesungen über die Ästhetik I* (13), pp. 80–81; Hegel, *Aesthetics: Lectures on Fine Art*, pp. 53–54: "Now this opposition does not arise for consciousness in the restricted sphere of moral action alone; it emerges in a thorough-going cleavage and opposition between what is *absolute* and what is external reality and existence. Taken quite abstractly, it is the opposition of universal and particular, when each is fixed over against the other on its own account in the same way; more concretely, it appears in nature as the opposition of the abstract law to the abundance of individual phenomena, each explicitly with its own character; in the spirit it appears as the contrast between the sensuous and the spiritual in man, as the battle of spirit against flesh, of duty for duty's sake, of the cold command against particular interest, warmth of heart, sensuous inclinations and impulses, against the individual disposition in general; as the harsh opposition between inner freedom and the necessity of external nature, further as the contradiction between the dead inherently empty concept, and the full concreteness of life, between theory or subjective thinking, and objective existence and experience. These are oppositions which have not been invented at all by the subtlety of reflection or the pedantry of philosophy; in numerous forms they have always preoccupied and troubled the human consciousness, even if it is modern culture that has first worked them out most sharply and driven them up to the peak of harshest contradiction. Spiritual culture, the modern intellect, produces this opposition in man which makes him an amphibious animal, because he now has to live in two worlds which contradict one another."

12. Hegel, *Vorlesungen über die Ästhetik II*, p. 220; Hegel, *Aesthetics: Lectures on Fine Art*, p. 593: "But in the modern world these flights are nothing more than 'apprenticeship', the education of the individual into the realities of the present, and thereby they acquire their true significance. For the end of such apprenticeship consists in this, that the subject sows his wild oats, builds himself with his wishes and opinions into harmony with subsisting relationships and their rationality, enters the concatenation of the world, and acquires for himself an appropriate attitude to it. However much he may have quarreled with the world, or been pushed about in it, in most cases at last he gets his girl and some sort of position, marries her, and becomes as good a Philistine as others. The woman takes charge of household management, children arrive, the adored wife, at first unique, an angel, behaves pretty much as all other wives do; the man's profession provides work and vexations, marriage brings domestic affliction—so here we have all the headaches of the rest of married folk."

13. On the literary background of this idea (and on the role that the literary examples play in Hegel's *Phenomenology* in general), see Allen Speight's extremely valuable study, *Hegel, Literature, and the Problem of Agency* (Modern European Philosophy; Cambridge: Cambridge University Press, 2001), xii, 154 pp.

14. See the discussion in Rutter, *Hegel on the Modern Arts*.

15. Hegel, *Vorlesungen über die Ästhetik II*, p. 240; Hegel, *Aesthetics: Lectures on Fine Art*, p. 609.

16. Rutter, *Hegel on the Modern Arts*.

17. Ibid.

18. That since Hegel's time, we often and almost unreflectedly use the language of social roles or even that of playing social roles to characterize this situation only illustrates how much of a gap has been instituted between such positions in social space and ourselves. Hegel himself does not speak of social roles; the idea that everything is a role analogous to that of the theater is twentieth-century sociological language for a phenomenon that is not so much an intrinsic feature as a historically inflected aspect of social life. That all the world is a stage is something that comes on the scene in times of social disruption and heightened self-consciousness.

19. About true comedy, Hegel says: "On these lines, an individual is only portrayed as laughable when it is obvious that he is not serious at all about the seriousness of his aim and will, so

that this seriousness always carries with it, in the eyes of the individual himself, its own destruction, because from beginning to end he cannot devote himself to any higher and universally valid interest which would bring him into a conflict of substance [i.e., with another such interest]." See Hegel, *Vorlesungen über die Ästhetik III*, 552–53; Hegel, *Aesthetics: Lectures on Fine Art*, p. 1220.

20. Hegel, *Vorlesungen über die Geschichte der Philosophie II*, p. 224.

21. On Hegel's reaction to the criticism, see Terry Pinkard, *Hegel: A Biography* (Cambridge: Cambridge University Press, 2000).

22. See Robert Stern, "Hegel's Doppelsatz: A Neutral Reading," *Journal of the History of Philosophy*, 44/2 (April 2006), 235–66. Stern's argument that the so-called *Doppelsatz* expresses merely a commitment to philosophy as a rational enterprise is partly correct— Hegel did indeed intend the assertion to be about philosophy as rigorous theory, as *Wissenschaft*—but it fails to take account of how Hegel also intended it to have this normative sense (which Stern denies it has). Stern is right to say, "Thus, something is 'actual' for Hegel if it is a self-maintaining system which can be understood in its own terms, without being seen as grounded in something else" (p. 258). Hegel takes that one step further and argues that it implies that *no* state can therefore be fully actual in that precise sense.

23. This raises an obvious question: As a basic stance, how is this different from Richard Rorty's idea of irony? Hegel's sense of irony differs from Rorty's in what is perhaps the obvious way: Whereas Rorty takes irony to be the stance of someone who realizes that there is no comprehensive conception of final ends that can be justified, Hegel thinks that since we can justify a comprehensive conception of "being at one with oneself" as the final end of life, we need not be ironic in the Rortyean sense about it. However, the way that final end is specified in our fragmented modern lives is itself not capable of a complete comprehensive formulation—is not, that is, one of the items listed in the *Encyclopedia of the Philosophical Sciences*— and thus not all aspects of our lives are best approached with the same confidence that we can attach to our more abstract, philosophical ideas. Moreover, for Hegel, metaphysical questions are the heart of the enterprise, whereas for Rorty, they are merely unsolvable puzzles that are most likely best ignored. See Richard Rorty, *Contingency, Irony, and Solidarity* (Cambridge: Cambridge University Press, 1989), xvi, 201 pp.

24. Hegel, *Die Philosophie der Geschichte: Vorlesungsmitschrift Heimann (Winter 1830/1831)*, p. 231.

25. Ibid., p. 128. This particular reference to the divisions among the German *Länder* is missing, so far as I can tell, from Karl Hegel's edition of the lectures.

26. Hegel, *Grundlinien der Philosophie des Rechts*, §103; Hegel, *Elements of the Philosophy of Right*, p. 131.

27. Hegel remarks in several different places about how philosophies that therefore countenance withdrawal from the world of public affairs flourish in those situations where it seems that only power and interest rule. One formulation is in the lectures on the philosophy of history, Hegel, *Vorlesungen über die Philosophie der Weltgeschichte: Berlin 1822/1823*, pp. 173–74; Hegel, *Lectures on the Philosophy of World History: Introduction, Reason in History*, p. 143; Hegel, *Vorlesungen über die Philosophie der Geschichte*, pp. 93–94; Hegel, *The Philosophy of History*, p. 69: "And in the development of the state itself, periods must occur in which the spirit of nobler natures is forced to flee from the present into ideal regions, and to find in them a reconciliation with itself which it can no longer enjoy in a world estranged within itself (*in sich entzweiten Wirklichkeit*)—for the reflective intellect attacks all those sacred and profound elements, which were artlessly introduced into the religion, laws and ethical mores of the peoples, and flattens them out into godless generalities, melting them into thin air (*verflacht und verflüchtigt*). Thought is then impelled to become thinking reason, and to pursue and accomplish in its own elements the undoing of that decay which had previously overtaken it."

28. On the crucial and irreplaceable importance for art in this role, see Rutter, *Hegel on the Modern Arts*.

29. This was the force of the appeal to moral "personality" that Kant made in more or less direct reference to Rousseau in Kant, *Religion within the Limits of Reason Alone*.

30. I take this to be more or less in agreement with the interpretation given in Sebastian Rödl, *Self-Consciousness* (Cambridge, Mass.: Harvard University Press, 2007).

31. See Hegel's denunciation in "Preface to the third edition (1830)," in Hegel, *Enzyklopädie der philosophischen Wissenschaften I*, pp. 33–34; Hegel et al., *The Encyclopaedia Logic, with the Zusätze: Part I of the Encyclopaedia of Philosophical Sciences with the Zusätze*, p. 19. There he speaks of those who wish to do this in matters of religion. It is an enraged passage that amounts to Hegel's attack on the emerging restoration regime (even if he himself would not have put the point of his attack quite so bluntly): "That personal attack, grounded upon very specific external details of religion, showed itself in the appalling presumption of those who were ready to excommunicate certain individuals from Christianity upon their own full authority, and thereby put upon them the seal of damnation in this world and in eternity.... One of the defamatory complaints made against a certain modern philosophy has been that in it the human individual posits himself as God, but compared with this complaint based on a false inference, the presumption in which one assumes the role of the world's judge, give one's verdict against the Christianity of individuals, and utters the sentence of inmost damnation upon them, is an actual presumption of quite another sort."

32. Hegel, *Grundlinien der Philosophie des Rechts*, §103; Hegel, *Elements of the Philosophy of Right*, p. 131.

33. I go into Hegel's discussion of who he took these figures to be in his 1807 *Phenomenology* in "Shapes of Active Reason: The Law of the Heart, Retrieved Virtue, and What Really Matters," in Kenneth R. Westphal, *The Blackwell Guide to Hegel's Phenomenology of Spirit* (Blackwell Guides to Great Works; Malden, Mass.: Wiley-Blackwell, 2009), xxvii, 325 pp.

34. Hegel, *Vorlesungen über die Philosophie der Geschichte*, p. 312; Hegel, *The Philosophy of History*, p. 256: "In the French Revolution, the republican constitution as a democracy thus never took hold, and tyranny, despotism raised its voice under the mask of freedom and equality."

35. Michael Hardimon's triumvirate of war, poverty, and divorce heads up the inventory and has become the basic building block of the Anglophone Hegel studies that do not see Hegel's project as some kind of rosy-tinted, overly optimistic view of reconciliation in modern life. See Hardimon, *Hegel's Social Philosophy: The Project of Reconciliation* (Modern European Philosophy; Cambridge: Cambridge University Press, 1994).

36. The alternative conception of democracy as "reasoned self-rule," which attends to the problem inherent in the nature of the bureaucracy necessary in a representative government (and how bureaucratic domination can possibly undermine such democratic self-rule), is made out convincingly by Henry Richardson, *Democratic Autonomy: Public Reasoning about the Ends of Policy* (Oxford Political Theory; New York: Oxford University Press, 2002). Richardson's study complements Kervégan's similar attempt to show how Hegel's distrust of purely bureaucratic solutions for democracy dovetails with many contemporary theories of the problems of representative democracy. See Jean-François Kervégan, *L'Effectif et le Rationnel: Hegel et l'esprit Objectif* (Bibliothèeque d'Histoire de la Philosophie Temps Modernes; Paris: J. Vrin, 2007).

37. This is the theme of, among others, Robert Pippin, "Authenticity in Painting: Remarks on Michael Fried's Art History," *Critical Inquiry*, 31/Spring (2005), 575–98; Pippin, *Hollywood Westerns and American Myth: The Importance of Howard Hawks and John Ford for Political Philosophy* (Castle Lectures in Ethics, Politics, and Economics; New Haven, Conn.: Yale University Press, 2010), x, 198 pp.; and Rutter, *Hegel on the Modern Arts*.

38. See Hegel, *Vorlesungen über die Philosophie der Geschichte*, p. 533; Hegel, *The Philosophy of History*, p. 450–51: "Robespierre set up the principle of virtue as supreme, and one can say that this man took virtue seriously. With him, *virtue* and *terror* were to be the ruling order, for subjective virtue, which governs merely on the basis of cast of mind, brings with it the most fearful tyranny. It exercises its power without legal formalities, and the punishment it inflicts is equally simple—death. This tyranny had to perish, for all inclinations, all inter-

ests, rationality itself revolted against this terribly consistent freedom, which in its concentrated form so fanatically came on the scene."

39. Hegel, *Enzyklopädie der philosophischen Wissenschaften I*, §6, p. 49; Hegel et al., *The Encyclopaedia Logic, with the Zusätze: Part I of the Encyclopaedia of Philosophical Sciences with the Zusätze*, p. 30.

40. Hegel and Henrich, *Philosophie des Rechts: Die Vorlesung von 1819/20 in einer Nachschrift*, p. 51.

41. The passage involves a well-known Hegelian play on the words for "doubt" (*Zweifel*) and "despair" (*Verzweiflung*). Hegel, *Phänomenologie des Geistes*, p. 71 (¶78): "This path can accordingly be regarded as the path of *doubt*, or, more properly, as the path of despair, for what transpires on that path is not what is usually understood as doubt, namely, as an undermining of this or that alleged truth which is then followed by the disappearance of the doubt, and which in turn then returns to the former truth in such a way that what is at stake is taken to be exactly what it was in the first place."

42. For a sympathetic account and defense of such a view, see Manfred Frank, *"Unendliche Annäherung": Die Anfänge der philosophischen Frühromantik* (Suhrkamp Taschenbuch Wissenschaft; Frankfurt am Main: Suhrkamp, 1997), 959 pp.

43. Hegel, *Enzyklopädie der philosophischen Wissenschaften III*, §441; Hegel et al., *Hegel's Philosophy of Mind: Being Part Three of the "Encyclopaedia of the Philosophical Sciences" (1830)*, p. 181.

44. Norman Malcolm, *Ludwig Wittgenstein, a Memoir* (London: Oxford University Press, 1958), p. 83.

45. For Hegel, religion is an attempt to make sense of the world as a whole and our place in that world. Thus, religion is also a form of thinking about things, and, since the whole can be grasped only in thought and not in sensory intuition, religion plays a fundamental role in Hegel's conception of idealism. Religion is form of reflecting on what ultimately matters to us that has to do with our feeling for where we stand in that whole. Religion is thus an attempt to bring the world into view for us as having a kind of sense, a place for us, but in a way that appeals to our emotional makeup as it is mediated by rite and ritual. For Hegel himself, it would make little sense to have a social setup lacking some form of more affective and less reflective, overtly conceptual attempts to think about the whole, and thus since the agent not only as subject but also as substance is crucial to this conception of reflection, it would have made little sense for him to think of a social world devoid of any religious outlook. In some of its forms, religion tries to come to grips with the general unintelligibility of our world in terms of grasping various contingent events—such as why a good person has suffered—as expressions of opaque acts of will by certain deities. On the other hand, the Christian religion, at least on Hegel's view, supposedly marked a kind of progress in religious comprehension in that it constructed a view of the world as a whole in which all was supposed to make sense in terms of God's loving plan for the world and in which that plan was also supposed to make sense to humans. For the Christian, such human suffering occurs only because there is a good reason for it—since God acts out of love for the world—even though that reason may not be apparent to the finite human beings who are subject to such suffering. Hegel's own view seems to be that, philosophically understood, the world simply is full of contingent events that have no further role to play in the world's goodness but that nonetheless human life itself remains for humans at least a *Selbstzweck*, an end in itself. In the last analysis, Hegel simply rejects the idea of there being a providential order for the world, even though he thinks that such an idea has an obviously intuitive appeal and is a first step on the path to constructing an overall conceptual grasp of the whole. In his views on religion, Hegel may have come up against the limits of his tendency to want to have things both ways: to want to maintain a religious outlook that is nonetheless fully circumscribed by the secular claims of philosophy.

46. Heinrich Heine, Terry P. Pinkard, and Howard Pollack-Milgate, *On the History of Religion and Philosophy in Germany and Other Writings* (Cambridge Texts in the History of Philosophy; Cambridge: Cambridge University Press, 2007), xli, 218 pp.

47. The most recent and well-argued attack from the point of view of Christian philosophy on Hegel's own account of his philosophy as genuinely Christian is William Desmond, *Hegel's God: A Counterfeit Double?* (Ashgate Studies in the History of Philosophical Theology; Aldershot, England: Ashgate, 2003), 222 pp.

48. There are many passages that can be cited here, but one in particular is the following: "[Religion has] the same end, the same content as philosophy, but it expresses the *truth* not in the *shape* of *truth*. Rather, it expresses it as *feeling*, as a *given*, as something held in faith, something intimated.—Immediate representation—one cannot stay put at religion—[it is] not *conceptually comprehended—that's the way it is—immediately* accepted, not as an *eternal* truth but in the mode of time-bound stories and historical truths." See Hegel, "Konzept Der Rede Beim Antritt Des Philosophischen Lehramtes an Der Universität Berlin," in Eva Moldenhauer and Karl Markus Michel, eds., *Enzyklopädie der philosophischen Wissenschaften III* (10; Frankfurt a. M.: Suhrkamp, 1969).

49. Hegel, *Vorlesungen über die Geschichte der Philosophie I*, p. 173.

50. Hegel, *Phänomenologie des Geistes* (3), p. 67 (¶72).

51. It is unlikely that Hegel himself would have liked the language of self-conscious "primates." However, he cannot claim to have been ignorant of the idea itself: "...the ape is a satire on humans, a satire which it must amuse him to see if he does not take himself too seriously but is willing to laugh at himself." See Hegel, *Enzyklopädie der philosophischen Wissenschaften II*, ed. Eva Moldenhauer and Karl Markus Michel (9) §368, p. 515.

52. Hegel's conception of divinity is thus to be distinguished from that of his student, Ludwig Feuerbach, who claimed that "we" were divine. For Hegel, that would make no sense. "We" did not create or order the universe, and so forth. On the other hand, "we" are also not simply projecting ourselves onto some fictional deity. Such a reduction of the religious point of view to the merely anthropological simply could not be satisfactory. There could be no "religion of humanity," even if the divine principle of reason is realized only in the activities of human communities reflecting on their highest concerns. A similar thesis to Feuerbach's is in H. S. Harris, *Hegel: Phenomenology and System* (Indianapolis, Ind.: Hackett, 1995), x, 118 pp.

53. For example, his statement in the 1807 *Phenomenology*: "However, the religious community's representational thought is not this *comprehending* thought. Rather, it has the content without its necessity and, instead of the form of the concept, it brings the natural relationships of father and son into the realm of pure consciousness. Since in that way it conducts itself *representationally* even within thought itself, the essence is indeed revealed to it, but the moments of this essence, in accordance with this synthetic representation, separate themselves in part from each other such that they are not related to each other through their own concept." See Hegel, *Phänomenologie des Geistes*, p. 560 (¶771).

54. Hegel, *Grundlinien der Philosophie des Rechts* (7) 20 vols., §270; Hegel, *Elements of the Philosophy of Right*, p. 295: "Indeed, since religion is that moment which integrates the state at the deepest level of the disposition [of its citizens], the state ought even to require all its citizens to belong to such a community—but to any community they please, for the state can have no say in the content [of religious belief] in so far as this relates to the internal dimension of representational thought. A state which is strong because its organization is fully developed can adopt a more liberal attitude in this respect, and may completely overlook individual matters which might affect it, or even tolerate communities whose religion does not recognize even their direct duties towards the state (although this naturally depends on the numbers concerned). It is able to do this by entrusting the members of such communities to civil society and its laws, and is content if they fulfill their direct duties towards it passively, for example by commutation or substitution [of an alternative service]."

55. In this respect, Hegel's often-cited journal entry from his Jena period probably expresses more of his outlook than one might otherwise think: "Early reading of the morning paper is a kind of realistic morning prayer. One orients one's stance toward the world or toward God or to the world itself, whatever it is. The former gives the same assurance as does a blessing, in that one knows where one stands." See Hegel, *Jenaer Schriften*, ed. Eva Moldenhauer and

Karl Markus Michel, 20 vols. (Theorie-Werkausgabe, 2; Frankfurt a. M.: Suhrkamp, 1969), p. 547.

56. Neuhouser argues that Hegel effectively integrates Rousseau's idea that certain kinds of dependence on others are the root of loss of freedom. In Neuhouser's description of the joint Hegel-Rousseau idea, dependence is the source of the subjection of one will to another. An overall social situation of dependence thus guarantees that individuals will be unfree since people will not opt for freedom over satisfaction (that is, over getting what they need). Thus, a structured dependence—dependence on the rule of law—is what is required. See Neuhouser, *Foundations of Hegel's Social Theory*.

57. Hegel's conception of combining a strong sense of historical situatedness with a commitment to an equally robust sense of truth has been both appropriated and criticized by the hermeneutic tradition in philosophy. On the difficulties of that appropriation, see Kristin Gjesdal, *Gadamer and the Legacy of German Idealism* (Modern European Philosophy; Cambridge: Cambridge University Press, 2009), xvii, 235 pp. Although highly critical of Gadamer, Gjesdal herself is also critical of Hegel, but she sees him, as does Gadamer, as a philosopher of a "closed" totality. She argues instead for the superiority of Herder and Schleiermacher in light of the "openness" of their systems. See also Kristin Gjesdal, "Hegel and Herder on Art, History, and Reason," *Philosophy and Literature*, 30/1 (April 2006), 17–32.

58. Hegel, *Phänomenologie des Geistes*, p. 585 (¶802).

59. "This universal spirit, the world-spirit, is not equivalent in meaning to 'God.' It is reason in the spirit as it exists in the world. God is the spirit in its [religious] community. It lives, is actual in it. The world-spirit is the system of these processes by means of which spirit produces for itself the genuine concept of itself." See Hegel, *Vorlesungen über die Philosophie der Weltgeschichte: Berlin 1822/1823*, p. 262 (Zusätze aus dem Wintersemester 1826/27).

60. Hegel, *Introduction to the Lectures on the History of Philosophy*, p. 10.

61. Hegel, *Enzyklopädie der philosophischen Wissenschaften I*, §31 Zusatz; Hegel et al., *The Encyclopaedia Logic, with the Zusätze: Part I of the Encyclopaedia of Philosophical Sciences with the Zusätze*, p. 69.

62. Ibid.

63. Ibid.

64. Kant, *Immanuel Kant's Critique of Pure Reason*, p. 665.

65. Hegel, Hoffmeister, and Nicolin, *Briefe von und an Hegel*, vol. 3, p. 261, #603, Weisse to Hegel, July 11, 1829. "You yourself, honored teacher, once orally indicated to me that you were totally convinced of the necessity of further progress and newer embodiments of the world-spirit, which would go further than the completed embodiment of science that you yourself had brought about. But you were not able to give me any further account of this."

66. "It is up to this point that the world-spirit has come.... This concrete Idea is the result of the *efforts on the part of spirit* throughout almost 2,500 years...its most serious work, that of making itself objective to itself and knowing itself." See Hegel, *Vorlesungen über die Geschichte der Philosophie III*, p. 455.

# BIBLIOGRAPHY

Aristotle, *The Nicomachean ethics*, trans. W. D. Urmson, J. O. Ross, and J. L. Ackrill (The World's Classics; New York: Oxford University Press, 1998), xxxvi, 283 pp.

Aristotle and McKeon, Richard, *The basic works of Aristotle* (New York: Random House, 1941), xxxix, 1487 pp.

Beiser, Frederick C., *Hegel* (Routledge Philosophers; New York: Routledge, 2005), xx, 353 pp.

Bonsiepen, Wolfgang, *Die Begründung einer Naturphilosophie bei Kant, Schelling, Fries und Hegel: Mathematische versus spekulative Naturphilosophie* (Philosophische Abhandlungen Bd. 70; Frankfurt am Main: V. Klostermann, 1997), 651 pp.

Brandom, Robert, *Making it explicit: Reasoning, representing, and discursive commitment* (Cambridge, Mass.: Harvard University Press, 1994), xxv, 741 pp.

——, "Holism and Idealism in Hegel's Phenomenology," in *Tales of the mighty dead: Historical essays in the metaphysics of intentionality* (Cambridge, Mass.: Harvard University Press, 2002).

——, *Tales of the mighty dead: Historical essays in the metaphysics of intentionality* (Cambridge, Mass.: Harvard University Press, 2002), x, 430 pp.

——, *Reason in philosophy: Animating ideas* (Cambridge, Mass.: Harvard University Press, 2009).

Brandom, Robert B., "Some pragmatist themes in Hegel's idealism: Negotiation and administration in Hegel's account of the structure and content of conceptual norms," *European Journal of Philosophy*, 7/2 (August 1999), 164–89.

Brandon, Robert N., *Concepts and methods in evolutionary biology* (Cambridge Studies in Philosophy and Biology; Cambridge: Cambridge University Press, 1996), xiv, 221 pp.

Brinkmann, Klaus E., *Idealism without limits: Hegel and the problem of objectivity* (New York: Springer, 2010).

Broadie, Sarah, *Ethics with Aristotle* (New York: Oxford University Press, 1991), xiii, 462 pp.

Desmond, William, *Hegel's god: A counterfeit double?* (Ashgate Studies in the History of Philosophical Theology; Aldershot, England: Ashgate, 2003), 222 pp.

Dworkin, Ronald, *Law's empire* (Cambridge, Mass.: Belknap, 1986), xiii, 470 pp.

Ferrarin, Alfredo, *Hegel and Aristotle* (Modern European Philosophy; Cambridge: Cambridge University Press, 2001), xxii, 442 pp.

Franco, Paul, *Hegel's philosophy of freedom* (New Haven, CT: Yale University Press, 1999), xviii, 391 pp.

Frank, Manfred, *"Unendliche Annäherung": Die Anfänge der philosophischen Frühromantik* (Suhrkamp Taschenbuch Wissenschaft; Frankfurt am Main: Suhrkamp, 1997), 959 pp.

Frankfurt, Harry G., *The importance of what we care about: Philosophical essays* (Cambridge: Cambridge University Press, 1988), x, 190 pp.

Franks, Paul W., *All or nothing: Systematicity, transcendental arguments, and skepticism in German idealism* (Cambridge, Mass.: Harvard University Press, 2005), viii, 440 pp.

Fried, Michael, *Absorption and theatricality: Painting and beholder in the age of Diderot* (Berkeley: University of California Press, 1980), xvii, 249 pp.

Gardner, Sebastian, "Critical notice of Richard Moran, authority and estrangement: An essay on self-knowledge," *Philosophical Review*, 113/2 (April 2004), 249–67.

——, "'The present situation of philosophy': The limits of naturalism and the interest of German idealism," in Espen Hammer (ed.), *German idealism: Contemporary perspectives* (London: Routledge, 2007).

Gjesdal, Kristin, "Hegel and Herder on art, history, and reason," *Philosophy and Literature*, 30/1 (April 2006), 17–32.

——, *Gadamer and the legacy of German idealism* (Modern European Philosophy; Cambridge: Cambridge University Press, 2009), xvii, 235 pp.

Hardimon, Michael O., *Hegel's social philosophy: The project of reconciliation* (Modern European Philosophy; Cambridge: Cambridge University Press, 1994), xiv, 278 pp.

Harris, H. S., *Hegel: Phenomenology and system* (Indianapolis, Ind.: Hackett, 1995), x, 118 pp.

Hegel, Georg Wilhelm F., "Konzept der Rede beim Antritt des philosophischen Lehramtes an der Universität Berlin," in Eva Moldenhauer and Karl Markus Michel (eds.), *Enzyklopädie der philosophischen Wissenschaften III* (10; Frankfurt a. M.: Suhrkamp, 1969).

——, *Phänomenologie des Geistes*, ed. Eva Moldenhauer and Karl Markus Michel, 20 vols. (Theorie-Werkausgabe, 3; Frankfurt a. M.: Suhrkamp, 1969).

——, *The philosophy of history* (New York: Dover, 1956), xvi, 457 pp.

——, *Enzyklopädie der philosophischen Wissenschaften I*, ed. Eva Moldenhauer and Karl Markus Michel, 20 vols. (Theorie-Werkausgabe, 8; Frankfurt a. M.: Suhrkamp, 1969).

——, *Enzyklopädie der philosophischen Wissenschaften II*, ed. Eva Moldenhauer and Karl Markus Michel, 20 vols. (Theorie-Werkausgabe, 9; Frankfurt a. M.: Suhrkamp, 1969).

——, *Enzyklopädie der philosophischen Wissenschaften III*, ed. Eva Moldenhauer and Karl Markus Michel, 20 vols. (Theorie-Werkausgabe, 10; Frankfurt a. M.: Suhrkamp, 1969).

——, *Grundlinien der Philosophie des Rechts*, ed. Eva Moldenhauer and Karl Markus Michel, 20 vols. (Theorie-Werkausgabe, 7; Frankfurt a. M.: Suhrkamp, 1969).

——, *Hegel's science of logic*, trans. A. V. Miller (Muirhead Library of Philosophy; London: Allen & Unwin; New York: Humanities Press, 1969), 845 pp.

——, *Jenaer Schriften*, ed. Eva Moldenhauer and Karl Markus Michel, 20 vols. (Theorie-Werkausgabe, 2; Frankfurt a. M.: Suhrkamp, 1969).

——, *Nürnberger und Heidelberger Schriften 1808–1817*, ed. Eva Moldenhauer and Karl Markus Michel, 20 vols. (Theorie-Werkausgabe, 4; Frankfurt a. M.: Suhrkamp, 1969).

——, *Vorlesungen über die Ästhetik I*, ed. Eva Moldenhauer and Karl Markus Michel, 20 vols. (Theorie-Werkausgabe, 13; Frankfurt a. M.: Suhrkamp, 1969).

——, *Vorlesungen über die Ästhetik II*, ed. Eva Moldenhauer and Karl Markus Michel, 20 vols. (Theorie-Werkausgabe, 14; Frankfurt a. M.: Suhrkamp, 1969).

——, *Vorlesungen über die Ästhetik III*, ed. Eva Moldenhauer and Karl Markus Michel, 20 vols. (Theorie-Werkausgabe, 15; Frankfurt a. M.: Suhrkamp, 1969).

——, *Vorlesungen über die Geschichte der Philosophie I*, ed. Eva Moldenhauer and Karl Markus Michel, 20 vols. (Theorie-Werkausgabe, 18; Frankfurt a. M.: Suhrkamp, 1969).

——, *Vorlesungen über die Geschichte der Philosophie II*, ed. Eva Moldenhauer and Karl Markus Michel, 20 vols. (Theorie-Werkausgabe, 19; Frankfurt am Main: Suhrkamp, 1969).

——, *Vorlesungen über die Geschichte der Philosophie III*, ed. Eva Moldenhauer and Karl Markus Michel, 20 vols. (Theorie-Werkausgabe, 20; Frankfurt a. M.: Suhrkamp, 1969).

——, *Vorlesungen über die Philosophie der Geschichte*, ed. Eva Moldenhauer and Karl Markus Michel, 20 vols. (Theorie-Werkausgabe, 12; Frankfurt a. M.: Suhrkamp, 1969).

——, *Wissenschaft der Logik I*, ed. Eva Moldenhauer and Karl Markus Michel, 20 vols. (Theorie-Werkausgabe, 5; Frankfurt a. M.: Suhrkamp, 1969).

——, *Wissenschaft der Logik II*, ed. Eva Moldenhauer and Karl Markus Michel, 20 vols. (Theorie-Werkausgabe, 6; Frankfurt a. M.: Suhrkamp, 1969).

——, *Hegel's philosophy of nature*, ed. Michael John Petry, 3 vols. (Muirhead Library of Philosophy; London: Allen & Unwin; New York: Humanities Press, 1970).

———, *Jenaer Schriften*, ed. Gerd Irrlitz (Philosophische Studientexte; Berlin: Akademie-Verlag, 1972), liii, 526 pp.

———, *Lectures on the philosophy of world history: Introduction, reason in history*, ed. Johannes Hoffmeister (Cambridge Studies in the History and Theory of Politics; Cambridge: Cambridge University Press, 1975), xxxviii, 252 pp.

———, *Hegel and the human spirit: A translation of the Jena lectures on the philosophy of spirit (1805–6) with commentary*, ed. Leo Rauch (Detroit, Mich.: Wayne State University Press, 1983), 183 pp.

———, *Introduction to the lectures on the history of philosophy*, trans. T. M. Knox and A. V. Miller (Oxford: Clarendon; New York: Oxford University Press, 1987), viii, 193 pp.

———, *Aesthetics: Lectures on fine art*, trans. T. M. Knox, 2 vols. (Oxford: Clarendon, 1988).

———, *Elements of the philosophy of right*, ed. Allen W. Wood, trans. Hugh Barr Nisbet (Cambridge Texts in the History of Political Thought; Cambridge: Cambridge University Press, 1991), lii, 514 pp.

———, *Vorlesungen über die Philosophie der Weltgeschichte: Berlin 1822/1823*, ed. Karl-Heinz Ilting, Hoo Nam Seelmann, and Karl Brehmer (Vorlesungen/Georg Wilhelm Friedrich Hegel; Hamburg: F. Meiner Verlag, 1996), x, 626 pp.

———, *Vorlesungen über die Philosophie der Kunst (1826)*, ed. Annemarie Gethmann-Siefert (Frankfurt a. M.: Felix Meiner, 2003).

———, *Philosophie der Kunst oder Ästhetik: nach Hegel, im Sommer 1826; Mitschrift Friedrich Carl Hermann Victor von Kehler* (Jena-Sophia: Studien und Editionen zum deutschen Idealismus und zur Frühromantik. Abteilung I, Editionen; München: Fink, 2004), xlix, 301 pp.

———, *Die Philosophie der Geschichte: Vorlesungsmitschrift Heimann (Winter 1830/1831)*, ed. Klaus Vieweg (Munich: Fink Verlag, 2005).

———, "Phenomenology of Spirit (translated by Terry Pinkard)," http://web.me.com/titpaul/ Site/Phenomenology_of_Spirit_page.html.

Hegel, Georg Wilhelm Friedrich, Butler, Clark, and Seiler, Christiane, *Hegel, the letters* (Bloomington: Indiana University Press, 1984), xiv, 740 pp.

Hegel, Georg Wilhelm Friedrich, and Henrich, Dieter, *Philosophie des Rechts: Die Vorlesung von 1819/20 in einer Nachschrift* (Frankfurt a. M.: Suhrkamp, 1983), 388 pp.

Hegel, Georg Wilhelm Friedrich, Hoffmeister, Johannes, and Nicolin, Friedhelm, *Briefe von und an Hegel* (Philosophische Bibliothek; Hamburg: F. Meiner, 1969).

Hegel, Georg Wilhelm Friedrich, and Hoppe, Hans-Georg, *Die Philosophie des Rechts: Vorlesung von 1821/22* (Originalausg., 1. Aufl. edn., Suhrkamp Taschenbuch Wissenschaft; Frankfurt am Main: Suhrkamp, 2005), 236 pp.

Hegel, Georg Wilhelm Friedrich, and Jaeschke, Walter, *Vorlesungen über die Geschichte der Philosophie* (Philosophische Bibliothek; Hamburg: F. Meiner Verlag, 1993).

Hegel, Georg Wilhelm Friedrich, and Miller, Arnold V., *Hegel's philosophy of nature: Being part two of the Encyclopedia of the philosophical sciences (1830), translated from Nicolin and Pöggeler's edition (1959), and from the Zusätze in Michelet's text (1847)* (Oxford: Clarendon; New York: Oxford University Press, 2004), xxxi, 450 pp.

Hegel, Georg Wilhelm Friedrich, Wannenmann, P., and Ruhr-Universität Bochum. Hegel-Archiv., *Lectures on natural right and political science: The first philosophy of right: Heidelberg, 1817–1818, with additions from the lectures of 1818–1819* (Berkeley: University of California Press, 1995), x, 356 pp.

Hegel, Georg Wilhelm Friedrich, and Williams, Robert R., *Georg Wilhelm Friedrich Hegel: Lectures on the philosophy of spirit 1827–8* (Hegel Lectures Series; Oxford: Oxford University Press, 2007), vi, 287 pp.

Hegel, Georg Wilhelm Friedrich, et al., *Hegel's philosophy of mind: Being part three of the "Encyclopaedia of the philosophical sciences" (1830)* (Oxford: Clarendon, 1971), xxii, 320 pp.

Hegel, Georg Wilhelm Friedrich, et al., *The encyclopaedia logic, with the Zusätze: Part I of the Encyclopaedia of philosophical sciences with the Zusätze* (Indianapolis, Ind.: Hackett, 1991), xlviii, 381 pp.

Hegel, Georg Wilhelm Friedrich, et al., *Vorlesungen über die Philosophie des Geistes: Berlin 1827/1828* (Vorlesungen/Georg Wilhelm Friedrich Hegel; Hamburg: F. Meiner, 1994), xxxviii, 321 pp.

Heine, Heinrich, Pinkard, Terry P., and Pollack-Milgate, Howard, *On the history of religion and philosophy in Germany and other writings* (Cambridge Texts in the History of Philosophy; Cambridge: Cambridge University Press, 2007), xli, 218 pp.

Honneth, Axel, *The struggle for recognition: The moral grammar of social conflicts* (Cambridge, Mass.: Polity, 1995), xxi, 215 pp.

Horstmann, Rolf-Peter, *Die Grenzen der Vernunft: Eine Untersuchung zu Zielen und Motiven des deutschen Idealismus* (Frankfurt a.M.: Anton Hain, 1991).

Houlgate, Stephen, *The opening of Hegel's logic: From being to infinity* (Purdue University Press Series in the History of Philosophy; West Lafayette, Ind.: Purdue University Press, 2006), xix, 456 pp.

Ilting, Karl-Heinz, Wannenmann, P., and Homeyer, C. G., *G. W. F. Hegel, die Philosophie des Rechts: Die Mitschriften Wannenmann (Heidelberg 1817/18) und Homeyer (Berlin 1818/19)* (Stuttgart: Klett-Cotta, 1983), 399 pp.

Irwin, T. H., "Who discovered the will?" *Philosophical Perspectives*, 6 (1992), 453–73.

Jaeggi, Rahel, *Entfremdung: Zur Aktualität eines sozialphilosophischen Problems* (Frankfurter Beiträge zur Soziologie und Sozialphilosophie; Frankfurt am Main: Campus, 2005), 267 pp.

Kant, I., "On the common saying: 'This may be true in theory, but it does not apply in practice'," in Hans Siegbert Reiss (ed.), *Kant: Political writings* (Cambridge Texts in the History of Political Thought; Cambridge: Cambridge University Press, 1991).

Kant, Immanuel, *Immanuel Kant's critique of pure reason*, trans. Norman Kemp Smith (London: Macmillan, 1929), xiii, 681 pp.

——, *Religion within the limits of reason alone* (The Cloister Library; New York: Harper, 1960) cxlv, 190, cxlvii–cliv pp.

——, *Grundlegung zur Metaphysik der Sitten*, ed. Karl Vorländer (3 Aufl. ed., Philosophische Bibliothek, Bd. 41; Hamburg: F. Meiner, 1965), xxvii, 100 pp.

——, *Kant: Political writings*, ed. Hans Siegbert Reiss (2nd enl. ed., Cambridge texts in the history of political thought; Cambridge: Cambridge University Press, 1991), xv, 311 pp.

Kervégan, Jean-François, *L'effectif et le rationnel: Hegel et l'esprit objectif* (Bibliothèque d'histoire de la philosophie temps modernes; Paris: J. Vrin, 2007), 407 pp.

Kojève, Alexandre, and Queneau, Raymond, *Introduction to the reading of Hegel* (New York: Basic Books, 1969), xiv, 287 pp.

Kraut, Richard, *Aristotle on the human good* (Princeton, N.J.: Princeton University Press, 1989), viii, 379 pp.

——, *Aristotle: Political philosophy* (Founders of Modern Political and Social Thought; Oxford: Oxford University Press, 2002), xii, 520 pp.

Kreines, James, "Hegel's Metaphysics: Changing the Debate," *Philosophy Compass*, 1/5 (September 2006), 466–80.

——, "The logic of life: Hegel's philosophical defense of teleological explanation of living beings," in Frederick C. Beiser (ed.), *The Cambridge companion to Hegel and nineteenth-century philosophy* (Cambridge: Cambridge University Press, 2008).

——, "Metaphysics without pre-critical monism: Hegel on lower-level natural kinds and the structure of reality," *Bulletin of the Hegel Society of Great Britain*, 57–58 (2008), 48–70.

Kukla, Rebecca, and Lance, Mark Norris, *"Yo!" and "lo!": The pragmatic topography of the space of reasons* (Cambridge, Mass.: Harvard University Press, 2009), xi, 239 pp.

Larmore, Charles E., *Les pratiques du moi* (Ethique et philosophie morale; Paris: Presses universitaires de France, 2004), 264 pp.

Lear, Gabriel Richardson, *Happy lives and the highest good: An essay on Aristotle's Nicomachean ethics* (Princeton, N.J.: Princeton University Press, 2004), viii, 238 pp.

Lear, Jonathan, *Open minded: Working out the logic of the soul* (Cambridge, Mass.: Harvard University Press, 1998), 345 pp.

Lehmann, Hartmut, *Die Entzauberung der Welt: Studien zu Themen von Max Weber* (Bausteine zu einer europäischen Religionsgeschichte im Zeitalter der Säkularisierung Bd. 11; Göttingen: Wallstein, 2009), 149 pp.

Longuenesse, Béatrice, *Hegel's critique of metaphysics* (Modern European Philosophy; Cambridge: Cambridge University Press, 2007), xxi, 246 pp.

Lovibond, Sabina, *Realism and imagination in ethics* (Minneapolis: University of Minnesota Press, 1983), 238 pp.

Luther, Martin, *Von der Freiheit eines Christenmenschen*, http://www.fordham.edu/halsall/source/luther-freiheit.html.

Macintyre, Alasdair C., *After virtue: A study in moral theory* (Notre Dame, Ind.: University of Notre Dame Press, 1981) ix, 252 pp.

——— , *Dependent rational animals: Why human beings need the virtues* (The Paul Carus Lecture Series; Chicago: Open Court, 1999), xiii, 172 pp.

Malcolm, Norman, *Ludwig Wittgenstein, a memoir* (London: Oxford University Press, 1958), 99 pp.

Mcdowell, John Henry, *Mind and world* (Cambridge, Mass.: Harvard University Press, 1994), x, 191 pp.

——— , *Having the world in view: Essays on Kant, Hegel, and Sellars* (Cambridge, Mass.: Harvard University Press, 2009), ix, 285 pp.

Menke, Christoph, *Tragödie im Sittlichen: Gerechtigkeit und Freiheit nach Hegel* (Frankfurt am Main: Suhrkamp, 1996), 334 pp.

——— , *Reflections of equality* (Cultural Memory in the Present; Stanford, Calif.: Stanford University Press, 2006), xii, 226 pp.

Merleau-Ponty, Maurice, *Phenomenology of perception* (Routledge Classics; London: Routledge, 2002), xxiv, 544 pp.

Meyer, Susan Sauvé, "Aristotle on the voluntary," 137–58, in Richard Kraut (ed.), *The Blackwell guide to Aristotle's Nicomachean ethics* (Malden, MA: Blackwell, 2006).

Moran, Richard, *Authority and estrangement: An essay on self-knowledge* (Princeton, N.J.: Princeton University Press, 2001), xxxviii, 202 pp.

Moyar, Dean, *Hegel's conscience* (New York: Oxford University Press, 2010).

Mure, G. R. G., *A study of Hegel's logic* (Oxford: Clarendon, 1950), viii, 375 pp.

Neuhouser, Frederick, *Foundations of Hegel's social theory: Actualizing freedom* (Cambridge, Mass.: Harvard University Press, 2000), xiii, 337 pp.

——— , "Desire, recognition, and the relation between bondsman and lord," 37–54, in Kenneth R. Westphal (ed.), *The Blackwell guide to Hegel's phenomenology of spirit* (Malden, Mass.: Wiley-Blackwell, 2009).

Norton, Robert Edward, *The beautiful soul: Aesthetic morality in the eighteenth century* (Ithaca, N.Y.: Cornell University Press, 1995), xi, 314 pp.

O'Neill, Onora, *Acting on principle: An essay on Kantian ethics* (New York: Columbia University Press, 1975), x, 155 pp.

Patterson, Orlando, *Freedom* (New York: Basic Books, 1991).

Pinkard, Terry P., *Hegel's dialectic: The explanation of possibility* (Philadelphia: Temple University Press, 1988), xi, 236 pp.

——— , *Hegel's phenomenology: The sociality of reason* (Cambridge: Cambridge University Press, 1994), vii, 451 pp.

——— , *Hegel: A biography* (Cambridge: Cambridge University Press, 2000), xx, 780 pp.

——— , "Hegel's *Phenomenology* and *Logic*: An overview," 161–79, in Karl Ameriks (ed.), *The Cambridge companion to German idealism* (Cambridge: Cambridge University Press, 2000).

——— , *German philosophy, 1760–1860: The legacy of idealism* (Cambridge: Cambridge University Press, 2002), x, 382 pp.

Pippin, Robert B., *Hegel's idealism: The satisfactions of self-consciousness* (Cambridge: Cambridge University Press, 1989), xii, 327 pp.

——— , "Review of Allen Wood, 'Hegel's Ethical Thought,'" *Zeitschrift für philosophische Forschung*, 47/3 (1993), 489–95.

————, "Authenticity in painting: Remarks on Michael Fried's art history," *Critical Inquiry*, 31/ Spring (2005), 575–98.

————, "Brandom's Hegel," *European Journal of Philosophy*, 13/3 (December 2005), 381–408.

————, "Concept and Intuition: On Distinguishability and Separability," *Hegel-Studien*, 40 (2005).

————, *Hegel's practical philosophy: Rational agency as ethical life* (Cambridge: Cambridge University Press, 2008), xi, 308 pp.

————, "Hegel on political philosophy and political actuality," *Inquiry: An Interdisciplinary Journal of Philosophy*, 53/5 (October 20, 2010), 401–16.

————, *Hegel on self-consciousness: Desire and death in Hegel's phenomenology of spirit* (Princeton, N.J.: Princeton University Press, 2010).

————, *Hollywood westerns and American myth: The importance of Howard Hawks and John Ford for political philosophy* (The Castle Lectures in Ethics, Politics, and Economics; New Haven, Conn.: Yale University Press, 2010), x, 198 pp.

Rand, Sebastian, "The importance and relevance of Hegel's philosophy of nature," *Review of Metaphysics*, 61/2 (December 2007), 379–400.

————, "Animal subjectivity and the nervous system in Hegel's philosophy of nature," *Revista Eletrônica Estudos Hegelianos* 11 (2010).

Redding, Paul, *Hegel's hermeneutics* (Ithaca, N.Y.: Cornell University Press, 1996), xvi, 262 pp.

————, *The logic of affect* (Ithaca, N.Y.: Cornell University Press, 1999), x, 204 pp.

————, *Analytic philosophy and the return of Hegelian thought* (Modern European Philosophy; Cambridge: Cambridge University Press, 2007), x, 252 pp.

Richardson, Henry S., *Democratic autonomy: Public reasoning about the ends of policy* (Oxford Political Theory; New York: Oxford University Press, 2002), xii, 316 pp.

Rödl, Sebastian, *Self-consciousness* (Cambridge, Mass.: Harvard University Press, 2007), xi, 207 pp.

Rorty, Richard, *Contingency, irony, and solidarity* (Cambridge: Cambridge University Press, 1989), xvi, 201 pp.

Rutter, Benjamin, *Hegel on the modern arts* (Cambridge: Cambridge University Press, 2011).

Schnädelbach, Herbert, Siep, Ludwig, and Drüe, Hermann, *Hegels Philosophie: Kommentare zu den Hauptwerken*, 3 vols. (Suhrkamp Taschenbuch Wissenschaft; Frankfurt am Main: Suhrkamp, 2000).

Sedgwick, Sally, "Reason and History: Kant versus Hegel," *Proceedings of the American Philosophical Association*, 84/2 (November 2010), 45–59.

————, "Longuenesse on Kant and the priority of the capacity to judge," *Inquiry: An Interdisciplinary Journal of Philosophy*, 43/1 (March 2000), 81–90.

————, "The state as organism: The metaphysical basis of Hegel's philosophy of right," *Southern Journal of Philosophy*, 39 (suppl.) (2001), 171–88.

————, "Hegel's critique of Kant: An overview," in Graham Bird (ed.), *A Companion to Kant* (Malden, MA: Blackwell, 2006).

Sellars, Wilfrid, *Science, perception, and reality* (International Library of Philosophy and Scientific Method; New York: Humanities Press, 1963), 366 pp.

Sennett, Richard, *The culture of the new capitalism* (Castle Lectures in Ethics, Politics, and Economics; New Haven, Conn.: Yale University Press, 2006), 214 pp.

Siep, Ludwig, *Anerkennung als Prinzip der praktischen Philosophie: Unters. zu Hegels Jenaer Philosophie d. Geistes* (Reihe Praktische Philosophie; Freiburg: Alber, 1979), 378 pp.

Speight, Allen, *Hegel, literature, and the problem of agency* (Modern European Philosophy; Cambridge: Cambridge University Press, 2001), xii, 154 pp.

Stekeler-Weithofer, Pirmin, *Philosophie des Selbstbewusstseins: Hegels System als Formanalyse von Wissen und Autonomie* (1. Aufl. edn., Suhrkamp Taschenbuch Wissenschaft; Frankfurt am Main: Suhrkamp, 2005), 447 pp.

Stern, Robert, *Routledge philosophy guidebook to Hegel and the phenomenology of spirit* (Routledge Philosophy Guidebooks; London: Routledge, 2002), xviii, 234 pp.

————, "Hegel's Doppelsatz: A neutral reading," *Journal of the History of Philosophy*, 44/2 (April 2006), 235–66.

————, "Hegel's idealism," in Frederick C. Beiser (ed.), *The Cambridge companion to Hegel and nineteenth-century philosophy* (Cambridge: Cambridge University Press, 2008).

Taylor, Charles, *Human agency and language* (Philosophical Papers; Cambridge: Cambridge University Press, 1985), viii, 294 pp.

Trilling, Lionel, *Sincerity and authenticity* (Cambridge, Mass.: Harvard University Press, 1972), 188 pp.

Westphal, Kenneth R., *Hegel's epistemology: A philosophical introduction to the phenomenology of spirit* (Indianapolis, Ind.: Hackett, 2003), xvi, 146 pp.

————, *The Blackwell guide to Hegel's phenomenology of spirit* (Blackwell Guides to Great Works; Malden, Mass.: Wiley-Blackwell, 2009), xxvii, 325 pp.

Williams, Bernard Arthur Owen, *Shame and necessity* (Sather Classical Lectures; Berkeley: University of California Press, 1993), xii, 254 pp.

————, *Truth & truthfulness: An essay in genealogy* (Princeton, N.J.: Princeton University Press, 2002), xi, 328 pp.

Williams, Robert R., *Recognition: Fichte and Hegel on the other* (SUNY Series in Hegelian Studies; Albany: State University of New York Press, 1992), xviii, 332 pp.

Wittgenstein, Ludwig, *Philosophical investigations—Philosophische Untersuchungen* (New York: Macmillan, 1953), x, 232 pp.

————, *Tractatus logico-philosophicus. The German text of Logisch-philosophische Abhandlung* (International Library of Philosophy and Scientific Method; London: Routledge & Kegan Paul; New York: Humanities Press, 1963), xxii, 166 pp.

Wolff, Michael, *Das Körper-Seele Problem: Kommentar zu Hegel, Enzyklopädie* (1830), §389 (Frankfurt a.M.: Klostermann, 1992).

Wood, Allen W., *Hegel's ethical thought* (Cambridge: Cambridge University Press, 1990), xxi, 293 pp.

Yeomans, Christopher, *Freedom and reflection: Hegel and the logic of agency* (London: Oxford University Press, 2011).

# INDEX

absorption, 59, 84, 107, 121, 123, 126, 132, 179
abstract, the
abstract meaning, 28, 50, 54, 55, 97, 107, 143,
    162–164
    abstract agency, 80n
    abstract being-for-itself 42n
    abstract certainty, 85n
    abstract freedom, 83n, 196n
    abstract Idea, 104, 109n, 113n, 143
    abstract (moral) good, 143
    abstract right 136–138, 142, 154, 158, 159
    abstract self-consciousness, 55, 61–62, 77n
    abstract spirit, 44n
    abstract subjectivity, 9, 14n, 96, 98, 103
action
    animal action and human action, 26
    as bodily activity of the soul, 29
    as caused by a substance, 98–99
    as caused by character, 115
    as responding to reasons as reasons, 26, 33, 183
    as translation of inner into outer, 32
    being fully "in" an action, 100, 174, 176
    desires and reasons, 66
    expressive and causal conceptions, 96–105
    voluntariness, 18, 90
    voluntarist conception, 31
    weakness of will as failure of practical
        knowledge, 94
actual, actuality (*Wirklichkeit*) 20, 31, 43, 47, 52,
    143, 177
    as effective, efficacious reality, 31, 143
Africa, 66, 81m 83, 194
agency, 18, 29–30, 45–46, 48, 57, 58, 59, 60, 61,
    62, 63, 80, 81, 89, 91, 92, 93, 95–97, 99–101,
    120, 157
    agency and recognition 90-
    agency, its goods 59–60, 93, 104–109, 190
    as "infinite worth" 64
    as knowing purposes as purposes, reasons as
        reasons 26, 56

as self-interpreting animal, 6, 10, 18, 23, 24, 57,
    95, 97, 99, 101, 105, 106, 115, 174, 190, 191,
    195, 196
alienation, 147–157, 184–185
amphibians 174, 176, 177, 178, 180, 181, 183, 195
Antigone, 128, 129
Aristotle, 10, 14, 17, 18, 26, 29, 30, 31, 33, 34, 40,
    42, 43, 44, 45, 47, 59, 74, 79, 83, 89, 90, 93,
    94, 96, 106, 108, 109, 110, 111, 112, 113,
    114, 115, 116, 124, 127, 133, 134, 135, 146,
    163, 168, 173, 180, 189
autonomy, see freedom

Beiser, Frederick, 14n, 34n, 38n
Brandom, Robert, 13n, 26, 39n, 40n, 76n, 83n,
    85n, 111n
Brandon, Robert, 22, 37n
Broadie, Sarah 74n, 109n
burgher, 154, 156, 158, 160, 162, 169, 181

character, 97–101, 102–104, 112, 115–116, 152, 169n
    character as destiny, 118
    character in democracy, 124–25
China, 66, 119, 165, 194
Christianity, 10, 68, 71, 83, 119, 135, 148, 165,
    178, 192, 193, 199
citizen, 123–125, 151, 158–165, 177, 180, 186
civil society, 153–156, 158–60
    as a spectacle, 156
    as society of burghers, not citizens, 158
conscience, 130, 140, 142, 152, 160, 185, 192
    as involving an antinomy, 140, 185

Darwin, Charles 22, 28, 37, 38, 57
democracy,
    as resting on organic view of nature, 126–127,
    151–52